T0369466

FTW
SELF DEFENSE

FTW

SELF DEFENSE

C. R. JAHN

iUniverse, Inc.
Bloomington

FTW SELF DEFENSE

iUniverse books may be ordered through booksellers or by contacting:

iUniverse
1663 Liberty Drive
Bloomington, IN 47403
www.iuniverse.com
1-800-Authors (1-800-288-4677)

ISBN: 978-1-4697-3255-8 (sc)
ISBN: 978-1-4697-3256-5 (ebk)

Printed in the United States of America

iUniverse rev. date: 01/03/2012

Contents

Dedication

I dedicate this book to mine enemies, without whom it never could have been written. Thank you for the lessons you have taught me.

INTRODUCTION

> *"The bad guys kill the bad guys. The bad guys kill the good guys. If you want to survive the bad guys, you have to have some bad in you—a lot actually. You have to know what they know."*
>
> Henry Rollins, *The Portable Henry Rollins* (p. 230)

This is not actually a "self defense" manual, *per se.* Perhaps it would be best if you didn't even think of this as a "self defense" manual at all, since my views frequently contradict established doctrine, official legalities, and even common sense. In fact, were you to actually apply these methods, you might well find yourself entangled in significant legal difficulties, and that would be bad. Do NOT take any legal advice from Captain Hook! This is really more of a rambling, tangential diatribe than anything else, and you should not take it too seriously. Perhaps you will be able to glean a few items that may prove useful, or you could view this book as an opportunity to look at the subject from a new perspective, or you could simply think of it as light entertainment. This is irrelevant to me. I am simply transcribing these words due to a compulsion I do not fully understand. Book wants to be written, and I'll be glad when it is finally done.

Let me now give you a general idea of what to expect before we get started. This book is far from perfect and I'm sure there is an error or two I've overlooked. I tend to go off topic to focus on detail or hypothetical situations. I repeat myself. Sometimes it seems as if I contradict myself because certain topics are complex and the rules change under specific circumstances. I occasionally revert to street slang or rural colloquialisms and tend to say "fuck" a lot more than I probably should. If you require linear precision and perfect grammar, as in a university textbook, you will be frustrated.

Primarily, my method consists of a philosophy, a "mindset" if you will. I have taken a lifetime of experience, observation, and research and distilled it into a concentrated form which is very easy for most folks to comprehend. Once comprehended it can be applied with minimal training, because these methods tend to be extremely simple and precision is generally not required. I arm you with basic concepts that you can utilize as you see fit in a way that is comfortable for you. Anyone can do this, regardless of body type, as it was specifically tailored to allow an individual who was small in stature and physically weak to defeat a significantly larger and stronger assailant. There are no takedowns, restraining holds, or sparring techniques in this system. You will learn how to stop someone from hurting you instantly. These techniques are unforgiving and vicious and often require the use of a tool. Due to these factors, it may be unlawful to actually implement them in certain jurisdictions, so please consider select tactics and tools "void where prohibited by law" and presented for academic study only.

Speaking of the law, well, one dirty little secret of self defense is that it is against the law to defend yourself in many places. In the United Kingdom, Canada, and Australia this is at its most extreme, but even in the United States there are places such as New York City, Chicago, and Washington DC where it is illegal for most law abiding citizens to fight back against victimization in any effective manner lest they be accused of "vigilantism" and "made an example of" via Draconian penalties, whereas the criminal who initiated the attack often is given opportunity to plead down to reduced charges and get early release. This is clearly insane, yet it is an established pattern in certain areas. If you reside in one of those areas the best self defense advice I can provide is: *move.* I do not say that lightly, and I shall go into greater detail in a later chapter. In any event, whenever I discuss a technique, tactic, or tool that may be of questionable legality I shall do my best to notify you of such, however, the law varies greatly between states and municipalities, I am not an attorney, I am unable to provide legal counsel on any matter, and legalities are really well beyond the scope of this book.

If you find my style of writing, occasional use of profanity, or assertions that the law is not on your side offensive, I strongly suggest that you put this book back on the shelf as it clearly is not the appropriate text for you. If, however, you are willing to examine new concepts from differing perspectives with an open mind, please feel free to read on.

Best Regards,

CAPTAIN HOOK

F.T.W. COMMENTARY

A brief summarization will follow each chapter. F.T.W. is an acronym which has multiple possible meanings. You can tell everyone it means "for the win" if you like. After all, F.T.W. Self Defense is all about winning. You never want to take second place in a streetfight.

Qualification Statement

Now, some of you are sure to scoff at Captain Hook, querying facetiously, "Oh, but what are your *qualifications* to write this book? Who was your *sifu*? Show us some *credentials*." And to those guys I just say: "suckit."

Here is the deal. I do not have a black belt or hold instructor rank in any formalized system. I have never been part of an elite Spec-ops unit. Heck, I didn't even take Ashida Kim's ninja correspondence course. So what "qualifies" me to write a book on personal protection? Not much, really.

Let's see, the first time I was stabbed on the street, I think I was about 4 years old. The other kid was carrying a serrated steak knife he had taken from his home and was maybe a year older than me—I didn't even know his name. I wasn't hurt too bad and it was a valuable lesson. I have been threatened and attacked with knives a number of times since then—more times than I even remember. It all sorta blends together after awhile.

I think the first time my Da showed me how to kill a man with a knife I was about 5. He was drunk, as he often was. After he got out of the military, he worked a series of jobs for several mob owned companies in Jersey and Upstate New York. He was pretty badassed, but not the easiest fellow to live with.

Experienced the first road rage incident in which I took fire at the age of 16. One of the town drunks was looking for a fight and decided to pick on a carload of teenaged girls we knew during a blizzard with icy roads. We thought maybe he should pick on us instead. He pulled over and produced a Mossberg shotgun which he then proceeded to fire at us. My Da's pickup took a few pellets of buckshot in the tailgate, but we were okay. I have probably been involved in more road rage incidents than anyone else on the planet because I used to be a real asshole, and I have developed some genuine expertise there. I also was the personal driver for an individual who had a number of enemies and have been involved in car chases which more than once devolved to demolition derby, so I know driving fairly well.

Entered the service immediately after high school, intending to make it my career, but that was cut short by a non service related injury, so no real story to tell there.

Worked as an overnight cashier at a truckstop next to a whorehouse after that. It was a real shithole with no cameras, no security, and no phone to call the police (except for the payphone outside). Saw lots of serious fights—not the bullshit fisticuffs drunk office drones who played high school football get in at the sports bar, but real fights where weapons were used and the loser left in an ambulance.

Shortly thereafter, I went to gaol a few times over minor stuff that I didn't even realize was illegal. Met some interesting folks in gaol, and kept in contact with some of them for years.

Was homeless for nearly two years, but rarely on the street. Slept in my car a lot, did some couch surfing at the trailer parks and the projects. Although I was never a drug addict or a gang member, I ended up hanging out with those guys off and on. Saw a lot of fucked up shit during that time.

Somehow ended up on the "Circle of Elders" of a tribe of lawless Hill Folk in the Adirondacks, which I suppose was sort of like a gang that didn't commit crimes . . . well, at least not for profit or in any organized way. There are a lot of bodies up in those Hills that no-one's gonna find, and even the State Police don't patrol those backroads, but they do know how to throw great parties and most of them were genuinely good people whom I respected and trusted.

I associated with a number of motorcycle clubs, some of which law enforcement like to describe as "outlaw motorcycle gangs" which in many cases is a misrepresentation if not an utter exaggeration. Not once did I ever see those guys with any of the meth or stolen motorcycle parts they are always accused of dealing in. Weed and unregistered handguns, sure, but the Bill of Rights says that's okay so fuck you if you don't like it.

Worked as a property manager for a few years in a low income apartment building that rented to welfare recipients. We didn't have problems with tenants using drugs . . . that would be an understatement. We had problems with tenants turning units into crackhouses or flop pads for junkies and gangbangers, then not being able to evict them in a timely manner due to New York law. I specialized in finding creative ways to drive out problem tenants, many of whom were drug addicts or violent felony offenders with weapons and lots of criminal friends.

I then moved to one of the most gang infested areas of the country, the Tidewater area of Virginia, where you heard gunfire every day and saw teenagers in gang colors open carrying cheap handguns stuck carelessly in their back pockets and waistbands on a regular basis. In some neighborhoods they would find a bullet riddled body on the sidewalk at least once a month, and no-one called it in until the next morning when the yuppies saw it on their commute to work. For about 5 years I worked as a store clerk in Oceanview and worked two night watchman jobs in Virginia Beach and Bad Newz. I had at least five idiots try to mug or carjack me there and had guns pulled on me at least a dozen times—only actually took fire once though (yet another road rage incident).

Now I'm in Denver, which has one of the largest and most visible homeless populations in the country, along with more than a few gangs. For about 4 years I worked for a private investigator who specialized in service of process, and I was sent into the projects and slums of Aurora, Five Points, Whittier, Lakewood, and Commerce City as part of my usual route. Spent another year working for a couple of towing companies that specialized in impounds and repos. Currently I am employed at another high risk job which I am not at liberty to discuss, and do freelance security at a variety of atypical venues. My business card says "Crisis Management." I have seen a lot of shit.

In the course of researching this book, I spent a few years learning everything I could about the best legal knives to carry as well as the most reliable inexpensive handguns. I am now pretty much an expert on Saturday Night Specials, and to be honest with you, some of them ain't half bad.

Aside from that, I haven't really got much in the way of credentials . . . I think maybe I'll just get a certificate suitable for framing from the "School of Hard Knocks" and put that on my wall. I'm no grandmaster and I ain't got no trophies, medals, or commendations. But I do have this laptop and a English degree from the Community College . . . so here's my book.

Required Reading

Normally, these lists are an appendix at the very end of the book. I'm putting this one at the front. Why? I want to eliminate confusion about what this book is and is not. Comparing it to other books may help achieve that goal.

First and foremost, this is not an entry level basic text for folks who are just starting to learn how to defend themselves. I'm not sure if this should even be considered a "self defense" book simply due to liability issues. Let's just call it a lightly entertaining diatribe filled with pseudo-philosophical discourse and hypothetical worst-case scenarios. You should already have the basics behind you and a firm grasp of legal and ethical concepts before reading this book.

Secondly, although I have written a prior self defense book and taught students privately on rare occasion, I have never considered myself an instructor. I have no intention of "teaching" you anything. All I am doing here is sharing my thoughts and observations. I have made many mistakes in the past and make no claims of perfection. What has worked for me may not work for you, nor may it be appropriate or even legal.

I am relatively small in stature and have a noticeable disability. This has made me a potential "target" on literally hundreds of occasions over the years. I have lived in some rather rough areas and associated with folks who eschewed civilized society to live by their own laws, which were invariably enforced with violence. I grew up in a violent household, in a violent community, and worked a number of jobs where violence was a regular occurrence. I have seen a lot of fucked up shit. This has all effected the way I now view conflict. It is not a game to me. If my verbal and nonverbal attempts at diplomacy and de-escalation fail and it looks as if I'm about to be pummeled and stomped by a much larger adversary, I'm not going to fuck around and pretend like I'm obligated to obey the dictates of society and either run away or play pattycakes with him in a grossly unfair sparring match. I'm going to take him out viciously and immediately, which means he will probably die and I will probably go to gaol. That is a choice which I have made. I do not advise you to emulate me in that, or any other, way.

I tell you this because there are consequences to your actions. Many authors, particularly of ultra-macho commando style combatives manuals popular during the last decade, fail to adequately address the very real legal and social repercussions of engaging in violence . . . and neither will I. This book is written from the perspective of an outlaw—and if you regularly interact with criminals and street people, many of them eschew legalities similarly, but for an entirely different reason. Therein lies the true distinction between a criminal and an outlaw: a criminal breaks the law in order to enrich himself and gain status, whereas an outlaw selectively ignores laws because he feels contempt for the hypocrites who write and enforce them. A responsible instructor will repeatedly reinforce what level of force you're permitted to use, when it is inappropriate to use force, and what weapons you are not allowed to carry or use. Captain Hook gives fuck all about that, especially if someone breaks Rule # 1, which is: "*Don't touch me.*" So it is in your best interest to take these essays with a grain of salt and look at them solely as a source of entertainment.

If you are truly serious about learning real world self defense, you need to heed the sage advice of respected and responsible instructors (which I, assuredly, am not), so I am recommending the following texts to you. Read them in order, if possible. If you have not read them already, I strongly urge you to put this book aside until you have done so. These books will keep you safe and, more importantly, keep you out of prison. They are the best books available regarding awareness, de-escalation, and legalities—extremely important subjects which I shall barely touch upon as the following authors have done a far better job than I could, and I shall occasional quote them (and many others) throughout this text rather than attempting to rephrase their eloquence in my own coarse words:

The Little Black Book of Violence by Lawrence Kane and Kris Wilder
This is an outstanding work directed at teens and young men. Best introductory text ever written, and this is from a guy who has read over 200 self defense manuals. Recently a condensed and well illustrated version of this book was released entitled, *How to Win a Fight,* and that is the version you want to buy multiple copies of as gifts to friends.

Cheap Shots, Ambushes, and Other Lessons by Marc MacYoung
This was the book that literally changed my life. A whole different way of looking at the subject combined with practical real world experience. Brilliant and concise.

The Gift of Fear by Gavin deBecker
I disagree with deBecker on several points, but this is the best book on intuition based awareness I've ever seen.

Violence, Blunders, and Fractured Jaws by Marc MacYoung
Street Sociology 102 will keep you from getting your ass kicked due to ignorance. 'Nuff said.

Meditations on Violence by Rory Miller
Facing Violence by Rory Miller
Rory's texts are not for beginners. You need to have a solid foundation before you can fully grasp these concepts, but he presents the matter in a very accessible manner. These are formatted like college textbooks and even experts with a lifetime of experience can learn something from these. Rory is brilliant as well as a gifted teacher. These books are groundbreaking and important.

Those 6 books should be the foundation of your defensive tactics, whatever style of fighting you choose to specialize in. Everyone can learn something from them, no matter what their level of training or experience may be. You might also want to check out my prior book, *Hardcore Self-Defense*, which talks a great deal about improvised weapons and developing the combat mindset, although it is far more controversial even than this text and also contained a few minor errors. Including this one, that makes 8 books you need to study. With these 8 books, you will learn more about self defense in a month of reading than most black belts have learned after 10 years of martial arts, and that is no exaggeration. I shit you not.

F.T.W. COMMENTARY

Although I fully endorse each of the books listed above and have spoken with their authors, please do not assume that they endorse myself, my methods, my advice, or this book you are now reading. They do not, nor would I expect them to. Each of those authors, as well as numerous other individuals to whom I shall later be attributing selected quotes, are well respected instructors and scholars, whereas I am an anti-social asshole who tells people to go ahead and disregard unconstitutional laws and smack the shit out of people who truly deserve it. Please do not make the mistake of assuming that I am in any way affiliated with these instructors aside from my admiration of their work.

The Fundamentals Of Personal Protection

"Wizard, there is only one rule about violence. Do whatever you must to make it stop."

Megan Lindholm, *Wizard of the Pigeons* (p. 262)

I am going to try to keep this as simple and concise as possible. Many instructors seem to be of the opinion that in order to defend yourself you need to be in peak physical condition with lightning reflexes, train constantly, and be heavily armed at all times. This is bullshit. Most people are unable to spend hours exercising and training every day, and few citizens carry a full sized fighting knife and high caliber handgun everywhere they go. This just is not a realistic expectation.

As the United States Army Special Forces motto says: "*Your mind is your primary weapon.*" That is no lie. Mindset is mandatory. If you lack the proper mindset you will be unable to adequately defend yourself from imminent violent attack. I have seen big strong men fold up and whimper like little bitches when threatened with a knife. I have seen karate black belts try to call a "time out" after getting their nose smashed into a bloody pulp in a roadhouse parking lot. I have also seen a five foot tall 100 pound girl kick the shit out of a drunk 300 pound trucker. I have heard stories of big healthy guys keel over and die from a seemingly superficial wound, and other stories of small guys who were still on their feet pissed off and fighting after taking multiple bullets to the torso. This is the importance of mindset. You can do this. Don't be a pussy.

The five primary principles of the FTW system (in order to be a genuine instructor you need to call what you teach a "system") are as follows:

BE OBSERVANT
DON'T BE AN ASSHOLE
AVOID CONFLICT
BE PREPARED TO DO WHAT NEEDS DOING
USE A TOOL

And that is pretty much it. Let us begin.

BE OBSERVANT

> *"You always want to know what's going on around you. Always. When you're walking or driving, you're constantly scanning, right sidewalk to the left sidewalk, left sidewalk to the right sidewalk. You just look for something out of the ordinary. Something that doesn't look right. And the best way to do it is—if it catches your eye, if it makes you take a second look, look at it a third time. Satisfy your curiosity."*
>
> anonymous, from *What Cops Know*, by Connie Fletcher (p. 20)

Fuck. This seems like a very simple concept, but in reality it can be extremely complex. There are multiple levels of awareness (as with the Cooper Color Codes) as well as distinct layers of awareness, some of which can be taught, some which can be conditioned, some which can only be acquired after years of experience, and some which you probably need to be born with. A few things are so subtle you practically need to have psychic powers to pick up on them, whereas others are glaringly obvious to anyone who knows the basics of what to look for. Observation skills can range from basic to highly advanced. You cannot learn them from a book. Total immersion into the target culture and a lifetime's exposure to violence will demand that you not only develop but fine tune these skills, as they are necessary for survival.

Marc MacYoung preaches the mantra of Awareness to all who will listen. He has an excellent website called "No Nonsense Self Defense" and wrote a book called *Cheap Shots, Ambushes, and Other Lessons* as well as another called *Violence, Blunders, and Fractured Jaws,* which go well beyond anything anyone else has ever written on the subject. Gavin de Becker preaches the mantra of Intuition to women and corporate security managers, and his seminal text entitled *The Gift of Fear* is the best book ever written on that subject. These three books are ESSENTIAL. I cannot stress that enough. Combined, they will give you an intermediate level of understanding how to be more observant. It will take years of constant practice to develop these skills. It requires dedication and sharpness of mind. Alcohol, marijuana, prescription medication, low blood sugar, high stress, and various distractions will prevent you from being fully aware of what is going on around you. Focus.

When I talk about subtleties that require an almost psychic level of perception, that is not mystical mumbo jumbo bullshit like "spiritual discernment" (as it is frequently misunderstood by the delusional). Pattern recognition (deja vu, in which you remember seeing a situation go down exactly like this before and you think you know what is about to happen next) is one example of this. Microexpressions (as with poker "tells") are another. Then there is the olfactory gland which can detect certain hormones and toxins which, although the scent is too faint to consciously recognize it, is identified on a much deeper level. A much different level is that of the highly trained fighter who seems to be able to anticipate his opponent's every move—but that requires a lot of training and right now we're just discussing passive observation skills rather than the zenlike state of *Mushin* ("without mind", "flow"). I believe that *mushin* is an essential element of success in the martial arts, but it is clearly beyond the scope of this book. Read the *Hakakure, Book of Five Rings, Art of War,* and the *Tao Te Ching* in order to better understand the elementary concepts that will help you to develop this level of unconscious movement. Basically, it comes after calmly accepting your mortality and becoming aware that you can die at any moment . . . and being okay with that. It is an advanced skill, based more upon philosophy than training, but regular training is necessary to develop it properly.

Basic levels of observation are far easier to convey via the written word. Often it is like the little ditty they used to sing on Sesame Street, "*Which of these things is different from the others? Which of these things does not belong?*" You're sitting there, zoning out, scanning a crowd, when all of a sudden someone pings your radar. You sharp focus and suddenly alarms start going off. THAT motherfucker is out of place here. THAT motherfucker is clearly up to no good. But why would anyone think such a thing? Here are a few clues:

CLOTHING

As the old maxim goes, "*Clothes make the man.*" While this is certainly not true, one's choice of clothing is a clear indication of how that individual wishes to be perceived by others. This can give you some idea as to the content of their character, as well as provide indicators of socio-economic status and profession. Gang members and wannabe tough guys frequently adopt a very specific mode of dress. While obvious gang colors may not be displayed, that particular style of dress will be recognized by other gang members as well as law enforcement (for example, sports jerseys of particular teams and unusually long white T-shirts). Someone wearing predominantly black clothing may be indicating they are a violent Juggalo, or they could be a mentally ill creeper freak, or they could just be a harmless goth who works in some corporate IT department—you need to look for subtle indicators such as accessories (belts, jewelry, etc) and hairstyles to get a better idea of what subculture they might belong to. An individual wearing clean but ill-fitting or mismatched clothing (pantlegs rolled up into unusually large cuffs, inappropriate colors or logos) is probably homeless, as they are regularly given free clothes which seldom fits. Someone who seems utterly unconcerned with their appearance (as well as hygiene) might well be schizophrenic or addicted to hard drugs, particularly crack. By their very nature, both "tough guys" and crazy street people are always potentially dangerous. Their danger level increases quite a bit if they obviously seem to be representing, hunting, lurking, or looking for trouble. Conversely, an individual who appears predatory but is wearing an Under Armor T-shirt and a leather basketweave belt is probably off duty law enforcement or former military (or a well meaning wannabe/fanboy), which indicates they are less of a potential threat.

SHOES

A very important subcategory of clothing, especially when dealing with scam artists and con men. You see, anyone can get a nice suit or fancy but out of style clothes from the Goodwill or thrift store for a few bucks or even for free. Shoes are a different matter. Nice shoes usually are priced significantly more than clothes and it is difficult to find nice shoes in the right size that match your outfit—particularly if you are a guy, because guys tend to wear shoes until they fall apart. So, being approached by a smiling fellow in a nice clean suit who is wearing battered raggedy shoes is an indication that he really is not quite as successful or respectable as he wishes to appear. Certain types of athletic shoes may indicate gang affiliation, particularly if they appear brand new with aftermarket colored laces. Doc Martens or combat boots may indicate a propensity towards violent behavior, particularly if again you are seeing the aftermarket colored laces. Battered steel toed boots show you that this person may well shatter your shin if he were to kick you, and exposed steel would indicate someone who gets angry and kicks stuff a lot. Engineer or harness boots might indicate a biker, and pointy toed cowboy boots could indicate someone who will kick or stomp you in a fight.

Birkenstocks or flip flops usually denote a harmless hippie. Shoes are expensive and difficult to replace. Many people only own one or two pairs of shoes. Always glance at the shoes. They can tell you a lot.

BODY MODIFICATIONS

Back in the day, tattoos used to mean something. Every tattoo had a story, and only military, bikers, musicians, and convicts typically had them. Nowadays they have mainstreamed to the point that most college kids have at least one, and the quality of art has greatly improved. Inferior artwork or shoddy craftsmanship nowadays typically indicates either the tattoo was done prior to 1990 or the individual in question is a criminal. A young guy with a bunch of crude tattoos done all in black either had them done at a friend's house for free or had them done in prison. Shitty tattoos on someone under 30 usually indicates either a gang member or a drug addict or some other sort of social deviant. Anyone with a little self respect and a paycheck can get a nice tattoo. Pay attention primarily to lack of quality and lack of color as indicators of potential trouble. Tattoos on the neck and knuckles should be looked at extra closely. Tattoos of weapons or unusual numerical codes are a clear danger sign. There are hundreds of different tattoos which have specific meanings within certain groups—but you go across the country and that same tattoo will have a different meaning there. Some tattoos which once had specific meanings are now fairly generic, such as barbed wire and the Maltese cross. Piercings, on the other hand, have no distinct meaning, and many harmless and rather nice people have extreme facial piercings. Expensive diamond earrings on a man may indicate rank in a criminal gang, or it may indicate he is gay—you need to look at a number of other aspects of his appearance before taking everything under consideration.

GAIT AND GESTICULATIONS

How people walk will tell you a lot about them. Some people seem hunched over, looking at the ground in front of them, taking small steps and keeping their arms close by their sides as if to take up as little space as possible. If they are plugged into an iPod they would make the perfect victim. Others are loud and boisterous both in their speech and in the way they swagger down the sidewalk, swaying side to side and swinging their arms around as if to proclaim that all the space within an arm's length (and everything therein) belongs to them. Then you get the punks who swagger in a challenging manner, and the pissed off tough guys who stomp around with clenched fists as if they're looking for any possible reason to punch some random passerby in the face. Finally, you get the distinctive staggers of individuals who are slightly drunk, quite drunk, shitfaced drunk, on various types of psychopharmaceutical (anti-depressants, anti-anxiety, anti-psychotic), fried on weed, tweaked on meth, cracked out of their mind, experiencing schizophrenic hallucinations, or having a psychotic episode. Different substances make users act in distinctive manners, and an experienced observer can look at some stranger walking down the street and tell you exactly what they are under the influence of, and this does include specific prescription pills as well as street drugs. Running is always a red flag, but is the guy running at you or past you? 90% of the time you see someone running they are either trying to get somewhere quickly or get away from somewhere quickly with no interest in bothering you . . . but that 10% exception you need to deal with decisively and brutally. Some people might be dressed like an outlaw biker or a goth or a death rocker or whatever subculture frightens citizens, but they present as level headed and squared away. Those people usually are not the problem. The guy in a 3 piece suit and expensive shoes who is grinding his teeth and twitching would be the one you ought to be keeping an eye on instead. Clothes are what you choose to wear or what circumstances dictate you wear, but the way you walk and move is a lot harder to fake.

FACIAL EXPRESSION

Most nonverbal communication is expressed via facial expressions. Some of these messages are quite clear, others can be extremely subtle, and a skilled manipulator will be able to fake emotions such as empathy or humility through false expressions. What some therapists and interrogators look for is something referred to as a "micro expression," where, in a fleeting unguarded moment, a deceitful person's true feelings are revealed. Facial expressions are usually unconscious manifestations of emotion and it takes incredible self control to hide or fake them, and such a ruse can seldom be sustained for any length of time and mistakes are frequently made. Salesmen, lawyers, investigators, and other con men are experts at this black art, but if you realize what they are doing it is easy to see through their act. Muggers act in a similar manner, feigning harmlessness as they approach, but they lack the skill of the salesman and something always gives them away. A few books or videos on non verbal communication will only convey the very basics, and this is a skill that will take years to cultivate so that it is accurate and reliable.

EYE CONTACT

Eye contact is one of the primary modes of non-verbal communication. Averted eye contact can indicate respect or submission, lingering eye contact can indicate strong interest, sustained eye contact can indicate dominance or a threat of violence. Wide eyes can indicate surprise or agitation, hooded eyes can indicate calmness or coldness, narrowed eyes can indicate irritation or anger. A stare is different from a glare, which is different from a gaze, which is different from someone who is unfocused and zoned out. If you are sensitive to these things, you can tell a LOT about an individual simply by glancing at their eyes for a moment. Be very aware of individuals behaving suspiciously who are wearing sunglasses which completely conceal their eyes, such as darkly tinted wraparounds or reflective mirrorshades, as not only can they hide emotions, but they also hide what or whom they are staring at, as well as evidence of drug use, illness, or psychosis. Seek out books on non-verbal communication to learn more about this complex topic, as a great deal has been written which is well beyond the scope of this book.

DISTANCE

In polite society, strangers are expected to keep a respectable distance between one another. Normal civilized people have respect for the unstated boundaries of others. Being forced together in a crowd is one thing, but when you are sitting on a long empty bench and someone decides to sit right next to you rather than a respectable distance away, that is a clear invasion of your personal space. You see street people and panhandlers closing the distance with people quite often. This is a test to see the limits of what they can get away with. You can be standing in the middle of an empty parking lot, and some fucking homeless will just have to pass within 6 inches of you, on your blindside, as he walks across it—that is just what they do, so don't flip out over it and commit a felony by faceplanting him into the asphalt, as 95% of them are relatively harmless. If someone wants a dollar or a cigarette, there is no need for them to approach within an arm's length of you, but they frequently edge closer and closer until they are practically nose to nose with you . . . and then they will start touching you, tentatively at first, maybe touching your jacket or briefly putting their hand on your shoulder . . . soon they will insist on shaking your hand or putting their arm around you or hugging you. If this progresses much farther they'll practically be fucking you up the ass. Rule #1 when dealing with street people is always: "*Don't Touch Me.*" They break Rule #1, that is a violation, a display of dominance, and a huge disrespect which street culture demands be reacted to immediately with extreme violence. Passively allowing a street person to repeatedly and intimately place his hands upon your person displays very clearly that you are a chump, a sucker, and a victim to whom he can get away with doing damn near anything he wants because you are a punk who ain't gonna do shit. Simple remedy to this is to tell them, straight up, to "Back the fuck off" before they inadvertently violate Rule #1 which mandates a hurtful physical correction. They may accuse you of being "rude", "racist", or even "scared", but you are doing it for their own good. You need to let them know immediately that closing the distance is unacceptable, either through words or through extending your own hand and touching *them*. That is a fundamental self defense technique which is seldom addressed. But as far as "observation" goes, you see someone closing the distance on others you just pinged him as a potential bad guy . . . or someone who is flirting a bit too aggressively.

ABILITY

Simply stated, is this individual a viable threat who clearly is capable of inflicting severe bodily harm upon your person with his bare hands, or is he a "walking wounded" with mobility issues or impaired health? A sick old man or frail person in a wheelchair does have the capability to harm you, but not nearly on the same level as a street thug. And an emaciated crackhead is dangerous, but less so than a steroid abusing gang member. Anyone can be a potential threat under the wrong circumstances, but the seriousness of that threat increases based upon: vitality, speed, musculature, and mass. Disability, injury, or illness reduces the potential threat level. Never underestimate a threat simply because of age, frailty, or disability. When a weak person strikes it is usually without warning, viciously, and with a weapon. Ability is just another factor you need to take under consideration.

HARDNESS

This one is not going to be easy to convey via the written word at all, so I'm not going to waste much time with this. Let us say that there are distinct levels of predation amongst street people, and when an apex predator arrives on the scene, the lightweights tend to cower or scatter. For want of a better term, the higher up the food chain you are, the "harder" you appear to others. This is clearly evident in the eyes, but more subtle signs frequently include: above average muscle tone, physical tension, confident posture, and a squared away appearance. Simply stated, these individuals seem to radiate malice and everyone on the street can feel the bad vibes. Most of them have spent years in prison. Many have multiple convictions for crimes of violence. Some have killed. There are many levels to this. A man who sleeps on the streets and eats out of dumpsters will be harder than the average homeless who lines up obediently for a hot meal and a cot every day; but he will probably not be as hard as the cold eyed crack dealer on the corner with an unlicensed pistol under his oversized T-shirt; and that guy will certainly not be as hard as the convict who was recently released from a maximum security facility after serving his full sentence for armed robbery. A truly hard man is serious and deadly. Fortunately, most of the guys committing petty crimes and strong arm muggings are punks and wannabes just a rung or two up from the addicts and scavengers. Your opponent's level of hardness will provide a clue how best to deal with him. The lesser the threat, the better they tend to respond to warnings. Greater threats require harsher warnings, up to presentation of a drawn weapon. If a hard threat has you on his radar and is closing the distance, sometimes the only thing you can do to prevent being scraped off the asphalt by EMS is to doubletap him in the chest without warning. Fortunately, unless you are a convenience store cashier, taxi driver, or drug dealer, you are unlikely to be confronted with this level of threat, and some familiarity with the signs of what to look for will enable you to recognize one of these guys so you can avoid him before he gets close enough to have an opportunity to hurt you.

CLIPS, BULGES, AND PRINTS

Nowadays, everybody seems to carry a knife. Usually these knives are just a tool for chores, in which case it will likely be in a leather pouch sheath on their belt or buried in their pocket. Guys who choose to carry knives as weapons often prefer to clip them to their front pants pocket. Sometimes these clips are flashy, shiny eye magnets, quite obviously intended to warn potential predators: "Lookit me, I got a knife!" without their even needing to draw it. More often, these clips are somewhat discrete, often thin and dull or blackened. If the other guy has a knife clipped to his front pocket, he is likely to draw it if threatened, angered, or possibly even annoyed. A verbal altercation that leads to a shove frequently ends in a stabbing nowadays. If you see a pocket clip, assume it is a knife, and expect it to be pulled and used against you should you end up fighting that person.

A lot of bad guys carry handguns. So do a lot of not so bad guys, good guys, and not so good guys. But some of the most dangerous armed individuals are not so much the bad guys (who are often somewhat professional in that they loosely adhere to vaguely defined rules of engagement), but the wannabe bad guys who carry a gun out of insecurity, adhere to no such rules, and feel a sometimes overpowering urge to impress others with their imagined badassitude. Disturbingly, you also need to worry about certain wannabe good guys, who similarly carry a gun out of insecurity, lack a proper understanding of the rules, and secretly long to point their gun at a vaguely defined bad guy. The scary thing is, both wannabe bad and good guys are frequently delusional and impulsive. This makes them more likely to pull their gun inappropriately with minimal provocation and fire it into a crowd or into another vehicle. So if you see the outline of a pistol clearly printing against someone's shirt, and that guy looks especially stupid or unusually pissed off, it is probably a real good idea to get the fuck out of there immediately, and try not to walk anywhere in their vicinity as you do so. It is unlikely that they are about to commit a robbery or go on a shooting spree, but stupid people in public places with loaded guns is always a bad combination. Avoid situations like that whenever possible.

WATCH THE HANDS!

Hands reach for, draw, and use weapons . . . unless the weapon is already in their hand. Where are his hands? Can you see both of them? Are they in his pockets, behind his back, or next to his leg with his body turned away from you? Okay, you see his hands, but are they empty? Are you sure? If the fingers are cupped or curled and you cannot see the palms he could be holding a weapon out of sight. This can be anything from a fixed blade to a derringer with other possibilities in between. If you cannot see his hands, especially if it seems as though they are being deliberately concealed, that is a high priority danger sign. Be very aware of their hands.

WORK RELATED GEAR

This is known as a mitigating circumstance. Sometimes I'm out in a parking lot and I see some scary looking pissed off guy with tattoos and I think, "*Fuck, that looks like a bad guy,*" but then I notice he has some work related gear on his belt or a patch on his shirt that indicates he is gainfully employed and I relax a bit. In many cases his shirt may identify him as an employee of the one of the stores adjacent to said parking lot. Let that be a lesson to you that not everyone who looks like a bad guy is a scumbag who does not work an honest job. And they have a right to be pissed off about it sometimes, because that is the nature of having a shitty job that requires you to punch a timeclock and labor on your feet all day for minimum wage while being verbally disrespected by some pudgy suit with soft little hands . . . but I digress. If the bad guy who dings your radar appears to be gainfully employed, that does not mean you can overlook him, it just means he gets a point in his favor making him less of a scumbag, which means he is probably more okay than another guy who looks and acts exactly like him but is NOT gainfully employed (quite possibly by choice, since every gangsta know dat work be fo' suckas). Sometimes you may see a scary looking guy with a goatee and long hair who has a pistol under his shirt. If that pistol is a quality brand in a decent holster and he is wearing a heavy duty doublestitched belt, he is probably a cop of some sort. This will be reinforced if he appears alert, sober, and is wearing new clothes and nice shoes. Subtle indicators like these can help put you at ease and prevent you from misidentifying someone as a threat and possibly making a serious mistake.

In conclusion, threat assessment is an art rather than a science, and you will only have seconds to process this data. It is an acquired skill that takes years to develop and you will make mistakes along the way. I am extremely good at this and my abilities far exceed those of most "experts" at threat assessment, but I am only about 90% accurate, which means 10% of the time I misread something which leads to a misinterpretation, so it is not a perfect science at all. Again, this is a very basic introduction to profiling through the interpretation of attire and mannerisms. Read MacYoung's and de Becker's books for more data.

DON'T BE AN ASSHOLE

> *"I won't be insulted, I won't be laid a hand on. I don't do these things to other people, and I require the same from them."*
>
> John Wayne, as "J. B. Books" from *The Shootist*

> "*Rudeness is a weak man's imitation of strength.*"
>
> Eric Hoffer, *The True Believer*

Holy fucking shit, I should not even need to be telling you this, but fuck—*citizens are frequently disrespectful to one another.* The worst offenders are privileged middle class norms who have been sheltered from violence their entire lives and learned how to interact with others from listening to public school teachers and watching popular television sitcoms. They do very well in certain isolated habitats, such as: corporate offices, government offices, educational facilities, hospitals, and large retail stores. These places are staffed with like-minded automatons who exist in an alternate reality. Such individuals enjoy playing games like "Let's pick on the weirdo" or "Let's offend others with unsolicited advice on personal matters." Then you have the privileged middle class jocks who played sports in high school, participated in a fraternity at college, and are accustomed to getting their way by intimidating others through yelling and making threats of violence, or having fun by bullying smaller individuals for entertainment. These two types of cretin, combined with similar types such as meddlesome do-gooders or self righteous hipsters, make up a significant portion of our population, by which I'm estimating about 25% . . . all of whom should probably be gassed for the greater good. These people have gotten away with, and been rewarded for, bad behavior all of their lives, because in their sheltered habitat it works quite nicely, in fact it is the established norm which is upheld through a number of unwritten and unstated rules. But the thing is, different places have different rules. Try pulling that shit in a low income community at the pub or even the supermarket where you are outnumbered by folks who will react to a snide comment with a punch to the face.

One thing I have noticed so many times it is an established pattern, is that in places where weapons are so restricted it is rare for anyone other than an off-duty policeman to have a concealed handgun, people tend to be a lot more rude if not outright aggressive towards total strangers. This does not just apply to predatory criminals but to everyone in the community. In weapon free zones, societal evolution reverts to the point that rudeness becomes a cultural norm and anyone who is frustrated or upset feels free to yell horrible insults at others—particularly if it is from the safety of their car or if they are surrounded by witnesses. Punks and bullies are greatly emboldened and feel free to approach, surround, shove, or even strike strangers as they also speak rudely to them, often roving in packs. Predatory criminals have a target rich environment and feel virtually invulnerable. Be aware that disarmed societies are a lot more rude and have much greater tolerance for casual rudeness—especially if you are moving from one of these places to, say, the South, where what might be considered polite banter in NYC will get you shot. When you cross borders the rules change.

If you are disrespectful to others, some people—even uninvolved people—can get very angry about this. How angry they become depends not only upon the nature and severity of your transgression, but upon how many societal lines you have crossed. This is a rather complex sociological concept, but the greater your degree of separation, demographically, the more incensed that person will become by your criticism. These degrees of separation can be the result of differences in: age, gender, race, religion, nationality, economic status, social class, disability, deviancy, or subculture. If the person you insult is from the exact same demographic as yourself, they will usually be more tolerant of your behavior since they are more likely to understand it and likely engage in it themselves. If the person you insult is of a different gender, sexual preference, or level of physical ability, it is likely you may be violating a societal taboo, which may make them feel self-righteous and turn uninvolved witnesses into allies willing to defend them. If the person you insult is of a different age, race, and economic class, you are insulting someone of a different culture and although your intentions may be innocent they will feel wronged, especially if there is any pre-existing tension or antipathy in that community between people who are different from one another, in which case a snide comment or unsolicited advice may be seen as a personal attack which they need to respond to via dramatic yelling or physical violence. So be extra careful when speaking with strangers who are different from you, especially if you are engaged in a verbal altercation with them, as it can escalate far more rapidly than anticipated.

Some people's immediate response to an insult will be violent. Some people will actually kill a stranger over an insult, or even a disrespectful stare. This does not just apply to inner city gangbangers. A lot of rural rednecks react in this manner as well. In fact, anyone under an overwhelming amount of stress can succumb to a temporary psychotic break. A few common things that can induce high levels of stress are financial trouble, relationship trouble, or employment trouble. If someone just spent their savings on a major car repair, got fired from work, and had their girlfriend dump them, well, they will be a tad unstable emotionally. If you do or say something which they find offensive, all that undirected rage and self hate they have bottled up inside will suddenly be directed at you. Their reaction will likely be disproportionate to the offence and you may die. Such stress is the primary underlying cause of most road rage incidents and barroom brawls—basically, one guy is so pissed off he is unconsciously looking for a fight and will use any excuse to start one. If no-one gives them that excuse, they may try to provoke you into giving them the "justification" they need to hurt you. I have seen this occur many times.

Don't. Be. An. Asshole. D.B.A.A. You might be surprised how many times you, yourself, may have violated this basic self defense rule. Let me give you a few common examples:

- Improper use of the horn in traffic
- Offensive or aggressive gestures in traffic

- Yelling insults at other drivers or pedestrians from your vehicle
- Driving aggressively (speeding, weaving, blocking, tailgaiting, brake checking)
- Complaining about the person ahead of you in line at the store
- Cutting in line
- Demanding that others "follow the rules" when you are unaffected by their actions
- Trespassing on someone's property
- Touching something that belongs to someone else
- Touching someone else
- Bumping someone in a crowd and failing to say "excuse me"
- Criticizing someone's appearance
- Making unfounded accusations based upon suspicion or prejudice
- Offering unsolicited advice on matters which are none of your business
- Making a joke at someone else's expense
- Mocking, snubbing, or dismissing others through tone or gesture
- Expecting that others submit to your demands
- Raising your voice or waving your arms in an aggressive manner
- Glaring, clenching fists, or looming in a menacing manner

Have you committed any of these infractions over the course of the last month? Be honest with yourself.

Somewhat related to this topic is the righteous indignation one experiences when someone thoughtlessly or willfully infringes on their rights in some way. A few common examples of this might include:

* Someone talking on their cellphone during a movie
* Someone bumping into your parked car while parallel parking
* Someone allowing their dog to crap on your lawn and not picking it up
* Someone cutting across your lawn
* Someone playing loud music late on a weeknight
* Someone handling an item on your property that is of minor value

These are clearly all infringements which an assertive individual would be well within their rights to loudly protest—after all, they are clearly right and the other person is clearly wrong. In many cases, such as blatant and willful repeat offenses, it will indeed be necessary to do something about it (I shall leave the nature of that "something" up to you). However, if it is an isolated event involving a stranger, you need to ask yourself if it is really worth the trouble should it escalate? Are you willing to pay the price for yelling at some unknown individual about whom you likely know very little? It is highly unlikely that you will actually cure them of their selfish behaviors, and it is likely you may never see them again. In many cases you are not trying to fix a problem, you are trying to gain smug satisfaction by putting that bastard in his place. Be honest with yourself. How do I deal with such events? It depends on numerous factors. Low blood sugar and lack of caffeine could make things get ugly very quickly. If, however, I'm in a somewhat pleasant mood and the offense in question is not terribly egregious, I am willing to overlook it in the common interest of maintaining tranquility. Fuck me again and we may be having words. It is very important what words you choose and what tone and volume is used, especially if dealing with a neighbor. Neighbors can be a pain in the ass and there is no easy or pleasant way of dealing with a bad one aside from putting him in the trunk of your car or moving to another location. Be especially diplomatic and courteous with neighbors. It is better to be on good terms with a bad neighbor than have him as an enemy nursing a grudge.

Pick your battles wisely and do not engage in unnecessary conflict. Sometimes it is necessary to be assertive with someone who is doing something which infringes on your rights or endangers your safety, but if it is only a minor inconvenience is it really that necessary for you to initiate a verbal altercation over it? I mean, if some stranger carelessly does something which annoys you or makes you need to wait for a few more minutes, is it really worth risking a fight over? Seriously, many fights between strangers occur after one demands that the other do or stop doing something, and the other fails to submit to this demand and responds with aggression. If it barely affects you and will be over soon it is probably not worth arguing about. Sometimes something as minor as politely knocking on someone's door can provoke them into killing you. Ever deal with someone who is tweaked out of their mind on meth? Total irrational rage fully directed at you for no discernable reason. Ever deal with a mean drunk who's been drinking whiskey all day? Not only will they hurt you, but they'll try to draw things out and make a game out of it. Ever deal with a passive aggressive sociopath? You will become their new hobby and they will devote hours of their free time every week to making your life a living hell. Even if they are somewhat normal and harmless you can still risk making an enemy who may harbor a grudge for years. Don't start shit with people unless you truly have no other choice. You are seldom obligated to correct the behaviors of others and it is a dangerous habit to get into. Excessive indignation will make you an asshole.

Excessive indignation is outrage, where righteousness becomes "self-righteousness," or as it is often called, "being a fucking do-gooder." Do-gooders feel compelled to mind everyone else's business and act like overgrown classroom monitors, calling 911 to complain about minor violations of the rules which they often reinterpret at their whim. They will get angry because they don't like your music, they don't like your car, they don't like your dog, they don't like your kids, they don't like your tacky lawn decorations, or whatever. They have a pathological compulsion to demand that others "obey the rules" as if they have been bestowed with some sort of official authority to enforce them. One writer has referred to such individuals as "mini sheriffs" and that is an apt description. I prefer the term "fucking do-gooder." Years ago there was an asshole in our neighborhood who would drive around yelling at people walking their dogs to demand they produce a poop bag or pooper scooper for his inspection, and since he had a thick German accent we called him the "Nazi Dogshit Patrol." Don't be like that guy. No-one likes that guy. Some folks will feel compelled to do something to that guy . . . he certainly seems to deserve it. Never assert false authority. You are too old to be a classroom monitor.

But, perhaps by far, the most common asshole related violation is *failure to mind your own business.* Seriously, if something does not concern you, whether it be a conversation, an argument, or someone hollering about something that appears to be insignificant, LEAVE IT THE FUCK ALONE. If it does not concern you, you have no business getting involved—and if you choose to do so, folks tend to get highly inflamed extremely quickly by a stranger's unsolicited and unwanted intrusion into their personal business. This especially applies if you see a man and woman arguing. If, as stated previously, there are multiple degrees of separation between your and their demographic, that constitutes a severe societal taboo that pretty much gives them "justification" to kill you where you stand without warning. This is one of the few situations where a stranger may immediately attempt to murder you simply for running your mouth . . . and you may even deserve it. I understand that all honorable men are rightfully revulsed by the thought of a man hitting a woman, but if it is her husband and they are of a different race and socio-economic background from you, and you have no lawful authority to intervene, as long as it is nothing more than shoving and slapping you just pass that bullshit by. It is not your job to save the world. The same thing may apply if you see a man being beaten. Do you know all the facts? Is it clearly obvious to you who the bad guy is? If the victim and attacker(s) are of the same culture and demographic it may be a complex issue. Sometimes it is obvious that an innocent man is being ratpacked by street punks, and if you want to step in and be a hero that's up to you, but, quite often, the guy getting the beat down did something to deserve it. It is possible he initiated the attack. It is possible he is being punished for theft or a sex crime. In some cases he may have even been a mugger who picked on the wrong guy. If you do feel compelled to get involved, state loudly and clearly, "Why are you beating that man?" If it is an educational or punitive beatdown they may even tell you. 50/50 chance you will be insulted or threatened, regardless of if it is justified. Again, if you try to save the world it usually is unappreciated, and in many cases even the victim will turn against you. You need to overcome the knee jerk reflex to stop violence wherever you see it unless you are lawfully obligated to do so. The courts do not treat vigilantism lightly, even if you are trying to be a "good Samaritan." If you use force against another person, regardless of the circumstances, expect to be charged with a crime.

Not being an asshole is a fundamental self defense tactic. It can be difficult for some people to learn this. I occasionally find myself relapsing into asshole mode if I am under stress and my blood sugar is low. Stay calm, cool, and collected. Keep your emotions in check. Try not to transgress against others and do your best to overlook minor transgressions upon yourself. This simple rule will keep you out of LOTS of trouble. Unfortunately, it took me nearly 40 years to master this basic technique and I am still learning. It takes dedication and practice. I even made a D.B.A.A. patch for my bike vest as a constant reminder to practice this essential technique. Don't be an asshole!

CONFLICT AVOIDANCE

> *"WAKE THE FUCK UP, PAL! Avoiding the fight is a goddamn technique, and not just a self-defense technique, either. It is an absolutely essential survival technique . . . . There are a lot of people in prison, and*

a lot more in graveyards, because a barroom brawl or streetfight got 'out of hand.' I don't think those people in prison wanted to go there, and I don't think those people in the graveyard wanted to die. They went to prison or were killed because they did not think beyond some machismo bullshit they were sold at some point in their lives."

Peyton Quinn, *A Bouncer's Guide to Barroom Brawling*

"To stand silent and aware while the suspect is taunting, insulting, and otherwise trying to distract you gives you a distinct advantage. You can read the person's body language and sense his energy if you don't focus on the abusive and derogatory behavior. It doesn't distract you from what the suspect is actually doing. This allows you to respond quicker and use less force to control him should he become violent. Often it permits you to deal with the situation without resorting to physical means at all."

Kerr Cuhulain, *Full Contact Magick* (p. 81)

I have a very loose and casual peripheral relationship with a network of extremely professional and highly skilled "experts" on personal protection. These guys are considered by thousands to be authorities on the subject matter—the "elite", if you will. Some of these guys have personal body counts in the dozens, and they know over a thousand ways to hurt people and break things. When it comes to self defense techniques for the real (civilian) world they all agree on one thing: your primary focus must be on conflict avoidance. I have also associated, in my checkered past, with a few individuals on the other side of the law who were professional killers, guys who the toughest badasses on the street knew to avoid messing with because they would die if they did. These guys told me the same thing: avoid stupid people, doing stupid things, in stupid places. If you aren't there to be targeted, you are safe . . . just don't do like one comedian did when challenged to a fight at the pub and say, "I'll meet you in the alley in 5 minutes . . . and if I'm not there, start without me," because that's not what I mean by not being there. He should not have been at that particular pub in the first place. I am not by any means advising you never to go out to have fun. There are many places you can go to have fun, some of which are less than reputable—strip clubs, for example. If you and your buddies want to have a night out at the tittie bar, perhaps it would be in your best interest to go to the upscale one with a well lit parking lot, uniformed doormen, clean bathrooms, well mixed drinks, and pretty girls. A bad tittie bar (yes, they exist) will be grimy and dimly lit with ugly girls and watered down drinks—they also are filled with petty criminals who may want to scam, rob, or beat you. Be advised that these criminals often include the bartender, doormen, and even the girls themselves (a "clip joint" is an example of this). Any bar is problematic after midnight, and often punks and predators lurk in the parking lot looking for someone who appears too drunk to drive, whereupon they will take away their keys—and their wallet, cellphone, watch, etc.—then they will beat him into a coma and drive off in his car. Drunks are easy targets, and every Friday and Saturday night many people get robbed coming home from the pub. You can avoid this by staying sober and being with a group of friends, or you could just leave the pub well before closing time.

If you see a scary guy acting weird, don't eyefuck him. That is a challenge and it will not go unnoticed. If you see a scary weirdo, AVOID HIM . . . unless for some reason that is a non-option, in which case you need to shift to "Condition Orange", which, in Cooper's Color Code is referred to as "specific alert," or as he clarified in Vol 13 #7 of his Commentaries, "In Orange you have determined upon a specific adversary and are prepared to take action which may result in his death, but you are not in a lethal mode."

If you are forced to interact with the scary weirdo, most self defense instructors advise their students to avoid eye contact, speak softly, make slow "patting" motions with your hands, and generally present as passive and submissive. I, on the other hand, look directly into their eyes and maintain eye contact until they either look away or attack (which seldom occurs). I generally do this with absolutely no expression on my face and either do not respond to their attempts to engage me in conversation or reply with monosyllabic answers. As Andrew Vachss would say, "*Look down or look hard.*"

Some instructors want you to acquiesce to minor requests or petulant demands made by these individuals in hopes that they will be satisfied and leave you alone. This sometimes works, but frequently you are being "tested" to see how far they can push you and how much they can get away with, and their demands will quickly become increasingly unreasonable and shrill, which is intended to take you off guard and make you freeze like a deer in the headlights, whereupon you will be attacked. Your answer to these requests, whether it be for a dollar, a cigarette, a ride in your car, an opportunity to shake your hand, or even the time should always be “No.” Be firm, yet polite, and never take your eyes off him or turn your back. No stranger who demands things from you on the street should ever be rewarded for that. The guys I give money to don’t ask for it. Asking me for money will get you an automatic “No”, especially if they’re intruding into my personal space.

“De-escalation” is not something you attempt on street people who approach and start interviewing you. They do not get that courtesy because they are not entitled to it. De-escalation is typically used in social situations where a misunderstanding gets out of hand and someone feels they “need” to fight you in order to save face because you, or someone with you, apparently “disrespected” them in some small way. In this case, it is often best to give them the benefit of a doubt and assume they may have taken offense through a legitimate misunderstanding combined with stupidity and alcohol. Sometimes a simple apology is all that is required to make the tension dissolve. Or, you could just leave, ignoring the woofing and insults he is shouting at your back. This is the intelligent and responsible thing for you to do. Myself, I think of what some of my biker friends like to say, "*You come to us with respect, you'll be treated with respect. You act like an asshole, you'll be treated like an asshole.*" Someone really needs to cross some serious lines before I’ll start yelling threats at them in a public place, and since I don’t make a practice of infringing upon the rights of others or acting like an obnoxious jerk, you sure as fuck better not start yelling threats at me. But I am usually rather taciturn and solemn when I am out, so if someone starts shit with me I know I'm not the one at fault. If, however, you are intoxicated, loud, clumsy, and sloppy, he might well have valid cause for offense and you might not have even realized you spilled his drink and stepped on his girlfriend's foot. You apologize for things like that and buy them fresh drinks and stop acting annoying.

Another form of de-escalation is when someone is rapidly spiraling out of control and it appears they are about to do something regrettable with severe consequences. Sometimes you may feel compelled to talk them down from this and snap them back to reality. This requires solid negotiator skills which you may not have. I am a very diplomatic individual and can frequently look at a situation as would a detached observer and calmly comment upon what the potential consequences of escalating the situation might entail. In well over a dozen instances I was able to prevent someone from committing homicide simply by offering understanding and a kind word which they needed at that time. It could've very easily gone the other way. Think of what might have happened if I was not there to intervene, but instead some jerk who was saying things like, "You ain't got the balls," or, "Do it, faggot." When someone is violently unstable—and that can happen to just about anyone under times of extreme stress—they are very susceptible to external influences. It is up to you to decide whether you want to defuse that IED (Intermittent Explosive Disorder) or detonate it, which can often be accomplished through positive or negative comments directed at him.

Words, tone, volume, cadence, gestures, and body language can all be used in combination to either decrease or increase the stress level of others. I used to have an unfortunate tendency to begin conversations with, "Hey, Fuckhead" when I was annoyed or upset. If they shouted something derogatory back, I would up the ante by shouting some sort of creatively bizarre insult or threat—which would either result in terror induced brainlock or uncontrollable rage. I seem to develop a form of situational Tourette Syndrome in rush hour traffic which compels me to impulsively shout horrible things at other motorists—hurtful, hateful words of which I am sometimes later greatly ashamed. After all, he probably is not a retarded cocksucker who fucks his mother, and it is not his fault he is a googly eyed, baldheaded cuntface. I really should feel more compassion towards handicapable minorities driving shitmobiles held together with duct tape. Sometimes I wish I was nicer. I would probably get shot at less.

Conflict avoidance can be a very complex subject if we were to analyze and dissect dozens of potential scenarios, which is well beyond the scope of this book. Instead, I am going to leave you with this classic bit of advice put forth by Peyton Quinn and since repeated by hundreds of others:

Don't deny it's happening
Don't insult them
Don't challenge them
Don't threaten them
Give them a face saving exit

If you can adhere to those 5 simple rules, I guarantee you will be able to walk away from 90% of all confrontations without having them needlessly escalate to physical altercations, which as we all know can further escalate to situations involving hospital and court. It has been estimated that out of a hundred potential situations, 80% can be avoided entirely simply through awareness, 19% you can talk your way out of one way or another, and only 1% of the time is the fight truly unavoidable. Avoiding pushing the other guy's buttons by insisting upon one upping him and getting in the last word. Not only does this prolong your contact with him, but it may compel him to attack you. Ignoring him can embolden and enrage him, also leading to an attack which will likely come from the blindside as you have rudely dismissed him. Just walk away from it. Usually it really is that simple.

BE PREPARED TO DO WHAT NEEDS DOING

> *"The Way of the Samurai is found in death. When it comes to either/or, there is only the quick choice of death. It is not particularly difficult. Be determined and advance . . . . (if) one is able to live as though his body were already dead, he gains freedom in the Way."*
>
> Yamamoto Tsunetomo, *Hagakure* (Wilson translation)

> *"If you go into the fight resolved to destroy your opponent no matter what the cost—if you go into battle truly committed to die for the opportunity to kill your enemy—his spirit will read it in your eyes and he will be crushed."*
>
> Forrest E. Morgan, *Living the Martial Way*

> *"Commit yourself violently and totally. Attack to destroy. Never fight anybody on equal terms."*
>
> Lt.Col. Anthony B. Herbert, *The Soldier's Handbook*

If you are involved in a confrontation with another individual, which escalates to a verbal altercation, which becomes hands on, there are significant risks involved with engaging in that activity:

- You could be injured
- You could be maimed or crippled or blinded
- You could be killed
- You could face criminal charges for injuring the other individual
- You could be sued in civil court for medical expenses or other damages
- You could be vilified in the press
- You could be alienated and shunned by coworkers and neighbors
- You could be fired from your job
- The other individual, or his family or friends, might seek revenge
- You could lose your right to own a firearm or engage in certain professions
- You could be incarcerated for months, years, or decades

These are all very realistic possible outcomes to engaging in a streetfight. This is not some hypothetical "what if" that you can just skim past, thinking, "Yeah, whatever, let me get to the good part where I learn to fuck people up." THIS

IS NOT A FUCKING GAME! If you get in a fight—a *real* fight, not some bullshit schoolyard shoving match that escalates to a slapfight before being broken up by others—I guarantee that at the very minimum you will risk arrest and prosecution, even if it was clearly self defense. See, criminals lie and snitch. You punch them in the face a few times and walk away thinking it is over, and they call 911 and report that you just attacked them "for no reason." If they really want to get you in trouble they may accuse you of a hate crime, accuse you of robbing them, or claim that you threatened them with a knife or gun (bonus points to their credibility if when police search you they actually find a knife or gun, even if it does not match the description). Or, they could call all their friends instead, telling *them* that you victimized him for no reason. I am familiar with many such cases. Usually less than a dozen friends are backing him up, but in a few cases that received nationwide media attention over a hundred individuals showed up and a riot ensued because they texted everyone in their contacts or posted on a social networking site, and these individuals forwarded it to everyone in their contacts, who apparently did the same. A veritable flash mob beatdown, if you will. There is always a risk, even if you did nothing wrong and no-one was seriously injured.

My Da taught me never to raise my hands to another man unless I intended to kill him. AVOID FIGHTING. Any use of force, however minor, can escalate rapidly. You need to be prepared for the consequences of your actions. Now, if you are over 6 feet tall and 250 pounds you are probably a fairly strong individual who is accustomed to others being intimidated by your size. You may think that you can just grab someone, lift them up and give them a little shake, and they will stop doing whatever it was you did not want them to do. That may work fine for you at the sports bar on a drunk yuppie in a polo shirt. Try that at a blue collar establishment and you're likely to get slit from asshole to eyeball before you have a chance to say "what the fuck?" Different cultures play by different rules, and what is considered harmless fun in one place is a killing offense in another. I should not have to be explaining this shit to you, but some people are so stupid they really think they have all the answers, and that their particular worldview is shared by every other person in what they consider "reality." Indeed, that may well be the dominant paradigm upon which our society's jurisprudence system is based, but it is not "reality." It is a bubble of false reality formed by sitcoms based loosely upon 1950s standards. That picture of reality is not shared by many others outside of the White Christian middle-class demographic. Many people outside your demographic will physically attack you over a disrespectful insult and will shank you in the belly over a little grabass. Here are a few more pertinent quotes from smarter folk than I:

> *"Being assertive will avoid problems; being aggressive will bring them on. The danger of using verbal aggression is that, while it works under normal circumstances, it can lull you into assuming that it will work in all situations."*
>
> Marc MacYoung and Chris Pfouts, *Safe in the City* (p. 281)

> *"ANYTIME YOU STEP INTO THE ARENA OF PHYSICAL VIOLENCE, YOU HAVE TO ACCEPT THAT IT MAY NOT END UNTIL*

> *EITHER YOU OR YOUR OPPONENT, MAYBE BOTH, ARE DEAD. I don't care if it's just a warning slap to someone—it can escalate! Anytime you are tempted to resort to violence, this is the bottom line: if you ain't ready to die for it or kill for it, don't do it."*
>
> Marc MacYoung, *A Professional's Guide to Ending Violence Quickly* (p. 13)

> *"Take some time right now and think. What do you want to achieve if you're attacked in a dark alley? Do you want to escape your attacker, bust him up, or subdue and hold him for the authorities? Will your objectives differ if there's more than one aggressor? What about age? Do you react differently if your antagonists are adolescents rather than adults? . . . Decide in advance. That way, when the threat materializes you won't hesitate in your response."*
>
> Forrest E. Morgan, *Living the Martial Way* (p. 80)

Now ask yourself, are you really willing to kill a man over an insult? More importantly, are you willing to die over it? Shit happens, things go sideways, what starts out as a verbal altercation frequently escalates to extreme violence, and sometimes people die. Over bullshit you probably could've walked away from if you were just able to keep your fucking mouth shut . . . but no, you had to get the last word and put that bastard in his place, didn't you? And now you need to explain to the judge why he should dismiss these felony charges. Good luck with that. As the maxim goes, *"Don't fight unless you're right,"* but I'm going to take that a bit further and posit that not only must you be right, but you really don't have any other option. Now, I am not telling you to be a pussy and run away, nor am I claiming that you have a "duty to retreat" on your property or at your place of business or anywhere else for that matter. I'm just saying don't throw that punch unless you're willing to take it all the way . . . and if you are going to hit someone, use a tool.

USE A TOOL

> *"The use of one's bare hands to defend against attack or to launch an attack has always been a desperation move, a method of last resort, by any people at any time and anywhere on this squalid little planet. It has only been rather recently in mankind's history that the habitual carrying of weapons has become something less than the universal norm."*
>
> Peyton Quinn

Your soft little hand is unlikely to drop someone with one punch, especially if they are twice your size, pissed off, or drunk . . . if they happen to be all three you will have a serious problem. You may have some martial arts training. You may even have a heavy bag at home that you practice on quite a bit. That is good. It is good to know how to punch properly. Do you know who can punch better than you? Professional fighters. Do you know what usually happens when a professional fighter drinks too much whiskey at the pub and gets in a brawl outside on the street? He breaks bones in his hand. So, the lesson to be learned here is not to hit people with your bare hand, and if you have no other choice don't slam your closed fist into someone's skull or teeth (palm heel, hammerfist, and elbow strike are your friend).

I love knucks. Brass knucks are great for administering physical corrections to dipshits. Most of the time when I've used them, all I needed to do was stare at the guy with no expression on my face while being real obvious about calmly reaching into my pocket, pulling them out for him to see, then slipping them onto my hand without bothering to hide what I was doing. This is a very nasty deterrent, and few people wanted to continue acting stupid after I calmly indicated I was carrying an illegal weapon and was casually unconcerned about the ramifications of using it on them. Few things better for getting your point across without killing the guy or waving an obvious weapon around in a public place. Very discrete, very effective, little effort required to produce extreme pain. Actually, grazing blows and grinding down with pressure are the preferred way to use knucks rather than a straight blast. Quick short jabs to the ribs work well too. There is an art to it. Only an amateur goes full retard and starts whaling away, creating a Jackson Pollack spatter effect on the walls and floor. Unfortunately, the world is full of amateurs and hundreds of people have had their teeth shattered by knucks, so they are now illegal practically everywhere. Remember, knucks were not designed to break other people's bones, but to prevent you from breaking yours. Even a trained fighter can break unprotected fingers in a streetfight, but with a properly fitted set of knucks with a padded brace a skinny teenager can punch an oak tree repeatedly with full force blows until he gets tired. Knucks are not really a weapon, they are more of a safety device . . . yet they remain illegal.

Some states specify that only "metallic" knucks are prohibited, which may mean that carbon fiber, G10 plastic, wood, and Lexan are okay—but often municipal ordinances go beyond what is prohibited by the state, and sometimes weasel words like "similar" or "of like kind" are used to allow police and prosecutors to call anything they want a weapon. So even plastic knucks are frequently prohibited. Usually the charge for simple possession is a misdemeanor, which typically means a maximum sentence of a year in gaol. If you get the max, "good time,' overcrowding, and other issues mean you will probably be in for no longer than 8 months. But you are not going to get the max for simple possession unless you have priors. You will probably get 20 days of grilled cheese sammich followed by a year of probation. That doesn't sound too bad for getting to carry a set of doublecool brass knucks to the pub, now does it? Now, a first offense with a set of knucks isn't that bad . . . unless they have spikes on them, or are engraved with "Hell's Hammer", or you have a set for either hand in addition to a razor. Scare the DA and he will insist on "making an example" of you. Just one set with no spikes is all you need. If it is legal to carry non-metallic knucks you probably ought to go that route instead, as they tend to be thinner, lighter, and appear less threatening to jurors.

Now, if risking a few months in gaol is not something you want to do, or if the thought of a gangster style paperweight in your pocket is objectionable for some reason, let me suggest the simple padlock. I have seen padlocks used as heavyweight one-finger knucks many times. They are popular weapons on the street and extremely effective. In fact, it seems fairly silly to break the law by carrying a prohibited item when a very similar legal option is readily available. Any padlock with a large enough shackle can be used, but the rounded body of a standard combination lock seems to fit the hand most comfortably. Just slip it in your front jeans pocket or your jacket pocket and you're good to go. Some guys recommend wearing lots of heavy rings, or even using a large carabiner as a set of legal knucks. Do not do this. Rings attract lots of the wrong kind of attention, and neither option adequately protects your fingers from injury, which is the primary function of knucks. Padlock protects your social finger and presses firmly into the palm of your hand as a brace. Padlock is what you want to use.

A few friends of mine love saps. There are many styles of sap. Most are small, semi-flexible, leather covered devices with a weighted end. To the casual observer they do not appear to be a weapon at all. Due to this, it is difficult to warn someone off by displaying a sap, as they likely will not regard it as a threat. So proper use of the sap entails smacking someone in the head with it immediately without warning. Depending on the type of sap, they will either be stunned or drop to the ground like a sack of potatoes. The most common sap is known as a "slapper" and has a wide flat surface area to better distribute impact to prevent serious injury. They were commonly issued to jailors and psych ward orderlies, who quickly discovered that they tended to work a lot better if you used the edge to strike with instead. Due to widespread misuse, they were discontinued and prohibited by the late 1960s. Most handmade saps are nothing more than narrow sacks filled with shot, which is referred to as a "sandclub." Depending on design, they can be very effective, and if the shot is not compacted they are unlikely to break bone. Now, another sap you sometimes see is called a "blackjack." This consists of a heavy lead weight at the end of a coil spring, which is a deadly combination. A properly designed blackjack will break bone with every blow. Legislators, of course, have deemed that all saps are in the same category as a blackjack, and in many states possession of a "blackjack" is prosecuted as a felony, even if it is a relatively harmless slapper sap. Although saps are incredibly effective I discourage folks from carrying them based upon risk of felony charges. Even the Perrin change wallet is prohibited under vaguely defined statutes in some states. It is a sad day when you can be sent to gaol for smacking a mugger with your change purse.

Again, the versatile padlock comes into play. There are about a dozen different ways to convert a padlock into a "knocker" that is just as devastating as a blackjack with fewer legal complications. The traditional method of creating a knocker is to roll a bandanna into a tight tube, then tie it through the shackle in a short secure loop. That way, simply by grasping the knot, you have a heavy steel weight hanging off the end of your fist, but all the witnesses see is you backhanding your opponent a few times. As a bonus, even if the lock is grabbed it is nearly impossible to pull it out of your grasp. Now, if you were instead to simply tie the lock at the end of your bandanna for more distance, not only could it be yanked away easily, but everyone within 50 feet will be able to see exactly what you are doing as you swing that lock around like a medieval ball and chain flail. Keep it short and sweet. My personal recommendation is for the round steel padlock made by Fortress, as it has no corners and will slip out of your pocket snag free. Now, if you live in a regime which has specifically prohibited "slungshots" by name, or has deemed them to be "similar or of like kind" to a blackjack, it will be illegal for you to tie a knot in your hankie. If you intend to be a good citizen and obey the law, you can pull that bandanna through the shackle and let both ends hang free of your pocket, which means you'll need to grab both ends tightly to ascertain your padlock doesn't go flying free. If it appears you are about to be contacted by law enforcement while in possession of such an item, simply grasp one end only, pulling the hanky free of the padlock, then drop it or stick it in another pocket and you are legal. Padlock on a bandanna is very popular with bikers and barroom brawlers, so if you see a knotted bandanna sticking out of someone's pocket that is what it is. This is one of the nastiest and most effective infighting weapons in common use.

Similar to the knocker, but legal practically everywhere, is the humble belt. For maximal effectiveness you want a wide leather belt with a heavy brass or pewter buckle. Now, when I say "buckle" I really mean "solid chunk of metal with a pointy stud on the back" rather than a traditional open faced buckle. If you don't have any pouches or clips on your belt, with a little bit of practice you can flip that buckle open and whip the belt free of the loops in about 2 seconds. You can put it to use instantly, or for best effect you can wrap the belt around your hand a few times so you have a more manageable length. The shorter the strap, the quicker the speed. I have beat people with belts many times. They are versatile and effective bludgeons. I have faced off multiple attackers armed with nothing but a belt on several occasions. I have knocked knives from people's hands with a belt. Once you have practiced to the point that you have familiarity with what a belt can and cannot do, you can launch wicked combination attacks which are nearly impossible to defend against, strike three opponents in rapid succession, and adjust the length of the strap at will. In *Hardcore Self Defense* an entire chapter is devoted to belt techniques, but I felt that information was so important to the martial arts community I posted that chapter in its entirety online, and I am aware that it has been reposted on several other sites and I have no problem with that. I think it is important for folks to realize the usefulness of the belt as a weapon. Frankly, I feel it is a better weapon for most people than a knife. Not only is there greater range, but there is far less risk of killing your opponent or spending years in prison as the result of an armed altercation. Few juries are going to send you to prison for smacking an assailant a few times with your belt. In fact, it is unlikely you would even be prosecuted under most circumstances. Belt is a great weapon. Take the time to learn how to use it as such. This is a great skill to have.

One of the nastiest one-punch fight stopping moves involves a loaded fist. Now, as with most techniques, there is a right way and a wrong way to do this. The traditional (wrong) method involves palming a roll of nickels, which adds mass and support to your punch, but it can also break your fingers. Using an extended fistload to augment hammerfist blows is far more effective. I saw a guy do this the right way at a truckstop about 25 years back. Scrawny homeless guy was being shoved around by a drunk 300 pound redneck, when suddenly he lit off a wild haymaker that came up from the floor and literally blew the other guy's face apart . . . then he ran away while the redneck sat on the floor and cried while his girlfriend screamed at me to call 911 while she was picking up his teeth. It turned out the raggedy man had a small pipe fitting in his hand, about 1" X 4" of galvanized steel with threaded ends, and he hit that guy right in the mouth full force with a reverse hammerfist. Devastating one punch stop. Now, although it is perfectly legal to carry a small piece of pipe in your pocket, that takes up a lot of space and, frankly, is a homeless weapon that isn't nearly as cool as knucks or even a padlock slungshot. However, an aluminum tactical flashlight will work almost as well and have other uses as well. Flashlight in the teeth is no joke, and it doesn't even need to have one of those fancy crenulated bezels either. Strike with the metal, don't use it as a traditional fistload.

Maybe, for some reason, you cannot even carry a tactical flashlight. Perhaps it is too heavy and you prefer the ghey little squeeze LED on your keyring instead. In that case you might want to hit the guy with your keys. Never hold keys so they stick out between your fingers, and don't throw them either. Just swing them from the lanyard, cord, or long leather fob they are attached to. If you only have 2 or 3 keys this won't do any good at all, but if you have 7 or 8 it will work quite nicely. I once knew a fellow who had over a dozen junk keys that didn't fit any locks affixed to a braided leather lanyard for this specific purpose. Very nasty weapon to be struck repeatedly in the face with. It will stun, lacerate, and possibly even blind—but make no mistake, this is a diversionary tactic or a means to repel unmotivated lightweights, and will do little good against someone seriously intent on hurting you. Think of it as a legal alternative to the telescopic coil-spring "steel whip."

A lot of guys tout their specially designed "tactical pens." Most of these pens are overpriced, are impractical to write with, are obviously designed as weapons, and will be confiscated at most security checkpoints. They are basically an over-rated, one-shot desperation weapon. You may as well use a $15 steel Jotter ballpoint which you can actually take through most checkpoints without a second glance. Sure, you can hammer your $150 tactical penlike object through a piece of wood to prove how great it is, but I think I'll pass, thanks. A Craftsman phillips head screwdriver only costs $5 and will do the same exact thing.

In the event that you have no weaponlike objects on your person, I advise you to pick something up and beat the fucker with it. I'm not going to waste much time going into improvised weapons here, as that topic was covered exhaustively and encyclopedically in my first book, *Hardcore Self Defense.* Here are a few things that may be in your immediate environment which will work nicely: beer bottle, glass mug, ashtray, billiard ball, rock, can of beans, unopened can of beer, coffee cup, assorted tools, scrap metal or wood. When I was in a "weapon free environment" I used: several pencils, a tube of toothpaste, and a sharpened pork chop bone. I have seen wire clotheshangers, extension cords, bungee cords, and even a Hot Wheels toy car used to hurt people so badly they required hospitalization. Weapons are everywhere. Where they do not exist they can be fabricated. If you are completely nekkid in a padded cell you still have your thumbs and teeth (which, incidentally, is why violent mental cases get the strait jacket and bite mask).

If you are a private citizen, minding your own business and causing no trouble, when some menacing individual unknown to you approaches and starts putting his hands on you in a threatening manner, are you thereby obligated to abide by the Marquis of Queensbury's rules for gentlemanly fisticuffs? Fuck, no . . . use a tool. If you are going to hit someone, do it right, do it hard, do it viciously, and preferably do it first. Put them the fuck down and do not stop hitting them until they stop trying to get back up. If they are getting back up they are still attacking, but if they aren't getting up it is time to stop hitting them and leave. A tool will make this much easier to accomplish. Without a tool you may find yourself rolling around on the asphalt for a half hour while he's headbutting you and trying to chew your nose off, and the rest of your day will probably suck. Always use a tool.

F.T.W. COMMENTARY

> *"When walking in open territory, bother no one. If someone bothers you, ask them to stop. If they don't stop, destroy them."*
>
> Anton LaVey

I have studied violence all my life. I am familiar with tens of thousands of case studies, have directly observed about a thousand violent incidents, and been involved with well over a hundred such incidents myself. Usually, if you are aware of the danger, it can be avoided. If it cannot be avoided, you can usually talk your way out of fighting one way or another, either through de-escalation or simply stating that you are clearly ready and willing to take things much farther than the aggressor. Remember that scene in Grand Torino when Clint Eastwood pointed his hand at the punks threatening him as if it were a gun? That instantly escalates your interaction to a death threat, but one which is technically legal and has plausible deniability—I have shut people up and instantly stopped road ragers with that gesture, but if you do that you have pretty much eliminated any further opportunity to de-escalate, and if the other guy just gets madder either he doesn't care if you have a gun or he has one of his own, which means you are now in very serious trouble. So don't bluff, and don't do something like this over meaningless bullshit. This is a clear warning that you will shoot someone without committing a felony by actually showing him your gun, which is inappropriate and illegal in nearly all confrontations. But I digress . . .

As I said, I've seen a lot of violence. Very little of it is truly random. There are precursors. For instance, well over half the violent situations I've been involved in started out as a road rage situation—and often I was at least partially at fault, either by having angered another motorist because I was disregarding the vehicle and traffic law, or was not intimidated by his aggressive driving, or because I escalated things by shouting a variety of expletives and adjectives which accurately described him in my eyes, and in retrospect was often inappropriate and even hurtful. Road rage is one of the most common precursors to "random" violence. Another is women. Some of the most dangerous situations I've ever been in started over a woman . . . or, rather, was started *by* a woman. Women sometimes start fights, even if they need to lie to make it happen. I have seen that lots of times. I have had women try to convince me to beat other men up, and I have had the reverse happen to me. I have had women flirt with me as bait in order to piss off their jealous boyfriend. I have also been with women who felt compelled to insult strangers for no reason. Then there are the times when the woman is not at fault at all, but some jealous drunk decides to insult or molest her in front of you. Be aware that violence often occurs around women. It also occurs around alcohol—especially when it is being consumed in massive quantities—and if you are drunk your judgement and awareness will be greatly impaired, and you will have less compunction about engaging in, or even initiating, casual violence over nothing. Cash transactions are another common cause of violence, especially when one person reneges on a deal, offers less money than promised, offers merchandise in other than stated condition, or mocks and belittles the condition of merchandise offered. If someone thinks they are being insulted or taken unfair advantage of, they may retaliate with violence. On the other hand, there are also rip offs, which sometimes happen with buying merchandise from strangers, such as through classified ads or websites like craigslist. Another common precursor to violence is trespass—either someone trespasses onto your property or you trespass on theirs, and a confrontation ensues. Aside from predatory, professional, and familial violence, the remainder of violent encounters truly are "random," with some stranger who is not motivated by profit or revenge simply starting shit with you because he is angry at the world and you happen to be a convenient target for him to focus on at that time. This can be anything from a bully at the pub to some crazy person wanting to attack you for braking on a crosswalk while trying to negotiate oncoming traffic at a busy intersection.

Don't start trouble. If you see trouble starting, leave. If you cannot avoid the confrontation, attempt to de-escalate and then leave. Words are not violence, ignore them. If you cannot leave without resorting to violence, hit first with your intent being to blind, maim, cripple, or kill with every strike until your opponent is on the ground and no longer trying to get back up. If his friends try to stop you from leaving, give them even worse treatment. Leave the area immediately. Don't allow yourself to be followed. If you are followed, consider it an attack and engage the enemy. If they do not disengage and retreat, destroy them. Never raise your hands over mere words unless they are obviously a prelude to an attack. Never allow your opponent to strike first. Use a tool to maximize damage thereby minimizing physical risk to yourself. Violence has many risks and long-term aftereffects. Never use violence lightly or unnecessarily. If you use violence, it must be immediate, vicious, and final. There is no other way.

THE NATURE OF THE BEAST

"The ability to act in spite of conscience or empathy is one characteristic associated with psychopaths. Robert D. Hare's insightful book Without Conscience *identifies several other features. Such people are:*

- *Glib and superficial*
- *Egocentric and grandiose*
- *Lacking remorse or guilt*
- *Deceitful and manipulative*
- *Impulsive*
- *In need of excitement*
- *Lacking responsibility*
- *Emotionally shallow"*

Gavin de Becker, *Gift of Fear* (p. 81)

I will likely upset a few folks with this particular chapter, and I make no apologies for that. Most violent crimes against strangers are committed by street people, by which I do not necessarily mean homeless, but punks, thugs, freaks, and grifters. Each group has its own defining characteristics and criminal subculture. There is a lot that can be told about these groups and various subgroups, pertaining to specific modus operandi and regional trends, but that is far beyond the scope of this book. I'm not performing a sociological study here, nor am I going to waste pages telling you common sense methods to avoid victimization. All I am going to do with this chapter is identify characteristics of the primary threats so you will have a better idea of what to look for so you can avoid these people, or failing that, at least be better informed about what type of threat you are dealing with.

Now, I realize that there are many types of "threat" other than the ones covered here, but I'm trying to be realistic and cover only serious random threats you're likely to encounter on the street. I will not discuss your drunk brother-in-law who never liked you and now is chasing you around the backyard with a BBQ fork, nor shall I discuss your psychotic girlfriend who will try to murder you in your sleep, nor shall we cover the office bully, the drunk guy at the sports bar who used to play high school football, or a group of ill behaved youths dressed in hip hop gear who actually come from good families and do not fully realize how disrespectful and obnoxious they might be presenting themselves as. These individuals, while they can all become a serious threat, are beyond the scope of this study.

I will be discussing the disadvantaged population a bit, and I expect to catch a bit of flack over that. Now, I know homeless people and interact with them regularly—I used to *be* homeless—one of my best friends lived under a bridge for years—please do not presume to tell me that I have "hobophobia" which is an irrational fear of the homeless, because that just ain't so. MOST street people really aren't homeless. If he is wearing clean clothes and doesn't have a sleeping bag he probably lives at a group home or in a Section 8 apartment. That guy with the shopping cart piled high with junk is homeless, that guy whose skin is so sunburnt it looks like leather and his shoes have holes in them is homeless, the guy you always see with an overloaded backpack and a dog is also homeless—but you know what I noticed about those guys? They will never approach you. Occasionally one may plant himself at the corner with a cardboard sign, but they will not aggressively demand money or attention. More often than not, they simply ignore everyone. The real threat comes from the drug addicted homeless who are barred from the shelters, and the ones who start drinking gin and juice for breakfast and are plastered and out of control by noon—you see these guys carrying giant sippy cups or gallon jugs filled with their inexpensive mixed drink of choice—often it is Kool Aid and vodka. They can be violent and unpredictable, especially when you add meth and mental illness to the equation. And then there are the muggers who may also happen to be homeless, or simply dress like them in order to blend in and appear less menacing. Many of these folks are transients who commit serious crimes before hopping on a bus or freight train, or stealing a car and relocating elsewhere. What I am trying to say is that I acknowledge the fact that most of the homeless and many street people (including addicts) are relatively harmless and present only a minimal potential threat to you. They don't all want to shank you, rape the wound, and give you hepatitis . . . actually, very fucking few will even consider doing that. Most street people are little more than an annoyance or an eyesore, and you do not need to panic or over-react if approached by one. If he pops up from hiding and lunges at you, that's another matter altogether, same thing goes if he makes a rapid bee-line towards you in a parking lot, corners you in a laundromat, or approaches you with a friend in a pincer movement. Those are threats, and will be discussed in more detail later.

A lot of well-meaning and frequently naive folks think of the homeless as a disadvantaged population deserving of whatever help we can provide them. It is their right to think that way and be charitable if they wish. This makes them better human beings than myself and I do not begrudge them that. I agree that most of the homeless, while they can be annoying and smelly and have no concept of how to interact with others in society, are generally harmless. But a few are really bad. Then there are the predators who are not homeless but pretend to be panhandlers in order to close with their victims without being regarded as a threat—in fact, most muggings start out that way. I have studied this for many years and I have seen some shit. I am aware of many homeless who have literally dragged women off into the bushes to rape them, and this sometimes includes charity workers whom they have known and interacted with for months. I, personally, know over a dozen women who have been mugged by homeless, whether it be a forcible purse snatching or an actually knifepoint robbery. Never make the mistake of thinking they are harmless. Even the ones you've known for years can suddenly turn on you if they're having a bad day. Street drugs and schizophrenia can do that to people.

Now, as I have been all like trying to evolve spiritually and shit, I shall try to avoid judging, pseudospeciating, or referring to Social Darwinism and Soylent Green in this section. I will just let the facts speak for themselves. Oh hell, what's a little pseudospeciation between friends? Utilizing pseudospeciation we can easily split most threats into 2 primary categories: "zombies" and "goblins.' Subclassifications are detailed below.

ZOMBIES

Zombies are low level threats. They tend to be low functioning with severe limitations in the areas of hygiene and self-control. If they are recognized as a threat they can usually be avoided or dissuaded with minimal effort. The problem with zombies is that they truly have nothing to lose and just don't care. If they are desperate for money, drugs, or human contact they may go to extremes. Many are crazed. Many have communicable diseases such as hepatitis. They tend to be depraved and beyond redemption. They also tend to be very good at working the system and sizing up potential marks. If you make and hold eye contact, it is generally considered by them to be either a challenge (to be responded to with verbal abuse or threats) or an invitation to engage you in conversation in hope of ingratiating themselves to you. Do not pity them. Pity shows weakness and makes you a target. When you are forced into a situation where you need to speak to a zombie, NEVER say "excuse me" or "please," and for fuck's sake don't call them "sir." I'm not being an asshole here because I am very serious when I'm telling you that the use of those words will tell that individual very clearly that you are a naive half-wit ripe for a long overdue victimization. Social workers who deal with street people everyday know never to say "excuse me" or "please" to them. Elevating them to an undeserved equal status will make them incredibly bold and they will commence putting their hands on you and start making increasingly unreasonable demands, because you just demonstrated that they can probably get away with anything they do to you, so in their eyes they practically own you. A request for spare change which gets them a dollar sometimes becomes an insistent demand for twenty dollars and the use of your cellphone and a ride in your car. Never back down from these people. Any small infringement that you permit will multiply exponentially: allow some homeless to sleep in your bushes one night with the understanding that he be gone tomorrow, and tomorrow he sets up a campsite, 3 days later his friends are living there, and by the end of the week they are living in your garage. A one time favor out of pity will suddenly turn into your daily obligation in their eyes, and if you tell them "No" they will fly into a rage. You cannot show kindness and compassion to those who will take undue advantage of it, and the reason most people are on the street in the first place is because they have alienated everyone in their family and gotten kicked out of every shelter due to their behaviors. They all understand "NO" and "GET OFF MY LAND" . . . and failure to accept those statements constitutes a clear threat and negotiation is not an option. Feel free to refer to them as "shitbag' and tell them "I need you to get the fuck out of my face before I seriously hurt you." If they are defiant in their continued infringement of your rights, all they will respond to is fear and pain. This is a hard truth, but it is a hard world. If you cannot Mace them or threaten them yourself, call the police they will come and do that for you so you do not need to risk breaking any laws or getting your hands dirty. Every situation is different and needs to be handled based upon the individual circumstances. There are no simple answers that will work all the time. Just remember that when you are interacting with street people, they are practically an entirely different species from you, and a whole new set of rules applies—start thinking of them as fellow human beings to be pitied or respected and you open yourself up to a world of shit. Avoid them.

SCAVENGERS

> *"They peep out from under cardboard crates, cursing me under their breath. They parade up and down the street day after day, year after year, screaming at invisible foes. Their hearts are pumping, but their brains are stalled. Their minds are warped from booze, neglect, religion, and war. They contribute nothing to society. Their unnecessary lives are carried out on a dead-end street."*
>
> Debbie Goad

Scavengers are a common sight in any city nowadays, raggedy men, often seen pushing a stolen shopping cart or a bicycle covered with partially filled trashbags, meandering through alleyways to paw through trash cans and dumpsters for recyclable metal and other discarded treasures. Some of them even have rusted out pickup trucks that they drive around. These individuals are usually harmless and unlikely to attack without provocation, but some will commit crimes of opportunity such as looking through an unlocked car or open garage. Scavengers also may set up a temporary camp on your property, which can develop into a serious problem should they decide to make it semi-permanent and claim it is now their "home."

Most scavengers are mentally ill. Many abuse alcohol or other drugs. All carry knives. Do not allow yourself to become sucked into a neverending conversation with one of these people. Do not insult or belittle them. Only confront or threaten them if they are trespassing on your property or mishandling your belongings (trash cans excepted). They are used to being ignored and dismissed, which should be your default reaction to them.

Some cities coddle the walking wounded, setting up feed stations and shelters and group homes for them, which provides support and sanctuary as well as a base of operations for them to retreat and recover. Many recently released convicts and fugitives take full advantage of these opportunities, often bussing cross country to cities with a well established support network for the homeless. Those who take advantage of these programs are often arrogant and surly, as a full stomach and a roof over their head gives them undeserved self esteem as well as a grandiose sense of entitlement, and they can get quite uppity and indignant when told that their antisocial behaviors are infringing upon the rights of others. In many cases this is due to a deficiency of vitamin Mace, which promotes good manners.

Some people flip out upon seeing a raggedy man pawing through their trash or sleeping under their bushes and might over-react as if he were a far more serious threat, which is the primary reason I have included them in this section. I am not telling you that scavengers present no threat, just that they tend to be a very minor one, and the exceptions to that rule typically are more accurately defined in one of the following categories.

CRAZIES

> *"They're going to make rules and wait for me to do something crazy and then they can come in and playact like they're sane. Then they want to handcuff me because they need my hands for something so they're*

representing my hands with it. They're representing my heart for that and they're representing my head for those things. They're cutting my hair and selling it for something and making pictures and books and changing my name and saying they're me in another perspective."

Charlie Manson

"I've looked into eyes that reveal nothing, eyes that scare the rest of the world. But all these people were innocent children once, before something descended on their sanity."

Marlin Marynick

There are a LOT of crazies in deep street, and most of them do not crawl through dumpsters or demand handouts. They just walk up and down the street screaming profanity, frequently mixed with scripture, and carry on loud conversations with their invisible friends. Sometimes they just shout abuse and meaningless threats at thin air. Stay the fuck away from these people. Many psychotics end up wandering the streets, whether they have family to live with or not. It is a compulsion. You will learn that these individuals have *many* compulsions, which they have very limited control over. They are crazy for real and operating on an entirely different wavelength in which they are convinced they are a very important person whom others should obey. Again, stay the fuck away from them and do not talk to them. They are completely unpredictable and will attack without cause or warning. I have seen them yell challenges and insults at every single person who passed by them over the course of several hours. I have seen them run out into the street to beat up automobiles. I have seen them find a funny hat and act as if it gave them magical powers. They are crazy. Stay the fuck away from them. If they start pestering you and won't leave you alone, DO NOT turn your back on them. Just pull out your Mace and give them the whole fucking can. It sucks that you are crazy, but you are required to behave in a semi-human manner in your interactions with others, so this is what you get. Fuck.

General rule of thumb is that the truly crazy folks out there: schizophrenics, psychotics, severe neurotics, etc, will try very hard to pass as normal. It is glaringly obvious that something is truly and disturbingly "off" about these individuals, and they know they are crazy, but they want to hide it from everyone, so they do their best to calm down and be polite. These people are crazy. Be courteous and respectful towards them, but do not engage them in conversation or turn your back on them, and do whatever you can to avoid agitating them in any way. Stress makes these individuals stabby. Now, that being said, many of the "crazies" you see walking down the street holding conversations with their invisible friend and acting out in a bizarre and alarming manner are fakers. You see, on the street crazy is respected since crazy people are genuinely fearless and are willing to cross lines that others will not. Knowing that crazy gets respect, a lot of weaklings who could never get respect otherwise pretend to be crazy so other street people leave them alone. Those jackoffs who wear old army fatigues and tell bullshit stories about all the people they killed during their Special Forces missions in Vietnam . . . when they were not even born until after that war was over . . . are a common example. Street preachers yelling scripture mixed with profanity and gibberish are another. Although they are not really crazy, they do start to believe their own lies after a while, and being accustomed to getting away with bad behaviors may well do something stupid like violate rule number one. Stay away from these individuals but don't take any shit from them. As Thomas Szasz is wont to say: no matter how crazy someone acts, they know when they are acting out in an injurious or offensive manner, and do so through their own free will. Compulsions can be resisted if one chooses to, but many are used to blaming their "illness" as an excuse. Do not pity these people, and never give them a free pass for blatant stupidity. I do not care if you are crazy: no-one is exempt from an ass whuppin. So fucking behave yourself and show a little respect. Thanks.

PARASITES

> *"These folks don't suffer from too little self-esteem, their problem is* too much *self-esteem; far more, in fact, than their accomplishments or capabilities would seem to merit. This is why they experience no shame whatsoever over their glaring ineptitude and uselessness; in fact, they flaunt it."*
>
> Boyd Rice, *Standing in Two Circles* (p. 139-140)

> *"Panhandlers, the homeless, street people . . . these people should not be objects of our pity. They are potential threats who must be recognized and avoided. Their need does not constitute a right to victimize you—and refusing to deal with them at the societal level produces disastrous, systemic consequences."*
>
> Phil Elmore, *Shorthand Empty Hand*

> *"You do not approach someone in a manner that makes THEM feel threatened. it doesn't matter what your intent is, it's how the person being approached treats it—their opinion is the one that matters. Sneaking up on someone and scoping them out, getting within their comfort zone, talking to them while scoping other things out, singling out a person/child esp female, following them, continuing to engage them in conversation when it's likely clear they have no interest . . . this is how you hunt."*
>
> Bladite

The parasite is the most common threat which you will be confronted with in any major city. Simply stated, these are panhandlers and beggars which are little more than an annoyance 90% of the time. Their litany is similar the nation over and usually starts with the phrase, "Excuse me, sir?" If you ignore them, shake your head, or say, "Sorry, I can't help you," they will usually leave you alone. I once studied linguistics and found that the following phrase conveys multiple discouraging messages: *"I ain't got nuttin' for ya."* Those words show that you are from the lower classes, do not have or will not give them money, and will use violence if provoked, yet remain non-confrontational. Frequently they will ask for "the time" or "a light" for their cigarette, which is nearly always a pretext for a request for cash. Sometimes they will dance around waving their arms in hope that you will turn towards them and make eye contact, whereupon they will immediately close the distance. Often they may make an insulting comment towards your lack of charity, which you should always ignore. You will not win a debating contest with a crazed street person, and it would be pointless to try. Using logic and reason with someone who believes that satellites are beaming messages into their brain will not work so well for you, but it will probably be the most interesting thing that has happened to him all day. Don't get sucked into his world.

Panhandling is deemed Constitutionally protected free speech in most jurisdictions unless certain lines are crossed, after which it becomes "aggressive panhandling" which is usually a petty offense punishable by a small fine, so many of these people give fuck all about the law if they can double their money through intimidation tactics. A few acts which have been prohibited under statute include: panhandling after dark, panhandling within 50 feet of an ATM, shouting abuse, touching others, following people shouting repeated demands for money. They can do this all day long in a busy parking lot, intimidating people into giving them dollars which they will yell angrily about because it is only a dollar and they need more than that. A skilled and intimidating aggressive panhandler can extort hundreds of dollars from passersby on a good day without legally crossing the line into "assault."

Assault occurs when an individual with the apparent ability to do you serious harm does or says something that indicates you may be in danger of being attacked. He does not need to actually state that he intends to strike you—simply closing the distance into your personal space, looming over you, following closely behind you, making sudden movements intended to startle, and shouting unintelligible nonsense is more than enough justification to believe one's safety may be at risk. This is usually considered a misdemeanor which means they can be summoned to appear in court and may even be arrested, but with crazy street people who are already overloading the system many policemen will simply let him go with a warning instead. Unless he actually places his hands on you, simple assault is considered a minor offense which is seldom taken seriously.

Mugging, or strongarm robbery as it is sometimes called, occurs when an individual touches you in any way and takes your money or property without permission. Actual violence is not usually required for this charge. Purse snatching and chain snatching are common examples of this. Another example is when you open your wallet to give a bum a dollar and instead he snatches your wallet and runs away. In more aggressive instances, someone may actually imply violence and proceed to shove, slap, or shake you until you give them money. These sorts of muggings sometimes appear to be aggressive panhandling but quickly escalate. In some cases you are practically ambushed the moment you park your car and open the door to get out, or he may stand between you and your car to prevent you from getting inside. Another indicator of a mugging is when you are rapidly approached by 2 or more individuals who spread out to surround you as they close in. The prelude to a mugging is always assault, and you are usually justified in drawing your weapon as a warning at this point. Attempted mugging is usually prosecuted as a felony and reduced to a misdemeanor unless the offender is already on probation or parole, in which case jail is virtually guaranteed. It is a pain in the ass either way, so very few panhandlers take things this far. Please note that as it relates to panhandlers this is really mugging by legal definition rather than the typical aggravated robbery (violent mugging) in which the victim is threatened with a weapon or savagely beaten. True aggravated robbery is the realm of an entirely different class of threat, but MANY (if not most) muggings and aggravated robberies begin under the pretext of panhandling. If they start insisting that they need to make a call on your cellphone (which deprives you of it) or demand that you drive them somewhere just a few blocks away, it is very possible that you are being set up to be robbed.

My default response to aggressive panhandling (when they continue after either being ignored or told to stop) is simply to tell them, "Fuck off or I will Mace you." That is the one and only warning they get. If they have not disengaged after 5 seconds they get the whole can. More on this tactic in a later chapter.

Some of you feel compassion for the homeless and want to help them, and that is very nice of you. The thing is, most panhandlers are *not* homeless and many are quite specific about exactly what kind of "help" they require. If you give them food, they will curse and throw it. If you give them coins, they will curse and throw them. They only want "paper money" and some will still complain if it is "only a dollar." Typically, the actual homeless seldom panhandle, and those who do will appreciate some food or coins. Many panhandlers may not be homeowners, but they live in a shelter or share a rented room with several others. A few actually rent an apartment and have their own car. You see, in some cities a professional panhandler can make well over $200 on a good day and rarely makes less than $50, even from only 4 hours of "work." That is more than most entry level laborer, food service, and retail jobs pay. If you want to know if a panhandler is homeless or not, the two primary indicators are a bedroll and unkempt clothes. Real homeless don't drink Starbucks coffee either, they all seem to carry a quart sized plastic cup like a 7-11 Big Gulp. If he is wearing freshly laundered clothing that actually matches and only has a daypack he is not homeless. If he is sitting in a lawn chair with an umbrella and a cooler and will not interrupt his cellphone conversation to accept your donation, just load your quarters into a wristbrace slingshot (that way he can pick them out of his cardboard sign at his convenience). Massad Ayoob recommended carrying a pair of dollar bills folded together and weighted with a couple of paperclips in one's front pocket to toss in the direction of aggressive panhandlers. I prefer dollar coins. If I think you look like you could use a dollar, I'll flip it in your direction. If you are screaming about the spiders in your head and acting like you want to go hands on, I'll bounce it off your forehead real hard, and then I'll pull out my Mace and ask if you want to drink it. Again, the most prudent policy is simply to stay away from them.

GOBLINS

Goblins are moderate to high level threats, dependant on their place in the food chain and if you are deemed a suitable target for them. Recognizing that an individual is potentially dangerous makes them less so. Being able to accurately identify and categorize the threat gives you a general idea of what to expect from them. Goblins are more dangerous than zombies because they will actively seek out and stalk potential targets and are difficult to dissuade once aroused. They are capable of unprovoked extremely violent acts, especially when acting with others. They are frequently armed with knives or pistols as well. Due to these facts, one should never confront or argue with a goblin without immediate access to a lethal weapon of some sort. You may well need to use it. Just remember: *"If you use your weapon your life is going to drastically change."* Are you prepared to pay the price? Are you prepared to fire the first shot and shoot those people to the ground? Are you prepared to spend the night in jail and testify about what you did in court? If not, perhaps you should just take Massad Ayoob's advice and carry a small wad of singles in your pocket held together with a cheap moneyclip to toss towards a potential mugger before you sprint away in terror, and leave that gun at home. Better not to have a gun at all than to pull it out if you're not prepared to pull the trigger and freeze due to a massive adrenal dump. That is why I typically advise folks to carry a blade instead, because the average untrained individual is less likely to draw a blade as an empty threat and more likely to actually use it if charged and taken to the ground, but you carry what you feel comfortable with.

ADDICTS

> *"Although it is true with criminals in general, you should really consider a street addict as someone from an entirely different planet. . . . We're talking someone who was conditioned from childhood that the way to get what he wants or needs is to batter and abuse the weak and take it from them. You are not a person to an addict; you are a source for what he needs . . . . he's got nothing to do except get high and watch for ways to get his drug money. In a real sense, his profession is being an addict and a thief. . . . In their*

> *world there are no boundaries except those enforced by violence . . ."*
>
> Marc MacYoung and Chris Pfouts, *Safe in the City* (p. 88, 90)

There are different types of addicts, and they all have their unique attributes depending upon the type of drug they favor and the means by which they administer it. There are differences between a crackhead and a tweaker and a junkie. There are also differences between snorters, smokers, and hypes. Not only do each of these subgroups appear and behave differently, but they all have their own subcultures which usually do not interact with one another. One could easily fill an entire chapter with clues to distinguish between different types of drug user, but I'm not going to waste my time with that because they're all pretty much the same to me. A few hints are: poor hygiene, emaciation, premature aging, rotten teeth, facial twitching, racoon eyes, bizarre gesticulations, unusual gait, a propensity for shouting nonsense, exaggerated glaring at all passersby, and extreme boldness. They usually are also by themselves, although on occasion they may have a sidekick for backup. Because their eyes look so freakish and depraved, they tend to favor dark wraparound shades to keep them hidden, as wild discolored eyes frighten people and they want to pass as normal. Tweakers tend to be lean and intense, with a vibe of barely controlled desperation as if they are vibrating like a tuning fork. They bounce around a lot, making everyone around them a bit nervous. Their eyes, voice, and movements can vary from sharp to hunted. Over time their skin, hair, and teeth may show signs of decay, and they tend to scratch and pick at their skin and scalp incessantly due to the impurities in the drugs irritating their pores as they sweat. Crackheads, on the other hand, often slur their speech as if drunk or their speech is so distorted it cannot be understood. Their movements tend to be jerky and uncontrolled, and they often exhibit tics as if from Tourettes or Parkinsons. Furthermore, crackheads stop caring about their appearance over time and will not bathe or change their clothes. Depending upon what state he is in at that moment, an addict can present as a low, moderate, high, or extremely high level threat. Again, these individuals are so unpredictable even they probably have no idea what they're going to do next.

Now, when I say "drugs" I'm referring to hard street drugs to which one can develop an addiction which leads them to commit crimes to obtain money for more drugs. Marijuana is not drugs, and party drugs like LSD and Ecstacy are not addictive, nor is PCP (which is currently losing popularity after a brief resurgence). The unholy trinity of addictive drugs are:

* Cocaine (flake, cut powder, and crack)
* Amphetamines (prescription pills, crystal, meth, crank, and ice)
* Opiates (prescription pills or heroin)

Now, of the three, junkies are usually the easiest to deal with. Opiates make you drowsy and careless, and if you are in withdrawal you'll experience nausea and cramps. They will sometimes commit robberies out of desperation, but, being less aggressive, they are far more likely to shoplift or commit smash and grab thefts from vehicles. Junkies are not typically violent, and when they do commit an act of violence it is often ineffectual.

Crackheads and tweakers, on the other hand, can be unusually brutal since they are usually out of their minds, full of wild energy, and have zero impulse control. Furthermore, they tend to have an extraordinary pain threshold. They will commit violent muggings, but rather than carefully select a mark and set them up with an interview, they just tend to step out of the shadows and brain them with a pipe, or run up to someone from behind and stab them. Too much coke or speed for too long will induce psychosis, and many addicts later claim to have had no memory of crimes they committed during a binge. Not only are their crimes usually completely unplanned, but they are not thinking clearly while they are committing them—this makes addicts extremely dangerous. By the time they are so far gone as to be burglarizing homes or robbing convenience stores they are usually completely out of control and will be killed or arrested very soon.

Never argue with an addict. Just give him whatever he wants, then shoot him the moment his guard is down. In a large number of cases, even after getting the money addicts have executed their victims anyway, right in front of multiple cameras with no mask. They cannot be reasoned with and can never be trusted not to kill you. There have been cases where, after getting the money and exiting the store an addict reopened the door to shoot the clerk almost as an afterthought. In other cases addicts have robbed the same store several times in the same week. Like I said, their brain is pretty much goo at this point, and you may as well be dealing with a hostile alien lifeform. Due to their propensity for extreme violence combined with self-induced brain damage, the addict is one of the highest levels of threat the average citizen can expect to be victimized by. These individuals are unpredictable and dangerous.

Also worthy of note is the state referred to as "Excited delirium" in which a user of CNS stimulants such as cocaine, methamphetamine, or PCP basically goes batshit and runs through the street attacking people at random and punching out plate glass windows. They have usually stripped off their shirts and are wild eyed and dripping with sweat. These individuals' brains are boiling and the chemicals in their bloodstream give them incredible speed and strength as well as invulnerability to pain and incredible endurance. These individuals are not trying to commit crimes in this state, they *become* the crime. Mace will not work, Taser will not work, knives will not work, bullets will not work either unless you hit them in the brain, spine, or heart. Don't even think about going hand to hand with an individual in this state. You are no longer dealing with anything remotely human and you will die. Individuals in this state are virtually unstoppable unless you pile 10 big guys on them or shoot them in the head. Think of them as "fast zombies." Fortunately, unless you work in EMS or LE your chances of encountering an individual in this state are incredibly slim. This is not necessarily due to an overdose. In some cases non drug using psychotics have entered this state, as have drug users with only minimal traces of the drug in their systems. So if you see a naked screaming guy running towards you punching holes in windows, get the fuck out of his way and call 911. I do not care if you are the badass outlaw who does not call the po-lice . . . it is your fucking civic duty to call 911 on naked screaming guy so he can get pulled off the street. Little kids and old people do not need to meet naked screaming guy who will bite them.

So you either call 911 or shoot him in the head, I don't particularly care which.

SLEAZEBAGS

> *"Thieves are usually those who have something and want more. They steal not for food but for flashier clothes, a better watch, a handsome car. They steal for money to spend on flash, on women or drugs."*
>
> Louis L'Amour, *Education of a Wandering Man* (p. 11)

> *"Declining to hear 'no' is a signal that someone is either seeking control or refusing to relinquish it. With strangers, even those with the best intentions, never, ever relent on the issue of 'no,' because it sets the stage for more efforts to control. If you let someone talk you out of the word 'no,' you might as well wear a sign that reads, 'You are in charge.'"*
>
> Gavin de Becker, *The Gift of Fear*

> *"To achieve this state of control, they employ a range of linguistic and behavioral methods, like rhetorical questions, shame tactics, lies. Looking you straight in the eye, challenging, making themselves taller than you, intimidating, testing. Assuming a preaching style, using blanketing statements, asking questions, acting as instructor, treating you as student, giving you no room to respond, defining the power dynamic between you."*
>
> Susan A. Phillips, *Wallbangin'*

On the street, Sleazebags are known by many different names, with "Player' and "Grifter" being a couple you may have heard. These guys are con men and scam artists. Some later graduate to becoming pimps, reverends, or political activists. Many actually go so far as to open a business or non profit charitable organization, even if the business or organization amounts to little more than a PO Box, email account, disposable cellphone, and a box of business cards. These guys are pathological liars who have devoted their entire lives to tricking people out of their money. They also trick women into giving them whatever they ask for, including a place to live rent free.

I have met and interacted with dozens of professional con men. They are expert manipulators, skilled salesmen, and practitioners of the black art of mind control. If you are unaware of the subtle tricks they use to convince marks to follow their instructions you can easily be misled, tricked, or scammed. You could even follow them willingly into a back alley so he will have the privacy he needs to mug you. If something sounds too good to be true, even if it seems foolproof, you are probably being set up to be scammed. All your alarms should start ringing if it seems as if you are being pressured to make an immediate decision without all your questions and concerns being adequately addressed. The one rule you need to always remember is that if you are ever being pressured to make a snap decision your answer should always be "No."

Some of these guys are incredibly dangerous and will think nothing of killing you if you get in their way or threaten their reputation—but if you are an average citizen with no desire to make trouble for them, or "get rich quick," or hire a prostitute, it is unlikely they will even give you as much as a passing glance. Their marks usually seek them out one way or another, and unless you have something that they want which they think they can trick you out of, or somehow manage to offend or disrespect them in some way, it is unlikely you'll ever have a confrontation with one of these guys. This section is posted simply so you know not to make fun of angry Black men in purple suits and funny hats, because some will then feel obligated to "make an example" of you to safeguard their reputation. This example often entails the judicious use of a razor or weighted walking stick. Leave these people alone and avoid interacting with them in any way. They are a moderate level threat.

PUNKS

> *"He is a walking time bomb that can be detonated at any moment by some tiny slight . . . Because he thinks someone's staring at him, he's ready to fight. (If) a motorist cuts him off . . . he speeds in pursuit intending to do the same to him."*
>
> Stanton E. Samenow, *Straight Talk about Criminals* (p. 69)

> *"Street criminals get a rush knowing they are feared, a response they define as "getting respect." They look at average people as wimpy suckers who are there to frighten, take from, and to hurt . . . When they see an easy target they react almost reflexively, giving little or no thought to the act."*
>
> Loren Christensen

"You think of earning money; he thinks of taking money. You think of romance; he thinks of rape. Criminal sophistication is almost totally lacking. He takes money: he doesn't plan in any real sense; he's not organized in his criminality. Even what to do with the money is not pre-planned."

Andrew Vachss

"He sounded tough . . . the way a car with a bad muffler sounded fast."

Andrew Vachss

A punk is basically an inexperienced wannabe thug. They are typically in the 13-23 age range and may either be affiliated with a gang or form their own. They seldom start trouble unless they either are armed with a handgun or have at least 2 friends backing them up. It is not uncommon to encounter punks in groups of 5 or more, and the larger their group becomes, the bolder they become. They are frequently loud and boisterous as well as incredibly rude to everyone around them. They usually wear distinctive clothing, frequently urban "hip hop" styles, regardless of their race or socioeconomic background. Extra long white T-shirts and shirts supporting specific athletic teams are common garb. Gangs composed of groups of White or Asian teens from affluent homes are sometimes encountered in the suburbs, and if they have weapons and a desire to "prove themselves" to their friends, they can be every bit as dangerous as ghetto gangbangers raised on government cheese.

Punks project a huge ego to compensate for their insecurities and secret feelings of inadequacy. They will think nothing of shouting insults at strangers for entertainment, and in the event someone talks back to them they will use that as "justification" to attack them. Frequently, they will set up situations in which a target is expected to react in a certain way, which they can use as an excuse to berate and threaten him in hopes of inducing fear prior to the attack for added entertainment. Usually the targets they select are young White men, but they seem to prefer those who appear timid or weak. They may also attack the elderly or disabled. They seldom will engage an individual who is larger and stronger than them unless they are armed or have a significant numerical advantage, due to the fact that cowardice is in a punk's nature. It is low-risk thrill violence for sport, and the cash rewards are often secondary. This willingness to form large groups for the purpose of savagely beating strangers recreationally is what makes punk motherfuckers a potentially serious threat. They are also extremely dangerous in the event they perpetrate an armed robbery due to inexperience and ignorance. Like the addict, they have a distressing tendency to execute people who cooperate without offering any resistance, either because they: feel the need to eliminate witnesses, want to experience what it feels like to kill someone, wish to enhance their reputation, or simply as the result of a negligent discharge.

The punk is easy to spot. He is the loud obnoxious guy wearing clown clothes who is walking down the sidewalk with a half dozen other guys dressed just like him. You should avoid him. If there is a confrontation you must be prepared to immediately switch to Condition Red and let the bodies hit the floor. Often, the punk motherfucker will see in your eyes that you just don't give a fuck and don't mind dying over this if he decides to get froggy, and he will back off and let you pass, woofing half-assed insults to convince his friends that he isn't really scared. You should not respond to these. Any time you confront a punk you need to be prepared to use extreme violence. You don't fuck around when facing a potential stomping, and I guarantee that at least one of them has a concealed handgun and several have knives. You need to be aware of the fact that even scrawny teenagers with big mouths in stupid clothes can kill you. Do not underestimate this particular threat. His ego will force him to attack you in order to save face if insulted in front of witnesses. They are most dangerous in packs.

Be advised that the punk is seldom encountered alone and is usually in a pack of 3 to 10. Sometimes much larger groups are encountered, which presents an extreme danger, even though most of those individuals are non-involved spectators. Be further advised that female punks are just as bad as their male counterparts, often deliberately escalating conflicts or even targeting victims themselves. The old rule "never hit a girl" does not apply to gangbangers, and never applies if they are attacking or are armed.

FREAKS

> *"These are people who are so damaged that they are beyond all fear and are damn near unpredictable . . . Most of these people are killing themselves with drugs, but that takes too long . . . They are no longer human beings. I don't know any other way to describe them. There is something about them that*

causes an instinctive reaction of "Wrong!" in normal people—not wrong in the sense of moral right and wrong, but wrong against nature and evolution . . ."

Marc MacYoung, *Violence, Blunders, and Fractured Jaws* (pp. 106-107)

"Know this: These predators like what they do and will keep on doing it—until we stop them."

Andrew Vachss

The freak pathology is sexual in nature, even if no overt sexual act occurs. Stabbing someone can be sexually gratifying to them, as can arson, sniping, stalking, or simply peeking in windows. There are over a hundred categories of freak. You will know them when you see them. For want of a better word, they tend to be somewhat creepy if not icky. Most are socially maladjusted to the point of virtual exile. The most dangerous ones are intelligent and able to successfully adapt and blend in without drawing undue attention to themselves. This category is so complex I will not attempt to delve into it here. They are high level threats to their specific targets due to their obsession and compulsions. Their targets frequently are limited to women, but children, elders, and the disabled are also at risk. The reader of this book is unlikely to be targeted, but a friend or family member might. Freaks seldom listen to reason and can never be trusted, making rehabilitation impossible. They need to be destroyed. The proper method of freak disposal is detailed in my prior book and shall not be covered here as it entailed a complete chapter. For more data on freaks, I'd advise looking at forensic psychology textbooks, "true crime" books about serial killers and sex offenders, or any of the "Burke" novels written by Andrew Vachss. Freakology is way beyond the scope of this book.

PREDATORS

> *"Violent criminals are like nothing the average person has ever experienced. They are psychopaths, which means they release their anger and get their kicks from senselessly hurting or killing other people. Many of them don't care whether they live or die. They may sound and look like anyone else, they are often friendly, but that's only so they can get what they want—control over others, then the injuries begin."*
>
> Sanford Strong, *Strong on Defense* (p. 30)

> *"The objective of the violent criminal is to control you, emotionally and physically. Everything he does—his threats and promises—is intended to terrify and control you . . . For most crime victims, their temporary cooperation backfired into full control over them."*
>
> Sanford Strong, *Strong on Defense* (p. 50)

Someone wiser than myself (whose name eludes me) once said something along the lines of: *"Overly permissive parents who fail to discipline their children end up with defiant brats who ignore anything they are told, point their finger at whatever it is they want, and scream demands and threats until they get it. As these brats become adults, that finger is often replaced by a gun."* That is a surprisingly apt allegory which describes the default predatory mindset perfectly: "Gimme MY money" or "I'm TAKING that pussy" are commonly heard phrases. They feel entitled to ownership of things that do not belong to them and are in the possession of someone weaker whom they can intimidate, hurt, or kill. Classic bipedal predatory behavior: "Dat shit be MINES."

There are many types of predator, the punk and freak being most common, but they are a few steps down from the top predators addressed in this section, which is why they are referred to as punks and freaks instead. These guys tend to have a superior level of physical fitness and a willingness to hurt innocent people to get what they want. They have a hardness about them and a coldness to their eyes which will distinguish them from other street people. Most of them have been in prison at least once for violent crimes, and many are older gang members. Typical age range for top level predators is 25-45. The predator you are most likely to come into contact with on the street is the professional armed robber. Fortunately, unless you are a cashier in a shop, a teller in a bank, or so wealthy you drive a luxury car and wear expensive jewelry, you are unlikely to face such a threat. Unlike the punk, the professional robber is experienced and used to being in control. He usually knows exactly what he wants, and if you refuse to comply with his demands you may be executed on the spot coldly and efficiently. Hand over your wallet, cash drawer, or car keys if you have a gun pointed in your face and do not argue or make any sudden movements. He should take what he asked for and leave quickly. If, instead, he tries to relocate you or bind you, that shows you are not dealing with a professional but a punk who does not know what he is doing, or a freak who is more interested in control and victimization than money. As the

Spetsnaz credo goes: *"Dont trust, don't beg, don't fear."* If a robber wants more from you than money, you need to kill him instantly or die trying, even if the only weapon you have is your thumbs and teeth. Never allow yourself to be isolated or bound. That is a non-option.

Oh, one thing that you might want to know about armed robbers is the appropriate way to interact with them in the event you happen to be present when a robbery occurs which does not directly involve you. According to the law as written and interpreted, it is not appropriate to draw your weapon in a store when someone is holding up the clerk—unless they turn their weapon on you. It is also not appropriate to draw your weapon on a bank robber in a bank (yes, you may carry your firearm into the bank, assuming there is no sign outside stating you may not), unless he draws it on you. Be aware that cameras are recording these events and multiple witnesses present will tell the police exactly what they saw you do. A lot of guys seem to think that it is okay to walk up behind the robber and set his hair on fire with their muzzle blast, but the law calls that homicide and you will be prosecuted rather than given a medal, so don't do that. Just stay well out of his way and strive to remain as inconspicuous as possible until he leaves. If he starts hurting people or ordering them into the back room, then it is probably legally permissible to shoot him in the back of the head, even though the law would prefer that he point his gun directly at you before you draw your own. This is why sensible folk often disregard ignorant nonsensical laws.

Aside from straight up armed robbery of stores, banks, taxicabs, pizza deliverymen, and people walking down the street, predators will also engage in carjackings and home invasions. Such crimes tend to be incredibly violent as well as sudden, and if you have not taken basic precautions such as locking your doors and having a weapon close at hand you are pretty much screwed. Counterambush techniques involve emptying your magazine at the threat(s) and reloading immediately, which requires training. More information about dealing with carjackers or home invaders in later chapters.

And that concludes *Deviant Anthropology 101: Introduction to Street Scum.*

F.T.W. COMMENTARY

"I am not arguing with you—I am telling you."

J. McN. Whistler

Most street people are not criminals, they are walking wounded with no interest in hassling you or anyone else. That includes scavengers and addicts as well as people on the dole who have given up on life and are just walking through a haze of drugs, alcohol, and mental illness. They may well be scumbags, but if they are not directly interacting with or interfering with you they should not be considered subhuman zombies. Your primary threat comes from muggers posing as panhandlers and packs of punks wandering through the club district after midnight. You cannot reason with a mugger or a punk—they will consider your attempt at de-escalation a display of weakness, which proves you are a suitable victim. Muggers and punks want easy victims, they do not want to die. Look them in the eye and speak your truth calmly and clearly—then feel free to show them the weapon in your hand. That is their one and only warning. I have said things like, "I will put one in your fuckin' head," or "I will gut you out like a deer," and meant it (be advised that simply uttering either phrase is punishable as a violent felony offense in jurisdictions which do not recognize your 1st Amendment right to free speech). If they refuse to either disperse or let you pass, start killing them rapidly and efficiently with the understanding that you probably will not be walking away from this. If you are able to, leave the area afterwards.

Empty Hand Techniques

> *"Your teeth are a most effective natural weapon. If, for example, you are immobilized by a bear-hug, bite into your opponent's shoulder. If a hand is over your mouth, bite it. If any portion of your opponent's body is touching your face, bite hard."*
>
> Joe Hyams, *Playboy's Book of Practical Self-Defense* (p. 27)

> *"The first rule of unarmed combat is to arm yourself."*
>
> C. R. Jahn, *Hardcore Self-Defense* (p. 41)

I'm not going to fuck around here.

There is really nothing stupider than engaging in unarmed combat with a criminal aggressor intent on causing you serious bodily harm, particularly if you are physically outmatched or he has friends backing him up. This is usually the case because criminal predators rarely pick fights in which they are evenly matched, and nearly all of them are pocketing a weapon of some sort, whether it be a boxcutter, a screwdriver, a short length of pipe, or a padlock on a bandanna. Fights on the street are settled with weapons, period. The only time you should ever intentionally refrain from using a weapon is when you are faced with someone who is obviously weaker than you and your sole intent is either to restrain or eject them, but that isn't really "fighting" at all, is it? And this book is not about "fighting" at all . . . it is about survival. If you want to learn how to "fight" start boxing at the gym several nights a week. I have no intention of teaching anyone how to fight.

Before you go hand to hand with a criminal attacker, pick up a tool or projectile of some kind and use it. Going empty handed against a violent assailant is neither "honorable" nor 'fair"—it is fucking stupid. But let's say you are in a situation that unfolds too quickly for you to arm yourself and the only option you have is to use your empty hands to keep the other guy from hurting you, what then? Well, with all due respect, if you are actually asking that question you're pretty much screwed. A few years of boxing or full contact jujitsu would really help you out here, and you ain't gonna acquire those skill from reading a book or watching a video. If you are in this situation and have failed to acquire the skill sets you need to prevail, there is only one option for you. You need to go totally batshit and fuck the other guy up hard. This goes double if he's twice your size or there's more than one of them. In order to do this effectively, you need to completely disregard the "rules' and just do the maximum amount of damage possible as quickly as you can. This will entail hitting the other guy first and hitting him in places that are considered "off limits," and no, I'm not talking about hitting him in the nuts—every guy expects a ball shot and half the time even if you do hit them it doesn't end the fight. I'm talking about the knee, the throat, and the eye. A successful strike to any of these areas will take the other guy out of the fight immediately and he will need to go to the emergency room in an ambulance—and if you don't leave the scene immediately you will probably be arrested and taken to jail. These are serious strikes with very real consequences—misuse them at your peril.

BLOWING OUT THE KNEE

This is a crippling move. If you execute it correctly the knee bursa capsule will rupture, ligaments will tear, and bones will dislocate. If you execute it incorrectly less severe injuries will result such as cracked cartilage and a displaced patella. A lot depends on how much weight your opponent has supported by that knee, at what angle the knee is bent, in what direction he is moving, and the direction and velocity of impact. The result of a successful knee strike will be your opponent falling to the ground, in agonizing pain and unable to walk or even stand. This will end the fight without need for inflicting further and more serious injuries, which is why I have listed it first. Injuries will be so severe that hospitalization, surgery, and months of physical therapy will be required and full range of motion may never be regained. Needless to say, your potential civil liability if found at fault could easily exceed twenty thousand dollars. This is not a move to be used lightly without justification.

I've heard a lot of theoretical nonsense regarding "how many pounds of pressure" is required to blow out a knee with a low thrusting side kick, but there are too many variables to say for sure. It is, however, estimated that your kick needs to produce at least 60 pounds of pressure for this to work. Try for 80. I have kicked people in the knees and been kicked in the knees—with boots—and nothing but bruising occurred. Trust me when I say that it is very difficult to focus that much energy on a low level moving target during a fight—and you'll only get one shot at this, because once he realizes you're targeting his knee joint he will either take care to protect it or go into overdrive and launch himself at you. Due to these facts, you want to try striking unexpectedly while he is immobile. This will entail a pre-emptive strike when you are certain a physical altercation is unavoidable. Yes, I just told you to hit him first. He who hits first usually wins.

The most favorable target is the outside of the knee joint, blasting straight through. The side hinge of either knee, from the outside towards the inside, is more likely to result in severe damage than any other attack. Low side stomping kick, preferably with heavy boots and impacting with the heel, is the best way of accomplishing this. Striking the side of the knee from inside towards the outside, or striking the kneecap from the front (especially if the leg is locked straight) can also work. Stomping side kicks are best, but a vicious snap kick delivered with a steel toed boot can do this as well.

Once your opponent is on the ground he is out of the fight unless he has a gun. I would advise leaving the area immediately unless you are forced to fight his friends or he really pissed you off and requires additional breakage. Be advised that once you kick someone who is on the ground and no longer presenting a threat, the law says that you are no longer defending yourself and are now the assailant, so if you proceed to kick his teeth out that is a felony charge.

CHOPPING THE THROAT

There are over two dozen ways I have been taught to attack the throat. Many of these are stunners, immobilizers, or sleepers. I don't teach those moves because they are complicated, risky, and require a lot of training to be reasonably effective. Plus, at 5' 7" and 150# with one hand, there is no way in hell I'm going to try restraining someone who is attacking me. Nearly everyone I have ever fought was approximately twice my size, with the average being 6' 1" and 230#, with a few being significantly larger than that. If I am forced to go hand-to-hand against a violent offender with that level of disparity of force, guess what? My first move is likely to be a killshot.

Now, before you get all indignant about how chopping someone across the throat is "overkill" or "not allowed," you need to understand that there are no rules outside of the ring, and an assault and battery by an attacker twice your size amounts to a threat of lethal force, against which the law permits you to shoot someone in the face. Now, tell me again why chopping someone in the throat under those circumstances is "chickenshit" or "heinous."

Another thing you need to know is, I have chopped people in the throat before—as well as been struck there myself—and nothing much happened aside from some choking and gagging. You need to hit HARD and follow through as if you expect your hand to blow through the back of his neck for this to work. Be advised that the throat is the most vulnerable area of the human body, and there are about a half dozen ways a significant injury to this area could result in death. If you hit someone here, there is a very high probability that they could die—perhaps within minutes, or it might occur hours later. But, as noted above, there is also the chance that no significant injury might occur. Remember, this is a moving target protected by the scalene muscles and possibly fat as well as the mandible. It is very possible your strike could be partially deflected or absorbed. It is also very possible your strike will miss its intended target entirely, as it is a natural reflex to protect the throat. Do not count on being able to strike your attacker in the throat effectively.

There are also over a dozen different ways to strike the throat from the front: multiple open hand strikes (i.e.: spearhand, V-hand, shuto, etc.), crushing chokes, clothesline style attacks, and the simple punch (often the result of a drunken roundhouse to the jaw which missed . . . oops). Any way you manage to strike the throat will do damage. I am going to keep things simple by referring only to the chop (shuto).

When you chop the throat, there are a number of tubes that can be crushed or ruptured, resulting in possible death. It is not unheard of for a single strike to this area to result in multiple injuries. This technique is so dangerous it must always be considered lethal—even though, realistically, you probably have less than a 50/50 chance of making it work. Here are just a few of the most vulnerable structures found in this region: *Thyroid Cartilage, Cricoid Cartilage, Carotid Artery, Jugular Vein*, and the *Vagus Nerve*. Now, a few other points which can be just as deadly but are less widely known include the: *Laryngeal Nerves, Phrenic Nerve, Hypoglossal Nerve*, and the *Carotid Sheath*. Lots of stuff to break here, and some of it can result in a slow death or a delayed reaction. You strike your opponent in the throat, he drops unconscious but appears to be breathing, and minutes later a misfiring nerve causes his epiglottis, vocal cords, or tongue to suddenly seal the airway; or a slow bleed within the carotid sheath can result in a hematoma which could cause death; or the lining of a contused blood vessel could slough off resulting in a clot that might kill him the next day. Again, this is an extremely vulnerable area and a lot can go wrong here—and if something goes wrong it may not be fixable, even if he is still alive by the time he reaches the ER and makes it into surgery. Never strike a man anywhere in the throat unless you intend to kill him.

Yes, I have seen videos of a few instructors claiming to be able to use "dim mak" to knock out an attacker harmlessly simply by chopping the side of the neck (rather than the front) in order to shock the *Vagus Nerve* into making the heart skip a few beats, thereby resulting in a temporary drop in blood pressure. The problem is that most of those instructors are frauds and liars, since their moves only work on obedient students who are practically hypnotized into believing that their infallible guru can execute this technique perfectly. Not only is there a very strong possibility that this magic knockout shot will not work, there remains the risk that it may work so well the heart does not resume beating automatically, or a blood clot could result. Never intentionally target the *Vagus Nerve* in hope of inducing a "harmless" knockout. It probably will not perform as advertised.

When you hit a man in the throat, hit him as hard as you possibly can—then hit him a second time if you can. This will stop the fight immediately, and there is a very high probability that he will leave in an ambulance. There is also a strong possibility that he could die. Again, this is a killing blow . . . when it works, which it may well not. Regardless, a strong blow to the throat which connects properly will stop the fight due to choking and gagging which interfere with breathing.

GOUGING THE EYE

This is one of the most vicious empty hand techniques one man can perpetrate upon another. Done correctly and effectively, the eye globe will rupture, spilling the *Vitreous Humour* and causing significant external hemorrhaging. It is excruciatingly painful and will stop the fight immediately. It will also result in permanent blindness. Done less effectively, the *Cornea* could be lacerated, resulting in spilling the *Aqueous Humour* which will result in permanent blindness if surgery is withheld or if infection is introduced. Alternately, the eye globe could become dismoored from the socket. Either result is correctable with immediate medical attention but will stop the fight immediately. Done ineffectively, the *Cornea* could be scratched or the eyelid could be scratched, resulting in pain and tearing similar in effect to a shot of pepperspray. Any successful attack to the eye will end the fight . . . unless your opponent goes batshit and tries to chew your face off, but fortunately that is a rare exception to the general rule.

There are over a dozen methods I am aware of to gouge the eye. By far, the most damaging method utilizes the thumbs. There are a few methods of doing this, but basically all that is required is that you jam your entire thumb as deep as you can directly into your opponent's eye socket—preferably through the eye globe, but as eyes tend to be resilient and squishy they have a tendency to shift under impact rather than rupture. When this occurs, the eye typically is pulled from the socket as the thumb is withdrawn, then hangs down the cheek suspended from the optic nerve and blood vessels. Although this appears incredibly gruesome, it is possible for the eye to be cleaned with saline and pressed back into the socket, whereupon vision may be restored within several days.

I am not going to titillate you with the finer points of eye gouging here, but having at least an eighth inch length of thumbnail and grinding the thumb while it is in the socket and popping it out suddenly will increase the probability of severe tissue destruction. How the thumb gets in the eye is up to you, but a straight shot similar to a punch works just fine. Please note that this subsection is titled "Gouging the EYE," and eye was not pluralized for a reason. There is absolutely no justification for gouging both eyes out of anyone's head. One eye is plenty damaging, and it is a guaranteed fight stopper if you do it right. The only time you should ever gouge both eyes is if you are grappling or being choked out and want to double your chances of making your strike work. Eyes are small moving targets, protected by skin and bone, and they are surprisingly durable even if they are extremely sensitive to touch.

In conclusion, you need to be aware that juries find the concept of deliberately blinding another human inexcusable—even if done in self defense—and after the prosecutor shows them a poster sized glossy photo in vivid color of the gaping bloody hole in that man's face, it is a virtual guarantee you are going to prison. That is why I posted the eye gouge last, even though it is, by far, the most effective one shot fight stopper you can use. You will probably be sentenced to as much time for gouging a man's eye out in a fight as you would for killing him with a chop to the throat, because it will be the difference between a maximum sentence for 1st degree battery or malicious wounding versus a fairly lenient sentence for manslaughter if you are not outright acquitted on the grounds of self defense. In fact, it is very possible you could do less time for killing a man than blinding him. That is just how the American legal system seems to work—through emotion rather than logic or reason. The eye gouge is the most effective move that exists—so effective it is practically forbidden and you will be punished for using it, even in defense of your life barring extreme mitigating and extenuating circumstances. You have been warned.

F.T.W. COMMENTARY

Fighting an unknown assailant emptyhanded on the street is one of the most foolhardy and ill advised stunts you can attempt, and if they are significantly larger, armed, or there is more than one of them, you will probably die. Fight accordingly and do as much damage as possible. You can't "tap out" in a streetfight and there is no such thing as "second place." Even the winner doesn"t always get to walk away. Never fight emptyhanded. There is always something that can be picked up and used to strike someone with. Barring that, slam him into walls, corners, the floor, the curb, down stairs, through closed windows, into traffic, slammed in doors, or you could even use Mr T's orange juicer technique in which he would drop people onto fire hydrants. Empty hands is a desperation move. If you have no weapons at all and it goes to the ground, chew his nose off. Empty handed combat is the worst possible scenario and you do not want to go there, ever.

Pepperspray Is Your Friend

"Assault is an act that creates an apprehension in another of an imminent, harmful, or offensive contact. The act consists of a threat of harm accompanied by an apparent, present ability to carry out the threat. Battery is a harmful or offensive touching of another."

Legal definition of Assault and Battery

"You are going to drink this whole can of Mace!"

Dwayne Chapman

Some folks refer to pepperspray as "kung fu in a can." I refer to it as canned manners. It is, essentially, a chemical bitch slap, and a very effective one at that.

Pepperspray is not a weapon. It sucks as a weapon. Bad guys can and will fight through it and hurt you if they can grab ahold of you while half blind and unable to breathe. It really pisses some people off. If you are actually being attacked, especially by an armed assailant, leave the pepperspray in your pocket. It is an inadequate defense versus serious threats.

Why then do I recommend it? Because you have a far greater probability of being harassed or annoyed than being violently attacked. Pepperspray is great for those problematic situations where it is inappropriate for you to draw a weapon, but it would be okay for you to shove and yell at someone. They are not actually "attacking" you, but they are getting in your personal space, looming over you, touching you, yelling at you, following you, making unreasonable demands, and refusing to go away after being told to do so. Unfortunately, society does not allow us to shoot people like that. If you pull out your knife and threaten them with it you can go to jail for that, or it could escalate to the point you actually do need to stab them. If you shove them it could similarly escalate to a wrestling match in the middle of a parking lot. You may even lose. He could gouge your eye and bite your nose off, and that would really suck. This is why I carry pepperspray. I don't like going hands on with street people or stupid fucks if it can be avoided, because I'm a little guy and nearly everyone who starts shit with me is twice my size, so if it goes hands on I'm getting stabby. Mace prevents this. I will make you drink my entire can of mace because I am a great humanitarian who wants to save your life.

Violent attacks are seldom ambushes. It is rare that some street person just blindsides a random passerby and shanks them in the kidney. No, there's this multi-stage process that a lotta folks refer to as the "interview." A street person will test you to see just how much he can safely get away with. All street people do this, regardless of what position they're at on the food chain. First, they spot you. If you appear to be a likely candidate, you will be approached and he will say something. Next, he will close the distance and say some more things. Then he will attempt to make light physical contact. If this is successful, he will become more insistent and demanding, and, depending on his levels of boldness and motivation, he may well attempt to take what he wants by force. You cannot placate or reason with street people—that shows weakness, and weakness is something to be exploited. They understand "NO," and they understand "BACK OFF"—failure to respect these lawful commands constitutes assault, and they need to be punished for it. They need to drink your Mace.

Typical scenario entails some scumbag street rat—not necessarily a homeless or a mental case, although this is more likely than not—approaching you in a friendly manner, as if you and he are buddies and he just needs you to help him out a little. If it makes you feel better about yourself to give money to the bums, I'm not gonna tell you you're a fool, but I damn well *will* tell you to leave your wallet in your pocket. Wallet has a lotta paper money in it, as well as your credit cards, and maybe he'll decide he wants it all and hit you in the face with a brick. No, if you wanna feed the animals, just fold over a couple of singles and give 'em a little weight with a paperclip so you can toss them better. Keep that in one of your pockets for when you go out. Me, I typically carry a couple of dollar coins which work even better—although I'm more selective about who receives those and at what velocity. But I digress. Anyhow, after the approach, either you give him a dollar or you don't—but now it is time for him to go away and bother someone else. Sometimes they just don't want to leave you alone. They will intrude into your personal space, looming over you and becoming louder and more insistent. If you think that turning your back and walking away will work, they'll be tailing right behind you at an unsafe distance. Be advised that a crazy will often attack as soon as you turn your back on him, so I strongly advise against this. Anyhow, you've got a street rat sticking to you like Velcro and refusing to leave you alone after you clearly told him to do so. What now? After all, he isn't actually attacking you. He may well be behaving in a threatening manner, all yelling and waving his grimy hands inches from your face, all like, *"I'm not touchin' yoo . . ."* Illegal to shoot him in the belly for that. Actually, it may even be illegal to hose him down with pepperspray, but that is irrelevant. Pepperspray is a minor charge, he deserves to drink it, and if it becomes an issue you're gonna lie.

Okay, bad joke, don't ever lie. Just bend the truth a little. More accurately, tell the truth as you interpreted it. We all know that 90% of communication is non-verbal, but try explaining that to a jury. The guy was clearly threatening you, but if he didn't actually grab you and vocalize those threats the jury is gonna say you "over-reacted" and will lock you in a cage and put a ding on yer permanent record saying you are a bad guy with anger issues who likes to oppress the less fortunate. That is unacceptable. Fortunately, it will probably be your word against his, and you are clean cut, respectful and articulate, whereas he is drunk, belligerent, and hasn't wiped his ass all month. So you tell the nice policeman that after you asked him to leave you alone he grabbed you by the shirt and wouldn't let you leave, then raised his clenched fist as though he was about to strike you, at which point you gave him the peppers. But, as long as you leave the area quickly and there are few witnesses and no cameras, this will likely be a non-issue as street rats seldom call po-lice when someone they were trying to mug Maces their dumb ass.

Pepperspray is great. No-one is allowed to put their hands on you. If someone approaches you in a threatening manner in a semi-secluded area, you don't even need to tell them to back off before you hose them down. This is the only weapon which is acceptable to use against someone who is not actually in the process of trying to kill you. Don't touch me, and back the fuck off. Pepperspray wears off. Lesson learned. Don't do it again.

Mace also works great on canines. I love dogs. I like dogs better than most people. Dogs tend to be innocent and honest and pure of heart. Sometimes they make mistakes. Sometimes they have been subjected to neglect and abuse. Sometimes they even become psychotic and will attack anyone they meet. I would feel awful if I needed to shoot a dog. One thing you need to know about dogs is they are incredibly tough. I have studied dog destruction techniques taught to special forces operatives, and let me tell you it is a lot easier to take out a sentry than a guard dog. I have read hundreds of cases where a dog was shot or stabbed or clubbed, and in many of those cases the dog got really pissed off and continued to attack. Ever try choking out a large dog like a Rottweiler? It does not work so well. Good luck slitting a dog's carotid through those thick waddles of fat. If you are attacked by a dog and do not have a high caliber handgun, your best bet is to blow out one of its knees with a kick to keep it from chasing you down, as that is pretty much the only reliable way of stopping it. Unless you have pepperspray. You see, canines are extremely vulnerable to pepperspray as their primary sense is smell, and if you overwhelm their olfactory gland things become very confusing for them. This is particularly easy because their nose is covered with moist mucus membranes and they typically attack with their mouth wide open. One good spray in the face will usually stop them in their tracks and they will lose all interest in biting you. And the best part is it wears off within an hour and they will be fine. This is your best possible option when dealing with a vicious dog. Extremely effective and has no lasting effects.

There are MANY varieties of pepperspray and they certainly are not created equal. When I refer to "pepperspray" that usually indicate concentrated cayenne pepper extract (oleoresin capsicum) mixed with a carrier agent of some sort. In a few cases CS tear gas is added to the mix to enhance the effects. It is extremely rare to find straight CS in spray dispensers anymore as studies have shown that OC is safer and more effective on the average subject. The addition of CS to OC (usually in combination with UV dye which is marketed as "3 in 1" or "triple action") is supposed to be more effective, but I've seen no indication of that. UV dye is an additive that is supposed to be visible under UV light for up to a week to aid in identification of your assailant. It will also get on your hands and dilute the contents of your spray can. Visible dye is even worse for obvious reasons. If some drunk street person assaults you and you hose him down with pepperspray, he will choke and puke and be miserable for about an hour . . . but then he will consider it a lesson learned and get on with his life. Do you think things will be different if he is purple? Let us think about this for a moment. Even if he has no intention of ratting you out for macing him he will show up at the shelter or halfway house later that evening and they will see that he is purple and will assume that he raped someone, or maybe he robbed a bank and got the dye pack. Officer Friendly drives by and sees Mister Purple he will think the same thing. Either situation will lead to police interrogation, and they will pressure him to tell the truth, and then he will lie about how you just maced him for no reason and give them your description as best he remembers it. Now you are in trouble. So DO NOT purchase spray with visible dye, and I would strongly urge you to avoid "invisible" UV dye as well. Don't do it.

There are many types of canisters sold under dozens of brand names. Most of these are crap. If you have never heard of the brand and it is manufactured in China or Mexico you have no idea what you are getting and it is unlikely to be a quality product. In fact, it may not even work at all—and by that I'm not necessarily saying that the formula is ineffectual, but that the nozzle is defective or there is inadequate pressure and nothing comes out. I have seen that happen with new cans right out of the packaging. Then there is the cannister design itself. Let me first tell you what you DO NOT want. You do not want pepperspray with a safety switch. These switches are tiny and difficult to manipulate under stress, and are usually used on cans with exposed actuator buttons—which is another feature you want to avoid to prevent accidental discharge. Another thing you do not want is an oversized can. 4 oz canisters are designed to be carried on a utility belt in a pouch, and 9 oz cans (and larger) are typically carried by idiots who think bigger is better. All you really need is a pocket sized 2 oz can, and in some cases you can even go smaller, but then you trade off ease of operation for comfort.

The BEST canisters have a flip-top cap over the actuator button and no safety. MACE and FOX are two popular brands that utilize this configuration. Both brands manufacture pocket-sized 2 oz cans as well.

MACE Pepper Foam is my default choice whenever someone asks me what spray to choose. It is effective and practically foolproof. Flip-top cap, small 2 oz size, wide clog free nozzle, and a foam based carrier that permits indoor use. The foam reduces effective range to within 6 feet, but it makes aiming simple and the weight of the foam prevents blowback or deflection in a light crosswind. It will only affect the person who is sprayed with it. The only negative is the round cylinder is awkward to carry in a pants pocket. Great product which I highly recommend to all novices. It requires zero training.

Kimber Pepperblaster, also marketed as the "Guardian Angel," is a 2 shot derringer which utilizes a small pyrotechnic charge to fire a massive glob of pepper gel at extremely high velocity. There is a flip safety inside the triggerguard which should be broken and removed for ease of use. It is available in 2 configurations. The original model was rectangular and resembled a pager, but was awkward to hold and aim. The improved model looks like a squirt gun, fits the hand perfectly, and even has sights. The gunlike version can be had in red plastic (less likely to get you shot by a bystander) or grey plastic (more menacing to the guy you're pointing it at). It works extremely well and hits hard enough to work on an attacker who is wearing a ski mask and sunglasses. Gel permits it to be used indoors. Not effected by most wind. Will only affect the person who is shot. The only negative is that this product is expensive, retailing at nearly

$50 in many stores. I recommend the Pepperblaster to anyone who wants the best product available, but it is not recommended for folks in an urban environment who need to use pepperspray on a regular basis.

ASP Palm Defender is the smallest and most concealable pepperspray dispenser on the market. It is an aluminum tube 4.5" long and just over a half inch thick weighing under 2 oz. It disappears in your pocket and is unlikely to discharge accidentally. It also is reloadable, and inert training canisters are available. The negatives are: this device is awkward to use and requires training, and the spray is dispersed in a cone shaped blast of fog which should never be discharged indoors or on a windy day. This product is also somewhat expensive, and ASP makes two larger versions (Key Defender and Street Defender) which you probably want to avoid. The tiny Palm Defender is ultra concealable and can be dropped in a shirt pocket or tucked in your sock. I would advise not attaching it to a keyring as intended, but if you are only attaching a house key and a car key that should be fine. Great for use against canines and for close range outdoor work. Device does not look like a weapon at all and completely disappears in your hand. Spray shoots out the bottom of your fist. Very unique and ingenious design. Recommended for experienced users only.

FOX Labs streamer is a great product for folks who need to use spray frequently in an outdoor area. Works well on canines and provides multiple shots before it loses pressure. Streamer is accurate and not affected by mild crosswind. Not intended for indoor use. If you use a streamer indoors there is less overspray than with a fogger, but it will contaminate the room or hallway where it is used and effect everyone therein. Do not use this at the pub.

MACE Pepper Gel is a product I have a love/hate relationship with. It is more accurate and has more range than the foam, and it covers your assailant with a thick slime which he cannot wipe off or throw back—but after each use it is necessary to clean the nozzle thoroughly under hot water or gel residue will harden and clog the pinhole sized nozzle . . . and the next time you try using this product it will not work. If it was not for the clogging issue this would be the perfect product. For experienced users only.

Guardian .75 oz fogger is a great product for EDC outdoors as it is a small, flat, black plastic canister with an integral pocket clip. Very easy to carry, even in jeans, and it is not noticeable to others. As a fogger, it cannot be used indoors without contaminating an entire area with choking mist for hours, and it is susceptible to light wind which can blow it off course or even back in your face. The really nasty thing about foggers is that they are great for Escape & Evasion, in that if you are being pursued through a hallway, stairwell, or even an alley, you can turn around and conjure an invisible wall of blinding, choking, puking unpleasantness that your adversaries will run directly into, quite possibly with mouth and eyes wide open while sucking in massive amounts of oxygen . . . and that will slow them down right quick and probably make them lose any interest in pursuing you further. On a windless day, you can project this cloud into an open field or on a sidewalk and it will remain in place for over a minute—in an enclosed area, though, it is pure hell. Negatives of this product include: a safety switch, exposed actuator button, not suitable for indoor use or use in even light wind.

Now that we have discussed the various types of pepperspray and their intended application (indoor, outdoor, concealment, etc), let's talk about when it is appropriate to use it. Fuck, I used to use it fairly regularly, going through a can every other month over the course of several years. Be polite, motherfucker, or I will spray you without warning. I will use it as a pe-emptive strike. And then I will walk away . . . unless you are coming after me, in which case I get to practice one of my favorite moves, the flying side kick, which I learned doesn't work very well most of the time in a real fight, but against someone who is half blind and can barely breathe it works pretty good . . . and it is funny. Here are the rules of effective pepperspray use:

1. NEVER hold up your spray as a "warning." This rarely ends well. Everyone knows that pepperspray is non-lethal and the effects wear off within an hour, so street people have little fear of it. It is an unpleasant annoyance at worst. You show them that can and they will know to hold their breath and close one eye as they charge you, or shield their face with their hand, or attempt to deflect the stream or grab the can from your hand . . . after which they will gleefully empty it into your face and kick in your ribs before stealing your wallet, cellphone, and whatever else may be in your pockets. Never let them see the can. Always use it without warning. Hold the button down for a full second if not longer. Right in the face.

2. Do not hesitate to use pepperspray as a physical correction for poor citizenship. If you violate the social contract by

intruding into my personal space, refusing to leave after being asked to do so, shouting demands and insults, then putting your fucking hands on me or acting as if you're about to do so, guess what motherfucker? You're gonna drink this entire can of Mace! What have we learned today about respecting the rights of others? Yeah, fuck you, too.

3. LEAVE THE AREA IMMEDIATELY. Even if there are witnesses and cameras. You are NOT fleeing prosecution, you are heading towards safety. If you were completely justified in your actions and you know that witnesses have a good description of you and your vehicle, I would advise contacting law enforcement to file a report so that your side of the story is on file and you will not have an arrest warrant put out on you. If there are no witnesses, then fuck him. Give that bastard a kick in the ribs if you want.

4. Feel good about what you did. Did you shoot, stab, or beat someone who probably deserved it today? No, you did not. If you did not have that Mace you very well might have needed to engage in hand to hand combat, and that would not have ended well at all. He might have died, and you might have been seriously injured—after all, most street people carry a shank of some sort, and quite a few have at least one flavor of hepatitis which they'd be eager to share. Never go hands on with a street person. Even if you "win" you lose. You are not equals, you owe him nothing, not respect and certainly not a wrestling match on the fucking concrete. He is still alive because of your humanitarian concern for the welfare of others . . . and perhaps he will strive to be more civil in future contacts with the human race. One can only hope.

5. Replace your Mace. You only get about 4 1-second bursts from the average 2 oz canister, but after the initial use pressure gradually seeps away, and a couple months later it may not work at all. Mace is cheap. Buy several cans at once. Expiry date is a suggestion—this stuff does not do bad, but it does gradually lose pressure. A can of Mace that does not work is worse than no can at all, as it is nothing but false confidence.

In conclusion, pepperspray should be your first line of defense, and the first tool you grab when you are not in fear for your life but some obnoxious individual has targeted you for harassment and refuses to leave you alone. Once he persists by closing the distance to shadow behind you, loom over you, or place his hands on your person, that constitutes the legal definition of "assault" and you can make him drink your whole can of Mace. Of course, if questioned by authorities or forced to testify in court it would be rather stupid of you to admit that you were annoyed by this individual rather than terrified and decided to punish him for his bad behavior . . . if you say that, you will eat the grilled cheese sammich for months and will be liable should the dirtbag pursue civil charges against you to demand compensation for his pain and suffering. This is one of those times that you need to lie and say you were "afraid for your safety," because if you do not claim you sprayed him to stop an impending attack you are stating that you used it inappropriately in violation of the law. If you Mace someone who is harassing you and tell po-lice he deserved it and should not have pissed you off, well, that guy goes free, you go to jail, and the judge will garnish thousands of dollars from your bank account to fund the dirtbag jackpot. Do not think it will not happen to you. There are attorneys who specialize in this type of lawsuit, and at risk of being accused of racism this is especially prevalent amongst the African-American community (which also could upgrade a simple assault to federal "hate crime" status). Although pepperspray is perhaps the least harmful of all possible uses of force, including empty hand techniques, it is not without the potential for severe legal consequences, so please use some common sense and never use it without a good reason. My rule was to always give one verbal warning to "back off," and if that warning was disregarded I considered it a prelude to an assault and acted accordingly. In my opinion, it is practically a condiment and wears off within an hour with no ill effects . . . unless it contains indelible purple dye, which I specifically told you not to buy. Pepperspray is simple, non-lethal option with temporary effects that do not require medical attention. That is why I recommend its use when so many other instructors do not. I do not consider it a "weapon" but a form of harsh social interaction. It will fail as a weapon and should never be used as such.

F.T.W. COMMENTARY

Mace is not a weapon at all . . . it is practically a condiment. Feel free to use it on anyone who annoys you—just don't ever use it indoors because that is stupid and inconsiderate. Mace wears off. Mace is educational. Macing people instead of beating, bludgeoning, stabbing, or shooting them is a humanitarian act. Mace makes the city a safer and friendlier place. Just don't use the Mace with visible dye, and try to get the foam if you can.

THE SUBTLE BLADE

"The blade must be your constant companion . . . . she should be at your side in whatever you do, always providing assistance, support, and confidence. Treat her well, keep her sharp, and she will be faithful to you to the end."

Don Santiago Rivera

A knife is primarily a tool intended to be used for chores. Use for defense is secondary, although blades excel as improvised weapons. People who carry a blade exclusively for defense generally carry a second blade for utilitarian purposes. Again, a knife is a tool primarily designed and used for a variety of utilitarian tasks. Do not forget this.

A lot of men and women in our contemporary civilized society regularly carry a knife of some sort on their person or keep one close at hand, sometimes with the stated intent being that it is for protection. An exposed pocketclip or sheath knife does seem to work well as dirtbag repellant, but in the event an attacker is not impressed by the fact that you are clearly armed, most of these folks have no idea how to use it as a weapon other than to wave it around as a threat or perhaps jab someone lightly to keep them away. Sometimes those ineffectual methods actually have the desired effect, but why rely on tactics that will only stop a pussy? The average mugger is not afraid of your knife.

There are a surprising, if not disturbing, number of books and videos available which purport to teach folks how to fight with a knife. Some instructors even teach seminars and a few actually run dedicated knifefighting schools. The ridiculous thing about all this is that the vast majority of those authors and instructors have never actually been in a knife fight. Most of them have never even displayed a knife as a warning. Yet they proclaim themselves "masters" because they dance around on a mat slapping other men with rubber training knives. Some of these guys use rigid training knives that will actually leave bruises, which is a step in the right direction. I am aware of very few instructors who have ever taught anything approaching "reality based' knife combatives. Two things I'm gonna say right now: knife dueling is not reality based, nor are "guaranteed" knife disarming techniques. Unfortunately, it seems as if 90% of all blade related training applies to dueling and disarms. If that is what your instructor is teaching you, he is probably a dumbass with his head in some Walter Mitty fantasyland. A knife should only be used as a weapon against an unarmed opponent or an opponent armed with a lightweight bludgeon. NEVER go knife against knife, and if at all possible try to avoid any situation where you feel that taking a knife away from an attacker is a viable option.

Seriously, I don't care how fast, strong, or skilled you might be. If you attempt to take a sharp knife away from an alert and energized opponent who is highly motivated to use it against you, the chances that you will be able to accomplish this successfully without a trip to the ER for stitches and fluids and tetanus shots are slim to none. At the very least you will get carved up a little. It is more likely you will get carved up a lot. You could permanently lose mobility in one of your arms or have your belly zipped open to splash its contents on the floor. You might even die. The chances of severe injury or death increase tenfold should you proceed to engage in a knife duel, with prison being the prize awarded to the winner when he is released from hospital. Do not waste your time training with this nonsense in the hope that it will actually work on the street. A streetfighter will not duel with you. Duels are for amateurs and showboaters. If you encounter a knife on the street it will either be a threat or an ambush, never a challenge (unless tequila is a factor).

SELECTING THE RIGHT KNIFE

Society does not like people to carry knives, and many states and municipalities have passed laws banning fixed blades or lockblades that exceed a certain length. One thing I'm going to stress is that you really want to avoid carrying a knife with an overly intimidating appearance, even if it is lawfully permitted for you to do so. This includes, but is by no means limited to, the following: double-edged daggers, sawback survival knives, kerambits, switchblades, and balisong "butterfly knives." We should probably add tantos, kwaikens, T-handled push knives, assisted openers, and crude looking shanklike knives to the list as well. It may technically be legal for you to carry any single edged blade under 3.5" in length, but if it appears unduly menacing to a policeman or a jury they will do everything within their power to lock you in a cage for as long as possible. Due to this well established fact, I strongly discourage you from investing in mean looking "tactical" folders with blackened blades, and instead carry a simple looking knife of the sort that an outdoorsman or craftsman would favor. Polished fittings and wood inlays look more sane and responsible than skullcrushing "glassbreaker" pommels and hooked bladecatcher quillions . . . skulls and questionable etchings are discouraged as well. If your knife looks like something your grandfather might've carried, it will look better to a jury. If it looks like something a meth addicted punk rocker might carry, it will frighten them and put the thought in their heads that perhaps you aren't as nice and law abiding as you claim.

I am of the steadfast opinion that the knife you choose to carry should be well designed, constructed of quality steel, competently ground, and sharp. Furthermore, it should look respectable, like something a gentleman might carry. A handmade custom or a top quality production knife is best. Don't buy or carry flea market junk. Many knives I see are garbage made in China or Pakistan that were purchased at retail price for under twenty bucks. Expect to spend at least fifty and possibly over a hundred bucks on your knife. Occasionally you can find reasonably priced quality cutlery at gun shows, and they are an excellent opportunity to handle a variety of knives that your local cutlery shops do not stock, but your best bet is a reputable online source such as bladeforums, where members continually sell and trade new and used knives and you can research the knife in detail as well as the seller's feedback. Be aware that many of the custom knives sold on eBay are not properly heat treated, and many commercial knives are knock-offs if not actual counterfeits of better quality products. I would avoid buying knives from eBay unless you really know exactly what you're looking for and are able to spot irregularities that most buyers would overlook.

LOCKBLADES

As far as I know, lockblade knives are not specifically prohibited anywhere in America as long as they do not exceed blade length statutes, but a few states have prohibited the use of sheaths which open the blade upon drawing, or carrying an open and locked folder in a sheath. New York is trying to interpret folders which can be flicked open through inertia as "gravity knives" and assisted openers as "switchblades." NYC specifically prohibits carrying knives openly and will arrest and imprison you if an officer sees a pocket clip. Some states, primarily in the NorthEast, have successfully prosecuted people found with a lockblade as a judge felt it was "of like kind" to a dagger, which is undefined in the code but defined by Webster as "a knife suitable for stabbing." If the lockblade happened to have other features such as a quillion hilt, finger groove handle, or a pointed pommel, they have been used by prosecutors to further damn the knife as a dagger. It should be noted that those features are typically found on cheap flea market knives rather than quality commercial folders. Research your state's laws online to find out what is permissible to carry as well as cases in which people have been convicted for possessing a prohibited knife. This will show "precedent" and it is important to be able to cite case law—especially in regards to permissible knives—as the definitions are usually not defined in the statute. This is intentional, so that police and prosecutors are free to make decisions on what is illegal at their whim. Again, certain jurisdictions do not want citizens to be able to lawfully carry a knife, and you may be arrested without just cause and subjected to malicious prosecution and unduly harsh sentencing for nothing more than simple possession of an item that is not specifically prohibited under the statute and that a reasonable man interpreting said statute would believe was lawful to carry on his person. Gun laws are very clear. Knife laws are deliberately vague and subject to creative interpretation. If you want to dispute a knife possession charge you can reasonably expect to spend thousands of dollars on legal fees which will not be reimbursed to you by the court if you are found not guilty, nor can you claim them as a deduction on your taxes or as a loss to your insurance. All that being said, it is typically a safer bet legally to carry a folding knife instead of a fixed blade.

Personally, I've never been a fan of folding knives, particularly small folding knives. One basic requirement that I have for lockblades is that they be able to be opened quickly, easily, and ambidextrously with one hand. This eliminates balisongs and side-opening switchblades (for me, anyway, as I are somewhat inept). It also eliminates knives with thumbstuds and thumb disks. Knives with thumbholes—especially oversized thumbholes—seem to work best for me. I am also a fan of tip-up carry, preferring that option to the more common tip-down configuration, but that is a matter of personal choice. Many knives have pocketclips which can be inverted as well as reversed, and that is a great option. Another requirement I have is that the knife be lightweight with a grippy non-slip handle. Final requirement is that it not be a fucking liner lock—there are numerous lock options out there, with the lockback being the most common and a personal favorite of mine, but somehow the linerlock became popular and I hate it, even though the design has greatly improved. The original linerlocks were flimsy and unreliable, and this remains the case on many Chinese imports. Furthermore, I do not want to have to put my finger in danger of being cut in order to unlock the blade. One of the few companies that provides all of the aforementioned options is Spyderco, as well as their bargain partner company Byrd.

I realize that most of y'all likely prefer a traditionally shaped straight blade with a small belly, as non-traditional configurations may be outside your comfort zone. The Endura with black FRN or G-10 plastic handle is an excellent choice for you. It is available with a plain, serrated, or combo edge, and there is also a version with the quick-opening "Wave" feature. The cutting edge is just under 3.5" in length, making it legal practically anywhere. The economy version of this knife is the Byrd Cara Cara. For those of you who require a smaller knife, the Delica is the same exact design with a 2.5" blade, and is so small it can fit in the coin pocket of your jeans. The economy version of this knife is the Byrd Meadowlark. But the folder I'm liking the best is the Hold Out III from Cold Steel which is based on their old Culloden sgian dubh design and has a very pointy 3" blade which can be either plain edged or serrated, and I recommend their serrations highly. It is very thin and super lightweight, and in my opinion the best sub 3.5" folder commercially available at this time.

Personally, I've always been partial to hawkbills, especially in regards to self defense. Whenever someone asks me to recommend a knife I tell them to get a Spyderco Tasman, which is the hawkbill in current production (prior versions being the Harpy and Merlin). The economy versions of these knives are the Byrd Crossbill and Hawkbill. I have seen larger versions of these knives, such as the Spyderhawk and Superhawk, but bigger is not necessarily better with this style of blade as most of the work is done with the tip. I will discuss the inherent superiority of the hawkbill design later in this chapter.

FIXED BLADES

Most places in America still permit law abiding citizens to carry a small, single-edged, fixed blade knife, although there are often restrictions. California says it is okay to carry a sheath knife openly, but it becomes a felony if it is concealed by your jacket. A few NorthEastern states won't even let you have one in your car. Most states allow you to have a blade length of 3.5", but a few insist that it be under 3" and will charge you over a fraction of an inch difference. Be aware of your state's laws, and if you live in a major metropolitan area be aware of the municipal statutes as well. Don't be stupid and ask a cop—most cops lack a full understanding of the laws they enforce and will be highly suspicious of anyone who asks them about anything which is potentially unlawful, especially weapon violations. If you decide to ask Officer Friendly what knives are legal to carry or telephone the local police station from your home phone or GPS equipped cellphone, you may well find yourself the subject of intense and unwelcome scrutiny. Look these answers up online for yourself, and don't carry anything that can get you charged with a felony. Misdemeanor is a slap on the wrist, which typically means a night in jail and a $500 fine, but you probably don't want to risk even that. With knives, try to stay legal if at all possible. If your jurisdiction practically prohibits knives, don't think, "Well, since a Sharpfinger is illegal I might as well carry a Smatchet since it's the same charge," because the DA will be a lot less likely to reduce the charge for carrying a concealed Smatchet—don't be a smartass or it will backfire.

For the purposes of this section I'm not going to discuss Smatchets at all, nor shall I discuss khukris, Bowies, or other short swords. I'm only going to talk about fixed knives that are generally permitted to be carried in most places, that being single edged blades between 3" and 3.5" in length.

My personal favorite at this time is the BUCK 116 Caper. With a 3.25" blade length, it is the smallest fixed blade BUCK has ever made. I especially like the snap flap sheath, which when stuck in one's back pocket looks identical to a lockblade sheath, and thereby is regarded as "harmless" by the populace at large. Unlike any of my other sheath knives, the BUCK 116 has never gotten a second glance. Even when I'm holding it in my hand the dropblade resembles an oversized Swiss Army Knife. It isn't very menacing at all. And that's why I like it. The sad thing is hat this knife was discontinued in the mid 1980s and now fetches collectable prices averaging eighty bucks for lightly used. If you've got the cash they come up on eBay several times a month, and I recommend them highly.

Many of my friends are fond of the Schrade Sharpfinger, and it is a great knife but you've gotta know that not all Sharpfingers are created equal. A while back, Schrade filed for bankruptcy and was bought by Taylor who is now making these knives in China from inferior steel with substandard quality control. Don't waste your money on a Taylor/Schrade knife as they are crap. If you want one of these knives, go on eBay and find an old made in USA knife under the Uncle Henry or Old Timer name, preferably an OT152 with the carbon steel blade which is capable of taking a finer edge than the UT152 stainless. Another brand which made a great version of the Sharpfinger was Rigid, calling theirs the MAX Edge Hunter. This is a "tactical" version with a blackened blade, checkered and grooved handle, and pointed pommel, and I found it to be a superior knife at a fair price. Condor Knife & Tool of El Salvador also makes a decent version with a blackened blade and wood scales, although the factory edge leaves much to be desired and it will likely need a good sharpening if not a professional regrind. Beware of the inferior knockoffs made under the Winchester and Kissing Crane brands, as they are garbage knives even worse than the Taylor LLC "Sharpfingers." The primary weakness of this design is the delicate tip which can snap if misused or abused. Another flaw is the poorly designed sheath, but there are many custom sheathmakers who can fabricate a better one from leather or Kydex.

A lesser known commercial fixed blade which is of superior quality yet remains inexpensive is the Marbles Trailcraft with a convex edge and a variety of handle options, including stag and checkered rubber. This is a great knife with a non-threatening 3" blade that is extremely sharp and about an inch and a half wide, which makes for an impressive wound channel if one were to twist it around a bit. Try it in corrugated cardboard and you'll see what I mean.

These three commercial knives are tried and true designs which are guaranteed to serve you well. If you'd prefer a skinner, a bird & trout, or a custom blade, be sure to do your research. A great looking knife with an inept grind or poor heat treat will be a waste of money. If you don't know knives just pick a BUCK 116, a USA Sharpfinger, or a Marbles Trailcraft and trust me when I say any of them is a great choice. If you do not care if your knife appears a bit weaponlike, go for a sgian dubh style blade, but be sure to pick out a good one as most eBay sgian dubhs are practically nonfunctional replicas.

SHEATHS

Folders are typically just dropped in or clipped to a pocket, so sheaths are not generally used for them. Fixed blades, however, require a sheath. Unfortunately, they usually come with a crappy belt sheath from the manufacturer which is designed to be worn openly, is a disgusting tan color that doesn't match your belt, and has a bothersome retaining strap that gets in the way. Cold Steel's new Kydex sheaths have a "Secure-ex" locking system which makes them complete garbage. You probably want to contact a local leathersmith or an online custom sheathmaker to have a sheath made to your specifications. This will not cost too much, but will involve you shipping your knife to him and paying for return postage. It seems like a huge hassle, but trust me when I tell you that it is well worth it. Quick release Kydex is a great alternative to leather which permits inverted carry, should you decide on a paracord shoulder harness, a neck rig, or an ankle rig. With wet molding and rare earth magnets a leather sheath can be fashioned for inverted carry as well.

Whatever design you choose, it should be open top with no snaps or straps. I like Kydex for IWB and shoulder rigs, and I prefer leather for horizontal SOB and pocket carry. Your sheath is a personal preference just as was your choice of blade shape and handle design.

There are alternatives to having a custom sheath made if you either lack funds or need it quick. Sometimes you can get lucky buying a used sheath from eBay, although it will probably require modification. You could try making your own sheath if you have access to the appropriate tools. A cheap concealable sheath can be fabricated by epoxying the original leather sheath inside a cheap IWB holster for a small pistol, then snipping off the excess leather. A pocket sheath can be improvised from folded cardboard wrapped in layers of duct tape.

NON-TYPICAL DESIGNS

I"ve carried a knife since I was five years old. I have owned, carried, and used literally hundreds of knives. I know quite a bit more than the average person about knives, yet I am wise enough to realize that I am FAR from an "expert"—especially when it comes to topics such as metallurgy, grinds, or even sharpening. As I said, at one time or another I have owned practically every type of knife, including several prohibited pilum ballistic knives (which I do not recommend unless you are partial to impractical and hazardous novelty items). Here are my observations and comments on a few alternatives to the standard fixed blades and lockblades.

PUSH-OUT KNIVES: These are called by a variety of names and come in several styles and configurations. Basically, they are a short, single-edged blade that is manually slid out of the handle by pressing on a lock button and sliding it forward. They are retracted in the same manner. The "Christy" keychain knife is a superior example of this design. Several inexpensive utility knives with plastic handles have used this principle as well (back in the 1980s, Cold Steel produced several versions with serrated blades). An inferior version which is frequently found in the hands of street punks is the disposable utility knife with breakaway blades—they are flimsy, but incredibly sharp and can be purchased from some stores for as little as a dollar. Push-out knives are safe to carry and easy to open with one hand. Many folks favor them over pocketknives. They are also cheap enough to buy extras to give away as gifts or keep as spares in the event you forget or misplace your primary knife. The low price makes them real nice throwaways.

STRAIGHT RAZOR: I love straight razors. They make great utility knives and the high carbon steel blades with the high hollow grind is so sharp it can cut through 1/4" thick leather with ease. Be advised that I am speaking of properly made traditional straight razors here. Most of the ones you'll find on eBay or at your local cutlery shop are little more than razorlike novelties that have semi-sharp stainless blades. You can often find usable razors in secondhand shops for under $20. If you try to find a nice one in an antique shop or on eBay you will probably be overcharged as it seems to have become a fad to collect these nowadays. The thing I like most about razors is that they are so slim and light that you can slip one in your front pants pocket or your sock and it disappears without a visible print. The curved monkey tang also allows easy one-handed opening. Most people seem to think the best way to use a razor is to extend the blade and slash with it, but that's not true—fold it back across your knuckles, press hard against your adversary's body, and slide across it to create a long deep incision. The simple "flip slap slash" of a lockout grip results in nothing more than shallow superficial cuts. It is extremely difficult to kill with a razor, and the fine incisions frequently heal without visible scarring, making this an excellent tool for terrorizing and punishing—which is why they have always been a favorite of gangsters and pimps. Due to their bad reputation for misuse, it is illegal to carry a concealed razor in nearly every state and they are usually in the same category as brass knuckles.

PUSH DAGGERS: These are incredibly nasty weapons which are designed specifically for stabbing people repeatedly and efficiently. They usually are double-edged and utilize a T-handle which is usually rubberized to better absorb impact. The blade extends from the front of one's clenched fist and is frequently beadblasted or blackened to reduce visibility. They require zero training to use effectively and intuitively—just punch your adversary with it as you would hit him with your fist and it will result in a deep stab wound wherever you impact. It is nearly impossible to dislodge such a weapon from someone's hand as he is unlikely to drop it under circumstances that would cause a traditional knife to slip from his grasp. The truly terrifying thing about the push dagger is that few people ever see it. You could stab a man to death in a room full of witnesses and everyone would say they saw you hitting him a few times but never saw a knife. Due to its genuinely fearsome design, these knives are specifically banned in most states, and where they are not banned you will certainly receive prejudicial treatment from police and the court. This is, by far, my favorite knife design and I used to own an extensive collection. They were once very popular with riverboat gamblers during the 1880s and enjoyed a resurgence in interest when Cold Steel released the first commercial version a century later. Cheap, dull, imported knives of this basic design can be found at flea markets everywhere, and street people have used sewing scissors and tire repair tools as improvised substitutes. All versions are deadly. Think of them as brass knuckles with a knife on the end.

LA GRIFFE: The original La Griffe was designed by Fred Perrin, and was a small, single-edged fixed blade with a rounded pistolgrip handle and a ring at the choil (between handle and blade). This is a brilliant design, allowing for maximal weapon retention as well as pinpoint accuracy. The LaGriffe design has been licensed to several manufacturers (notably: Emerson, Spyderco, Boker, and Cold Steel), and many knock-offs and copies are also available. There are numerous variations on this design in a number of blade lengths and configurations, with and without scales. The Emerson design has been the most popular, incorporating a hawkbill blade and a thin skeletonized handle—it is intended to be carried in a Kydex sheath suspended from a ball chain or paracord under one's shirt as a deep concealment piece. Boker has several versions, including a miniaturized version marketed as the "Shark," which is akin to the OSS thumb dagger and is intended for front pocket carry. These are dedicated self defense blades not intended for utilitarian use which are designed specifically for concealment. This is one of my favorite knife designs and I recommend it highly.

KERAMBIT: This is a traditional Indonesian weapon that has gained sudden popularity in recent years after being featured in several action movies. It is, basically, a short clawlike blade attached to a handle with a knuckle-ring at the pommel. Very vicious weapon that can crush skulls and disembowel enemy combatants in skilled hands—but like the nunchaku craze of the 1970s the average idiot who buys a kerambit injures himself with it in short order, usually after spinning it around on his finger. These were originally a fixed blade weapon, but then several companies released expensive lockblade versions with pocketclips, which were invariably followed by inexpensive knockoffs, which in turn were followed by Chinese knockoffs of the knockoffs being sold at flea markets for $15. Now everyone has a kerambit because they are doublecool and apparently make great boxcutters. Everyone except me, because frankly I prefer Spyderco hawkbills to evil knuckle claw that makes cops angry. Even in places that kerambits are technically legal I would advise very strongly against actually carrying one.

PIKAL KNIFE: This is an odd design based around Silat techniques which presents an upswept blade with a sharpened top rather than bottom edge, like a reverse hawkbill. It is primarily used in the reverse ("icepick") grip to rip and strip and can be extremely effective in trained hands. The key word here being "trained." Silat, Kali, and other complex blade arts are not something you can practice on your own without professional level instruction. These are very advanced concepts well beyond the scope of this chapter. In short, don't select a pikal style knife unless you intend to seek further training, and if you see one of these in the hands of an opponent he probably is a lot better at carving people up than you are as these knives are not very common except among Silat students.

DAGGER: A true dagger is a pointed double-edged knife. Small versions are sometimes referred to as a "boot knife." Most of the daggers I have seen had 440C stainless steel blades that dulled rapidly, and nearly every boot knife I've seen on the street has been made of Chinese or Pakistani mystery steel that was dull as a butterknife. If a dagger is made from inferior steel and is poorly ground it will invariably be dull. You are better off obeying the law and abiding by convention and sticking with a quality single-edge utility blade which is far more likely to be sharp enough to actually cut paper with. The only daggers I've seen that were sharp enough to cut with were professionally reground unless they were custom knives to begin with. Seriously, several Gerber MK-I and MK-II daggers I've owned were dull new from the factory, and that is not the only commercial brand I've noticed this trend with. Daggers are typically ground to be pointy rather than sharp. By that logic you may as well carry an icepick. A properly ground dagger, however, can be pure hell in the hands of someone who has trained how to use it. Personally, I prefer the *sgian dubh* design, which is basically a hiltless, single-edged boot knife. The discontinued Cold Steel "Culloden" and "Mini-Culloden" were the best commercially produced examples of this type of knife.

SGIAN DUBH: This is one of my favorite designs. Translated from the Gaelic it means "black knife" and was a small hideout knife tucked in a garter or worn under a tunic. It is a small, flat, single-edged knife with a very pointy tip. Jimping on the spine for use of the saber grip is traditional. Most of these knives appear very similar with 3" to 5" blades and black handles. A lot of the ones on the market are non-functional replicas made in India or China, which are either crudely ground or have a fake gem set in the pommel. Custom sgian dubhs can cost hundreds of dollars, but frequently go on sale near the holidays and are reasonably priced secondhand. The Cold

Steel Mini-Culloden was a very well made and inexpensive commercial version with a Kydex sheath and a rubberized grip, and although it has been discontinued they still come up on eBay regularly. Avoid the Braveheart they replaced it with, as it has a crappy chisel grind and a retarded Secure-ex sheath which locks the blade in place preventing a quick draw.

SWITCHBLADE: Frankly, switchblades never really did that much for me once the novelty wore off and I realized they were flimsy knives with dull blades. Nowadays, along with the cheap flea market crap, there are some fairly high quality knives being produced—but they usually start at over $150 and can run to several hundred if not more. The thing I dislike about switchblades is that most of them have tiny round buttons that need to be located by feel and pressed firmly in order for the knife to open, and if you are under high stress and need to deploy that blade immediately this can be a serious problem. The only switchblade I can endorse for personal protection is the Microtech series of double-action Out-The-Front knives. These knives typically start at over $200 with the average price being closer to $300 so they are a substantial investment—and Microtech customer service notoriously sucks (they will also refuse to repair or return knives sent to them by civilians other than law enforcement officers or licensed dealers). Frankly, I discourage you from investing in a Microtech unless you have a large disposable income for toys, but the fact remains that they are the best OTF available with the most durable design, most user friendly actuator button, and the sharpest blade. But for fuck's sake always clean the blade off before retracting it. Simply opening a parcel and failing to remove the cellophane tape residue from the blade can gum up the mechanism and make it fail—just think what congealed blood would do. Next to the Troodon/Scarab/Ultratech OTFs, my next recommendation might be for a HK Tumult which is half the price and less than half the quality. If you really want to try out a OTF but want to spend under a hundred bucks, the only cheap switchblade worth buying is the AKC Concord series which is Italian made and utilizes 440C steel blades for about $75. You can buy cheapo OTFs for less money, but you really get what you pay for. It may look like a $300 Microtech Scarab at a tenth of the price, but you get dull mystery steel that won't take an edge and poor lockup with a blade that rattles when you shake it—trust me when I say that those Chinese flea market switchblades aren't even good letter openers and you would be throwing your money away.

CHEF'S KNIFE: Kitchen cutlery is very popular among street people. Next to a Saturday Night Special it is probably the deadliest weapon you will ever encounter in the hands of an adversary. Why? Because not only are these knives longer than most daggers and hunting knives, they also tend to be a lot sharper. The grind and steel of kitchen cutlery is intended to hold a sharp edge for a long time after much use. In fact, when someone buys new knives and tosses their old ones in the trash or donates them to a thrift store they usually are still sharp enough to slice a roll of paper towels down to the cardboard tube—and that means it can cut your arm down to the bone. During a few months long ago when I was penniless and homeless, I carried a Chicago Cutlery chef's knife with a 8" blade in a sheath I made from cardboard and duct tape and it was as good as any fancy Bowie knife—plus, due to the weight of the blade and smooth texture of the walnut handle, I could throw that knife accurately and make it stick every single time. Of course, I could only do that from 3 feet away, but that would give you quite an advantage of surprise if confronted with an assailant who also had a knife and was closing the distance. Chef's knives are the only knives I've had good luck sticking in targets consistently, but this requires weeks of practice and it is extremely ill advised to do in an actual combat situation unless you have a second knife in reserve.

USING THE KNIFE AS A WEAPON

> *"There is one unquestionable rule in knife fighting: never get into a knife fight. There are no winners in edged weapon contests—only losers to varying degrees."*
>
> Fred Rexer, Jr., *The Brass Knuckle Bible*

> *"The knife, it must be remembered, is a universal phenomenon. It exists in some form or other in every culture of the world. When used for personal protection, the techniques for its deployment vary as much as one culture varies from another."*
>
> James Loriega, *Sevillian Steel* (p. 2)

There are many styles of knifefighting. Some styles seem needlessly complex, overly ritualized, or have little connection with the reality of life in a modern urban environment or reality in general. In short, roughly 90% of the written data I have seen pertaining to this subject appears to have been written by individuals who have never actually used a blade against a realistic training target, let alone an actual opponent. My Dad taught me how to kill a man with a knife when I was 8 years old, and I have read every book written on the subject of knifefighting and taken multiple seminars. I have worn out and broken multiple knives on a variety of training targets, I have pulled knives on people, I have used knives on people, I have had knives used on me, and I have seen the results of knives on many others. I know very well what a knife can and cannot do, and I'm not about to give you bogus advice based on nothing more than theory and conjecture. My method will not only work, but you can learn it very quickly.

THE RULES OF KNIFEFIGHTING:

1. Have a knife, preferably a long, sharp, pointy one.
2. Do not drop your knife.
3. Do not throw your knife.
4. Do not hesitate to use your knife.
5. If the other guy also has a knife, switch to a distance weapon. Never fight knife versus knife

BASIC KNIFEFIGHTING TECHNIQUE #1: Draw and open your knife without dropping it. Show the open knife to your adversary. Tell him to go away.

BASIC KNIFEFIGHTING TECHNIQUE #2: If your adversary refuses to leave and instead advances, without hesitation slash him across the face. It is best to target the forehead. If he is reaching for you, slash his palm and fingers. If he grabs you by the arm or clothing, slice or stab his inner forearm. If he grabs you by the throat or takes you to the ground, stab him a single time in the torso, stirring and twisting the blade inside him until he lets go.

That is ALL the average person needs to know about knifefighting . . . oh, except the part where if the other guy has a knife you shoot him or run away. Knife dueling is great to train in if you are a martial artist, stage performer, or historical reenactor, but going knife versus knife in real life is practically suicidal. Look up the term "Pyrrhic victory."

Knives are poor weapons. They are typically illegal to use as a weapon, and a prosecutor will always treat a man who uses a knife different from a man who uses a licensed handgun for self defense. Even if you never open the blade and simply use your folded knife as a fistload bludgeon, you still will be arrested and prosecuted for assault with a deadly weapon. Use of a knife as a weapon will make a huge mess, splashing the possibly infectious blood of your attacker everywhere, including all over your clothes which will alarm others. Knives have extremely limited range, inferior to nearly all other weapon types. Knives have minimal stopping power, and an individual who has been cut or stabbed repeatedly can continue to attack you, possibly with a knife of his own. The best features of a knife are that it is lightweight, easy to carry, typically legal to possess, far more effective than empty hands, and it has hundreds of legitimate and useful purposes aside from stabbing people. I advise everyone to carry a knife at all times due to their usefulness, but it should be your last choice as a weapon. Indeed, the only time you should ever consider using a knife for self defense is if you have nothing else available, including improvised weapons. Far too many things can go terribly wrong if you use a knife for self defense.

You will not learn how to fight with a knife from reading a book, watching a DVD, or even taking courses with an instructor. In fact, many "knifefighting" courses will provide you with extremely dangerous misinformation. In reality, you never want to go knife versus knife—and in a hellish bizarro world scenario in which you do end up dueling with a knife you certainly fucking well better not try to "spar" with your opponent by circling around and trading cuts—no, you close with and destroy him by slamming your blade deep into his vitals while immobilizing his weapon arm while riding him to the ground where you will slam the handle back and forth like you're running the gears of a race car at the track to do as much internal damage as possible. Needless to say, no instructors train their students in this manner.

You need to learn how to make actual cuts, which is impossible to do with a training knife. The absolute best way to learn how to cut is to get a job as a meatcutter and cut steaks and chops from refrigerated carcasses 40 hours a week for over a year—then you will be a master. Seriously, studying anatomy may show you where to cut, but meatcutting will teach you HOW to cut, and there is a lot to be learned. The subtleties of cutting simply cannot be articulated in words or conveyed via demonstration—it must be experienced, again and again and again. If you are unable to make such a drastic career change for the sake of your art, you will need to practice on a variety of improvised targets made from cardboard cartons, carpet remnants, and old jackets. Styrofoam and pool noodles cut far too easily to provide realistic results. You need fibrous targets that offer resistance in order to see how seemingly minor changes in angle or pressure can drastically alter the length and depth of your cuts. This training will also greatly improve accuracy, which will be abysmal with no practice at all.

PRACTICAL KNIFEFIGHTING 101

> *". . . the greatest advantage of the edged weapon is that it need only touch you to do damage. Contact usually means cutting . . . . The edged weapon requires very little speed and even less strength to do its job."*
>
> Richard Ryan, *Master of the Blade* (p. 18)

So you have decided you want to learn how to knifefight. Okay, does the other guy have a knife? Is it already in his hand and open? If so, please stop now and re-read this chapter, noting that not once but several times I have repeated that you NEVER are to go knife versus knife. If the other guy's knife is still in its sheath that rule may not apply, depending on your speed and level of motivation. Knife is a lousy weapon. It is only used to give you an advantage over a much larger unarmed opponent when there is a clear disparity of force. Let me share with you now the fundamental techniques:

LESSON 1, DRAWING: The first thing you need to master is drawing and opening the blade. Do this slowly at least a dozen times every day, focusing on maintaining a firm grip as you draw, open, and grasp the knife. Speed will come naturally over time. Do not practice for speed, practice for smoothness. It needs to develop naturally over time to the point that you can have your open knife in your hand without even thinking about it. Using it everyday for chores and simple tasks is the key to mastering this. You might be surprised how common it is for folks to fumble their knife during the draw or the opening, particularly if they are trying to be quick or opening under stress. Trust me when I say that a smooth draw, clean opening, and firm grip accomplished in one second is far superior to a incomplete opening and weak grip accomplished in a fraction of a second. It is far more important for you to have that knife in your hand securely rather than instantly, even if it takes you twice as long. Dropping the knife is bad. Every time you drop your knife in practice (and you will), immediately stop training and punish yourself by doing a set of 50 pushups. This will help remind you not to be stupid. Drawing is the core of knifefighting. If you have not mastered the draw you have no business practicing more advanced techniques.

LESSON 2, THE GRIP: There are well over a dozen different grips that I am aware of. I only teach one: the natural grip (also known as the "hammer" grip). The reason for this is that it is an incredibly secure grip and you are unlikely to have the knife dislodged from your hand upon impact, as can be the case with a saber or pinch grip. It also requires less skill to use than the reverse ("icepick") grip. This is the best possible grip for close range stabs to the torso and simple slashes. This is the only grip you need to use, although the "experts" will decry it as amateurish and insist you not only need to learn multiple grips but constantly transition between them as you attack—this complicates things and greatly increases the probability that you will drop your knife. Natural grip is best.

LESSON 3, PRESENTATION: This is the primary method of utilizing a knife for self defense—you show it to the guy who is threatening you as a warning that you are armed and he needs to back off or risk getting cut. Like many things, there is a right way and a wrong way to execute this technique. One example of improper technique is to shriek in a high pitched, girlish voice, "get away from meeeeee!" while waving your tactical folder at arm's length like a spasmodic with a magic wand. Another example of what not to do would be to draw your knife, then immediately freeze into a pale clammy statue as you are overwhelmed by the effects of a full adrenal dump. Fuck. Pull your knife and open it, then hold it close to your side, all calm-like, and you may not need to say a word to make him go away. If he freezes up and looks at you, it is up to you what to say then—words need to be yours and they need to be true, so I ain't gonna provide you with a script here. I told one guy, "I will gut you out like a fucking deer," and told another guy, "Motherfucker, I will kill you." This is against the law. You can be charged for this. NEVER pull a knife or any other weapon as an empty threat, because if he calls your bluff either you will need to stab him anyway, you will be forced to run away like a pussy, or he will beat the shit out of you and stab you with your own knife. That can and does happen when people pull weapons they had no intention of actually using. If you are too chickenshit to actually cut him, he will read it in your eyes and know you've got no heart and he can do whatever he wants to you. If you aren't willing to actually use it, don't pull it—fuck, you probably shouldn't even carry it in the first place.

PRACTICAL KNIFEFIGHTING 201

> *"When I pin that foot—as well as shoving a knife into his eyeball—he loses his balance. He goes down very quickly . . . . A quick jab is all you need. We're not*

> *trying to kill this adversary. We're trying to dissuade him from attacking us further. To say that this is a humanitarian act—to puncture someone's eye . . . is a little bit far-fetched. But compared to what you could do with a knife, yes—it is humanitarian. You are trying not to kill."*
>
> James Keating, from the COMTECH video, *Reverse Grip Knifefighting* (0:34, 0:50)

So you have mastered the fundamentals and want to learn more advanced methods of using your knife as a weapon. The following is everything you really need to know:

LESSON 4, THE CLAW OF DOOM: Sorry, just couldn't help myself. Ever since I was introduced to "Crafty Monkey Steals the Peach" in an Ashida Kim book I always wanted to develop a deadly technique with a melodramatic title of my very own . . . please permit me this small indulgence. As I stated previously, the hawkbill is one of my favorite blade designs for personal protection and it is my default recommendation for women and novices. Why? Ease of use and reduced psychological stigma. Let me discuss this briefly. A traditional knife can be used to slash or to stab. These are not necessarily intuitive movements, especially if you are in a grapple, and most civilized individuals react with horror and revulsion to the very thought of stabbing another human being, even if that person is attacking them. The hawkbill is so unique in design it can barely be considered a "knife" at all—it is, for all practical purposes, a talon. It does not cut with the edge, but rips with the tip. Using the hawkbill is an exercise in simplicity: press your fist against your attacker's torso, rotate the tip forward so it penetrates his clothing, and slide downward while maintaining pressure. This is nothing at all like the mechanics involved with a slash or stab and will result in a long, deep laceration that will require dozens of stitches to repair. Unless you have trained for increased penetration, it is rare for these cuts to be more than an inch deep, and if you stick to the torso and upper limbs as targets it is nearly impossible to accidentally kill someone with this type of knife. Due to the reduced risk of mortality and the lack of commitment and training required for use, an individual who would freeze up at the thought of stabbing someone usually has no problem using the "Claw of Doom" to slice them open like a fish. Unlike a razor or a well sharpened knife, these ragged cuts will hurt like hell and produce an instant pain response discouraging continued hostilities. Usually only a single rip across the chest or ribs is enough to make an attacker disengage and stagger away—but do not count on that as a guarantee. In the event that a proper hawkbill lockblade is unavailable to you, a linoleum knife, pruning knife, or even an old churchkey style can opener can be used in a similar fashion.

LESSON 5, THE SLASH: Slashing is usually less than lethal, provided a major artery is not severed. Most major arteries are buried deep under muscle and sinew, the exceptions being the throat and the inside of the arms. As long as you avoid targeting the throat and the inside of the arms with slashes you probably will not kill your adversary. That is why I recommend slashes over stabs—because a body on the ground is bad news and you will probably go to prison for that, self defense or no. If you are defending yourself against attack and slash your assailant across the chest or back of the hand, he probably is not going to report you to police and may not even need to go to the hospital. Slashes to the face are considered "maiming" and tend to be punished more severely than cuts to the body and limbs. Individuals who have their faces sliced open are also far more likely to go to the ER for stitches, and it is mandatory for the hospital to notify police when knife wounds come in, and someone who you cut across the face will probably co-operate with police investigators in order to "get even' with you for scarring him for life. So, although the face is a great target, the consequences of maiming or blinding someone are high, and I recommend limiting slashes to the arms and torso. Be advised that hard "power slashes' to the arms can sever tendons and nerves, which means that arm will be out of commission for a long time, and may even be permanently paralyzed, resulting in a dead "flail arm' which surgeons often end up amputating. But if that arm happened to be holding a weapon that he was about to hurt you with, well, fuck him.

LESSON 6, THE STAB: Stabbing someone is serious business. If you stab someone, even in the arm, they will probably need to go to the ER to stop the bleeding. If you stab them in the torso they can die—either within minutes due to exsanguination or days later due to infection (peritonitis often results when the bowel is ruptured). One low risk technique that gets folk's attention is a light jab—basically, you poke them with the point of your knife and immediately retract it. This typically hurts a bit, bleeds a little, and lets them know you are serious about cutting them, especially if you are calmly circling them and inquiring if they'd "like some more," or advising them that was "just a taste" of what they're about to get if they keep fucking up. If they press the attack, playtime is over and you need to kill them. They were warned. Terminate the threat by inserting the blade into its torso all the way to the hilt. It is best to aim for the centerline up under the sternum if possible, but anywhere in that area is good enough for starters. What a lot of guys do is imitate a sewing machine, resulting an a dozen inaccurate half-assed stabs that are all over the torso and only go partway in, leaving clean narrow wound channels that sometimes self seal. This makes a huge mess and is largely ineffectual without training and targeting. You only need to stab the fucker once, maybe twice—just do it correctly. Again, stick the blade in the middle of the torso all the way to the hilt as hard as you can, then try to get it even deeper via tissue compression, aiming at an upward angle towards the heart, liver, and lungs. Once it is in as deep as you can get it, twist the handle sharply to rotate the blade in a clockwise manner, then twist it back counterclockwise. This enlarges the wound channel for better drainage. Finish by pumping the handle. By this, I mean slam it in all 4 directions to stir it around (sometimes referred to as "running the gears"). This creates extensive trauma within the body cavity with the intent being to slice and lacerate as many blood vessels and organs as possible. This single stab wound will thus be far more damaging than a flurry of glancing strikes, and as a bonus it will look less horrendous to a jury . . . after all, you only stabbed him once.

LESSON 7, ADVANCED TECHNIQUES: These are just a few random moves above and beyond the typical slash and stab. First up is the "job in the face." I know I said to avoid cutting people's faces but this is okay because it is only the forehead, and folks seem to care less about that. Quick snap cut or power slash right across the forehead is a fairly low risk move and tends to end the fight immediately because scalp wounds bleed like hell and all that blood will run directly into his eyes. This is a classic streetfighter's trick which has been used hundreds of times with great success. The next move is the basic pommel strike. This is typically considered a non-lethal attack unless you are one of those freaks who likes to carry around a medieval style dagger with a huge spike on the butt. If you are in grappling range feel free to use the pommel of your knife to pound a divot into his skull to make him let go of you. If you have a lockblade, the closed knife can be used to load a hammerfist as an impact tool to strike the face and jaw. This is a low risk move that can scatter his teeth across the floor like Chicklets. Be advised that a closed knife is still considered a "knife" and you will be charged with assault with a deadly weapon. The final move is often referred to as "defanging the snake" and is designed to make him open his hand and drop his weapon. This occurs via massive tissue disruption. You can stab your blade completely through the forearm by inserting it firmly between the radius and ulna, then twisting sharply. This frequently severs the nerve which controls the hand. Another method involves laying the edge nearly flat against the forearm and cutting inwards at an acute angle along the bone, effectively peeling a large chunk of meat away from the bone in a strip. This is a lot more effective than a standard cut to the forearm which sometimes immobilizes only one muscle. There are multiple layers of muscle all around the forearm, and a strip cut ensures total immobility. Both methods of defanging the snake are crippling blows and recovery is not expected.

LESSON 8, EXPERT TECHNIQUES: A lot of instructors teach new students multiple grips from the very first class. As the natural grip is the best and most useful, multiple grips can be confusing and counterproductive to the novice. Even more awkward is shifting from one grip to another. An expert has trained shifting grips every day for months, until the knife flows effortlessly from natural to reverse grip with a minimal twitch of the fingers. This takes time and dedication, and you will drop your knife during practice. Start out with a butterknife or a drone trainer until you get the hang of it, and remember to immediately do your 50 pushups every time that knife hits the floor—this is not a fucking game. I have a love/hate relationship with the reverse (icepick) grip. I can draw my blade this way instantly and strike with pinpoint accuracy. I can cut patterns in the air quicker than your eyes can follow, creating a flashing barrier of steel comparable to an agricultural combine. I can stab so hard that I can penetrate a damp phonebook with ease . . . but range is limited to targets immediately in my face, like 14" away, which basically requires you to either initiate a sneak attack or chase the guy down and jump on him, making it primarily an offensive rather than defensive tactic. With the natural grip I can easily double my effective range, or triple it through lunges or running stabs and slashes. Another commonly taught grip is the "saber" grip, in which one's thumb rides the spine of the blade. This can provide extreme accuracy for light jabs, such as to the eye or throat, but you will drop your knife if you try using this grip to batter your way through a ribcage. Many instructors, who apparently have never even stabbed a tree in their lives, claim that the saber grip is superior to the natural grip, which it clearly is not. One extremely nasty move has been referred to as the "rip cut." Basically, this is a stab that is followed up by pulling down on the blade, resulting in an extremely deep cut of the sort that butchers use to process a side of beef. This is especially devastating as a disemboweling technique, and can be executed horizontally as well as vertically. The final technique I'm going to discuss involves "quick kill" targeting. A lot of bullshit has been written about this, particularly that they are guaranteed kills and there is even a "timetable of death" counting down how many seconds it takes for someone to bleed out after you stab them there. Sometimes you get lucky, sometimes you don't, and the major arteries are often only nicked rather than severed if not missed completely. I am not going to go into detail here, just get an anatomy chart of the circulatory system and locate the abdominal aorta (midline), renal artery (kidney), and subclavian artery (between clavicle and scapula next to neck)—those are the primary kill targets. The default kill target is, of course, the exposed carotid. Secondary targets, known as "bleeders," are the brachial and femoral arteries. Immobilizing targets include the Achilles tendon, the hamstring, and the IT (iliotibial) band, as well as major muscle groups of the upper arms, shoulders, and chest.

There you have it, everything you need to know about how to fight with a knife in only several pages. Most instructors could easily expand every page I have written into a complete chapter, then add in a stack of diagrams and photos for filler to create an entire book, but you don't need all that. If you wish to seek training in the blade arts, practically everything you will learn will be an expansion upon these basic concepts, or it will be overly complex shit that works great with a training partner, but not when adrenaline is affecting your fine motor skills. Keep things as simple as possible, but above all, *avoid using your knife as a weapon!* Seriously, use a bludgeon or a gun instead. Knife is a utility tool that can be called upon as a very effective improvised weapon should you find yourself without a bludgeon or gun. Knife should never be your primary weapon, always a secondary or backup. Only freaks and badguys use a knife as their primary—usually because it is scary and quiet. Knife is a bad choice of weapon unless it is a short sword style chopper like a Smatchet. It is most effective against unarmed individuals.

F.T.W. COMMENTARY

> *"Haven't you ever wondered what it would be like? What would be the feeling of a real blade entering another man's body? That initial resistance—and that sudden giving? The surprise on another man's face!"*

"The Villainous Master" in *By the Sword* (1991)

A knife can be used to frighten or intimidate because it is sharp, pointy, and silent. The only noise a knife makes are the howls of your adversary. The primary problem with the blade is that using one is extremely messy, which is why hitmen who favor blades wear raincoats or coveralls that they can strip off and bag shortly after use. You will not have that luxury and your porous clothing will be soaked with blood, as will your hands, hair, and face, because when you stab people they tend to squirt. If you are wearing light colored clothing and are in a semi-populated area where you would be likely to be spotted by others, this could be problematic. Furthermore, unless you have a high degree of skill both at accurately striking a moving target and at inflicting deep long cuts under layers of clothing, the blade has relatively low stopping power. Even if a lethal strike is delivered, that individual can remain on his feet fighting or chasing you for several minutes until his BP bottoms out and he drops. For those reasons I dissuade folks from relying upon a blade as their primary weapon, but in many cases it will be the ONLY weapon available to them. It is the best counter-rape tool available to women. It will enable a small and weak individual to "win" a fistfight against a much larger and stronger opponent or even multiple opponents who have decided to beat him. It is a very poor choice against an armed opponent unless it is unexpected and from behind.

THE CONCEALED HANDGUN

"Every morning that you get out of bed and strap on your sidearm, you're halfway to jail."

Robert Bailey, *Private Heat* p. 25

THE WAY OF THE GUN

The concealed handgun is the most effective self defense tool available to you, bar none. However, it is also the self defense tool most likely to get you locked in a cage should you use or even display it. Unless you are a policeman or are related to the judge, you run a serious risk of being convicted of a crime simply for drawing your weapon and telling an attacker to go away. That is a fact. Let me tell you another fact. In some states, particularly the Yankee NorthEast, it is a felony for a law abiding citizen with a clean record and no criminal intent to so much as own a handgun without an official permission slip issued by the state at their whim. I'm not talking about felony to carry concealed, I'm saying they will put you in prison for open carry, keeping a gun in the glovebox of your car, or even keeping an unloaded pistol locked in the trunk of your car. I could take up an entire chapter with how Draconian and unConstitutional certain gun control laws are, but I'm not going to waste either of our time. The laws are constantly changing and you need to research those laws for yourself. You are a fool if you think that ignorance of the law and a clean record will keep you out of prison. Many of those regimes have a one year mandatory minimum but can sentence you to years should they so wish. So if you choose to carry in violation of the law you need to be fully aware of the risk you are taking. It is no joke. Innocent people have been destroyed arbitrarily and capriciously with no legal recourse. It is downright unAmerican and the founding fathers are spinning in their graves, but that is the New World Order for you. Guvmint sez guns are bad and if you have an unlicensed gun you are a dangerous criminal. If you want to carry, you should get a license. If no licences are issued to citizens in your county you need to move. Seriously.

If you decide to become a gun owner, the most important thing you need to do before anything else is to familiarize yourself with the basic rules of safe gun handling, then you need to completely familiarize yourself with the gun itself. The vast majority of accidental shootings, negligent discharges, and inappropriate usage of a firearm to settle domestic disputes seem to occur in areas in which firearm ownership is discouraged or prohibited, as well as in urban environments where there is little opportunity to target shoot. That is because the people there lack experience with firearms and are profoundly ignorant of them. They are like powerful magical totems and objects of fascination and legend rather than the simple tools that responsible gun owners see them as. This fascination seems to increase exponentially as alcohol and drugs are added to the equation. Gun is a simple mechanical device, but it is extremely unforgiving if misused and you cannot take a bullet back once fired . . . it ain't gonna stop until it hits something, and maybe not even then. Keep your booger picker off the bang switch and never sweep the dangerous end past anything you do not wish to destroy. It was not my intent to cover gun safety in this book, but as it might be negligent of me not to do so, I shall refer you to Col. Jeff Cooper's four basics of gun safety, which follow:

1. All guns are always loaded. Even if they are not, treat them as if they are.
2. Never let the muzzle cover anything you are not willing to destroy. (For those who insist that this particular gun is unloaded, see Rule 1.)
3. Keep your finger off the trigger till your sights are on the target. This is the Golden Rule. Its violation is directly responsible for about 60 percent of inadvertent discharges.
4. Identify your target, and what is behind it. Never shoot at anything that you have not positively identified.

Now, a lot of folks would have you believe that a handgun is like a magic wand that will instantly make bad guys cower in terror or flee the moment you point it at them. Sometimes it actually does happen like that, but usually that isn't the case. You need to be prepared to squeeze that trigger if you plan on carrying a gun, because a gun without the will to use it is n nothing but an empty threat, and most criminals will be able to tell through your body language and the tone of your voice if you are bluffing or not. Even if you aren't bluffing you may end up getting rushed anyhow. Usually a grab for your gun is preceded by a bit of "disarming" conversation as the goblin slowly closes the distance. He may say he was only joking around and had no intention of harming you, he may accuse you of being rude as well as a racist, he may claim that you are unlawfully threatening him and he will call the police, he may state that your gun is not real or is not loaded, or he may flat out say that you just don't have the balls to use it. If he says any of those things while either approaching you, circling you, dawdling, or doing anything other than rapidly backpeddling as he leaves the area, you probably need to put one in his belly. Now, please note that I did not tell you to shoot an unarmed man who is not in the process of beating you to death. This is all hypothetical. From the hundreds of case studies that I have either read or observed personally in which this sort of passive-aggressive predatory behavior occurred, it was a setup for a brutal and unexpected attack. Now, this attack did not always occur but the goblin was definitely considering his options and weighing out the possibilities. If you pull a gun on an attacker and he fails to immediately leave the area, guess what? Yep, he is still attacking. It may be a slow motion attack, it may be nothing more than a strategic reassessment, but he still remains a very real threat to you. If he approaches, no matter how slowly or what words are coming out of his lie hole, you need to shoot him. If you decide to retreat and he follows, you need to shoot him. If it is a stalemate of sorts but he does not seem particularly motivated to leave and for whatever reason you cannot, perhaps a single "warning shot" is in order, preferably into the ground near his feet.

Gunfighting tactics are way beyond the scope of this chapter. Besides, realistically it is probable that you will be rushed and will not even be able to acquire a sight picture, let alone maintain a proper shooting stance. Hell, you may not even be able to draw your weapon before he's on you. Here is my complete course on combat pistolcraft in three easy steps: 1. Draw your gun without dropping it on the ground or shooting yourself in the leg. 2. Keep gun close to your side where it will be difficult for your attacker to grab. If necessary, use your other hand or elbow to push him away. Take a couple steps back if you need to create some distance. 3. If he closes the distance, shoot him. If he tackles you, press the muzzle against his torso and fire until your weapon is empty. Simple shit. Your ability to hit a bullseye at 50 feet or reload quickly is nice to have, but you need an entire different skill set for what basically amounts to hand-to-hand combat, which marksmanship at the range under strictly controlled circumstances certainly is not. Marksmanship is only good if your attacker is more than 30 feet away, in which case he probably would not be attacking you. Most "gunfights" occur within 8 feet. Frequently low light conditions and grappling are involved. Train to draw, and be willing to shoot. Range time is good, but it is unlikely to help you much on the street as a civilian.

Be advised that flashing lights and loud noises will probably result in multiple armed policemen responding to numerous 911 calls complaining about your activities, so you should already have some idea of how you might want to deal with that possibility. As Forest Gump might say, "A policeman is like a box of chocolates, you never know what one you'll get." Regardless of whether you get a good cop or a bad one, they will be responding to a "shots fired" call with guns drawn and pointed at you. They might shoot you, especially if you do something to frighten them. Once you have dealt with the attacker you'll probably need to deal with the cops as well. It is virtually guaranteed they will arrest you, so that is our best case scenario. If you choose to remain at the scene until police show up it is best if the gun is no longer in your hand, you refrain from saying anything other than "that is the guy who attacked me, I have a valid CCW permit, I'm having chest pains and think I need to go to the hospital, I will give a full statement once I've consulted with my attorney." It is up to you whether you stick around to allow them to arrest you and then give a possibly incriminating statement, which will likely not be verbatim and possibly twisted in such a way to make it seem as if you did something wrong, without legal counsel present. Many policemen would accuse you of "hiding something" and pressure you to incriminate yourself, but please consider what would happen if your roles were reversed and instead he were being investigated for a shooting. If a policeman shoots someone he is usually told to take the rest of the day off to recuperate mentally, and the next day, possibly later, he will answer a few routine questions while accompanied by his attorney and union representative to safeguard his rights and put a stop to any flagrant abuses. But little people don't get treated nice. Little people get bullied, threatened, yelled at, and their Constitutional rights are disregarded . . . after which the policeman will lie about what happened and everyone knows that a policeman's word carries far more weight than that of a lowly citizen. Leave the scene and lawyer up. If police arrive before you can leave, say you are having chest pains. Adrenaline causes huge increases in blood pressure and if you are in your 40s you probably will experience chest pains. It will remove you from their clutches, if only temporarily. Be advised that not only will they seize your firearm but you will be searched and they will seize other things as well, including your cellphone from which they will attempt to pull data including but not limited to: any calls you made within the past hour, as well as contacts, photos, GPS data, and if you have a smartphone they'll look at internet history and password protected documents as well—all legal for them to do at this time. But I digress . . . .

In short, what I wish to convey to you, is that while it is fine for the average citizen to carry a concealed handgun every day of his life since, statistically, it is unlikely it will ever be drawn let alone fired in an altercation, there is a very high probability you will get in serious trouble if it is. At a bare minimum this trouble will entail your name and address being posted in the local newspaper where it will be seen by your coworkers and neighbors as well as many thousands of dollars in legal fees . . . and that is the best case scenario. Depending on the jurisdiction as well as the sanity of your particular judge, it could easily be far worse. Revocation of your pistol permit is likely. A felony conviction is probable, even if you are able to avoid incarceration via a plea arrangement. But if you do not have all your paperwork in order, or there is any possibility something improper may have transpired, or holy hell you were prohibited from carrying or even owning the firearm in question (possibly because your county refuses to approve permit applications), well, here's your Grilled Cheese Sammich, and while your cellmate Bubba has no interest in raping you, he snores and wets the bed. That will be your life for the next 3-10 years. Gun = jail. If you choose to carry a gun, even if you can do so legally and never get liquored up or pull it in anger, you need to consult with a GOOD criminal attorney who specializes in self defense cases, pay him a retainer, and keep his card with you at all times. You'd better program his number into your phone as well. Have your girlfriend program it into her phone too. Get the name and number of a reputable bondsman and do the same. The time to do this is NOW. Do not procrastinate. After the fact will be far too late as the amount of stress you will be under may well prove overwhelming and you will not be thinking clearly. Establish a plan well in advance and pray you never need to implement it. Those nutters on the forums seem to think that if they decide to walk through the ghetto after midnight on a Saturday night, and some street thug accosts them, they "get" to shoot him as if it is a prize they win, and spout pat slogans like "Better to be judged by 12 than carried by 6" without a clue of what it is like actually to *be* judged—and most cases never even make it before a jury anyway, DA offers you a choice of 5 years probation or take a chance with the jury and risk 10 years of prison. That is a big risk, and the legal fees to take that to trial and prepare an appeal afterwards would probably mean your family would lose their house and everything they own to pay for this, after which you might end up in prison anyway. I'm not gonna tell you what to do here. That choice is yours to make alone.

Now that I have very plainly stated why I feel a handgun can prove more of a detriment than an asset in a typical self defense scenario once legal ramifications come into play, if you decide to carry anyway I want you to forget all that. Do NOT disregard it, just put it out of your mind during your day to day activities and it certainly must be the last thing on your mind should ever you be faced with a situation in which you might need to use it. Anxiety and second thoughts will lead to fear and possibly even inaction. You need to focus exclusively on the threat. At that moment, nothing else matters. FTW! You can deal with the bureaucratic bullshit after you deal with more immediate concerns. And if you get away clean, you may not even need to deal with that either. (Just joking . . . sort of.).

The internet badasses all have their opinions on what gun you "need" to carry on your person every day. A few seem to think you need multiple guns. Badass number one insists that you carry a .45 ACP 1911, as nothing else will do. Badass number two says Glock is best and even though the cops carry .40 caliber, 10mm is a lot better, especially with that superhot Buffalo Bore ammo. Badass number three says wheelguns never jam and anything less than a .357 is for pussies. Badass number four obviously hasn't paid any attention to the original topic and says the best possible concealed handgun is of course an AR-15 pistol with a red dot sight. Now, do you want to listen to the internet badasses or would you prefer to listen to me? It's okay if you like them better. It doesn't hurt my feelings none. I think all of those guns have their place, but everyday concealed carry just isn't one of them. My personal recommendations for folks who ask include the following: Lightweight .38 Special snubbie, Bersa Thunder .380, Ruger LCP .380, NAA mini .22 Magnum, and the Beretta Jetfire .25 ACP. Those are the default recommendations when someone is looking into purchasing a gun for concealed carry, and which one they choose will be determined by a number of factors, with their personal preference being foremost.

I'm gonna try to simplify this as best I can. It has not been easy for me. I have spent the past 3 years researching this chapter and this is, like, my tenth draft . . . from scratch. It would have been easy to have filled up over a hundred pages with data, but I wanted to write a self defense book, not a gun book. I have decided to leave a LOT of information out. For example, you do not need to know the exact weight and hammer configuration of every alloy framed snubnosed revolver made in the past century, nor do you require the velocity of a dozen types of .22 Magnum ammunition when fired from a 1" barrel. I am going to try to keep this as brief as possible. If you require further clarification the data is widely available, and much of it is even somewhat accurate. And we proceed . . . .

THE SNUBBIE

In the event you are somewhat unfamiliar with handguns, the best choice for you will be a double-action revolver. This is the simplest handgun design commonly available. It is so easy to use most novices can figure it out without even looking at the manual. Push the catch and the cylinder swings out for loading or unloading, pull the trigger and it goes bang. This should be your first handgun. For many people it is their only handgun.

For concealed carry, you want a lightweight, alloy-framed revolver with a short barrel. If this is your first revolver and you have no unusual health issues such as severe arthritis or carpal tunnel syndrome, you want a .38 Special revolver. I recommend the .38 Special over all other calibers for a variety of reasons, foremost being that .32 Long is underpowered and the impressive energy of the .357 (as well as the newfangled .327) is lost when fired from a short barrel, leaving you with twice the recoil but little more energy than the .38 +P. The only positive thing I can say about a snubbie chambered in .357 or .327 is that it gives you more versatility if you are short on ammo. Some folks like the .22 Magnum, and although I'm a fan of that cartridge I am not a fan of it out of a J-frame snubbie—too little power combined with complaints of timing issues in those revolvers chambered for it. .32 H&R Magnum is acceptable, but it is overpriced and scarce—have fun finding some if ever there is a shortage. Recently, .380 ACP revolvers have been introduced by Charter Arms, but they are the same size as a .38 Special revolver with less power. .38 Special is possibly the most widely available handgun round. You can find it at Wal*Mart, you can find it at the corner store, you can even find it at garage sales . . . and it is cheap. Loaded properly, such as in premium defensive ammo like Gold Dot +P or Golden Saber +P, it is a devastating manstopper. Loaded poorly, such as in wadcutter target ammo, not so much. Loaded improperly, such as with inbred Bubba's kitchen table reloads, it can literally blow apart the cylinder of your gun resulting in serious injury. So, the lesson to be learned here is never buy reloads, regardless of how much money you might save. Some reloads are great, but most are not, and a few are downright dangerous. Stay away from old, damaged, or corroded ammo as well. It may work, but it may misfire. You want to stick with new commercial ammo, preferably made in the USA. Quality control at many foreign plants is spotty at best.

Exotic ammunition is super cool. I know a few guys who collect it and briefly started collecting it myself. There is all sorts of fancy ammo out there: prefragmented, multi-strike, tracer, exploding, incendiary, armor piercing, and even poisoned. Frankly, this stuff tends to be expensive as hell and rarely performs as advertised. Some of it doesn't even fire. The double-crimped metal piercing rounds are so hot they can crack the frame of your gun. Some of it is illegal even to store in your safe let alone load into your carry piece. Aside from the reliable and effective Glaser Safety Slug (which typically results in a septic wound cavity as well as loss of ballistic evidence), I strongly advise you to pass on any temptation you may have to load your carry piece with dubious ninja gadgetry.

While you can save a few bucks by purchasing a heavy steel-framed revolver, those are best suited for the nightstand or the glovebox. If you want to carry a steel-framed revolver you'll either need a belt holster or a shoulder rig, both of which are not suited for everyday concealed carry. If all that is available to you is a steel-framed snubbie, possibly because it was a gift, I'd recommend a decent quality leather IWB clip-on holster without a thumb-break. ACE Case makes some very nice suede holsters that are very reasonably priced. You don't want nylon, and I'd advise against tuckable holsters that utilize J-hooks. If it does have a snap strap, take a pair of scissors and snip it off. Those things get in the way, are difficult to manipulate under stress, and even if you do succeed in unsnapping it there is still a chance the snap could snag the gun while you are drawing it. IWB is very convenient, but if it is windy or if you have been doing some sitting or bending your weapon will end up exposed to others at some point. Be very aware of that, especially if you look like a thug or do not have all your papers in order, because some busybody will see it and feel it is their civic duty to dime you to 911, describing you as "a crazy man with a gun" and the responding officers will react to that call accordingly. Avoid steel frames if at all possible. They are just too heavy.

There are a variety of lightweight alloys and polymers which make small revolvers so light they can be carried in a jacket or pant pocket without noticeably sagging. Aluminum is most popular, with titanium and polymer coming up next.

Scandium is the lightest, but at twice the cost of aluminum it is hardly worth it when you consider it is only a couple of ounces less. Your choice to make. What you do need to realize is that alloys are weaker than steel, and the metallurgy of the alloys on vintage Airweights was not up to modern standards, so if you are purchasing a pre-owned gun, particularly a vintage Smith or Colt, be certain to examine it carefully for hairline cracks, warps, or stretching. While an alloy snubbie with a cracked or stretched frame can probably be fired, it cannot be done so safely, and it cannot be expected to fire an entire box of ammo without snapping or seizing up. If it is free, keep it for a spare, but don't carry it and certainly don't pay anything for it. Alloy frames cannot be repaired, and a vintage Smith with a cracked frame is worth the price of a handful of scavenged parts. Don't get ripped off.

The lightweight snubbie is intended for pocket carry, but you need a pocket holster in order to keep it properly orientated in your pocket as well as free from lint and corrosive sweat. You do not need to spend a lot on a pocket holster, but you want to avoid the cheap nylon and polyester crap. The best ones I've found are the "sticky" synthetics such as the DeSantis Nemesis or the stickier Super Fly. WRB makes a very good knock-off version for about half the price. The Remora is a super sticky pocket holster that can double as a clipless IWB holster. Pocket holster is a mandatory purchase, and the best way to carry a lightweight snub, but be aware that sometimes they will pull free of your pocket still attached to your gun. Don't panic—a simple flick of the wrist will usually get it off, or you could simply fire through it with no worries that it will somehow plug the barrel.

There are dozens of configurations of snubbie, it being a classic and popular design. There are 5 shot versions and six shot versions. Some hold even more rounds, particularly if they are chambered for a smaller caliber such as .32 or .22. You can get fixed sights, adjustable sights, low profile sights, Tritium night sights, or even a laser designator. Grips can be slender wood, oversized wood, compact rubber, finger grooved rubber, or exotic materials such as stag. Finish can be brushed alloy, black alloy, colored alloy, or black polymer; and steel versions can be blued, parkerized, nickeled, or brushed stainless. Many options are available, and usually you can have your gun customized to meet your particular needs. The only option you really want to avoid is porting. This is a recoil brake created by drilling holes in the top of the barrel on either side of the sight to direct the gasses upwards, thereby reducing muzzle flip. The problem with this concept becomes obvious if you fire it at night and a 2 foot tall blinding sheet of flame destroys your night vision. Just say no to barrel porting. This isn't a target pistol, it is a defensive carry piece.

Perhaps the most important configuration to be aware of is hammer design. The classic "Chief's Special" design consists of a traditional exposed hammer with full sized spur. This allows ease of cocking and decocking for accurate single-action shots. The problem with this design is that the hammer spur can snag on clothing, particularly if it is being drawn from a pocket. In order to prevent this, some owners elect to "bob" the spur, either partially or entirely. The next configuration is the "shaved" or "concealed" hammer version. The hammer may either be partially exposed or flush with the frame, but there is no spur whatsoever, nor can it be manually cocked even if you can get your thumb on it because there is no internal notch for single-action use. These guns are DAO, or double-action only. Another popular DAO version is the "Centennial" style, in which the hammer is completely enclosed within a humpback style frame and you cannot see it moving at all. While this keeps lint and debris out of the internal mechanism and permits one to fire from within a pocket without fear of jamming, it also could contribute to a negligent discharge in the hands of an inexperienced and untrained shooter; furthermore, the stiff DAO trigger pull results in involuntary hand and wrist movements which will adversely affect accuracy beyond 10 feet, making them close range pieces only. The final version is the "Bodyguard" style, in which the hammer is shrouded but partially exposed. This allows one to fire from inside one's pocket as well as providing an option for accurate single-action fire, but these guns are recommended for experienced shooters only. In the new Smith & Wesson version, the 438/638, the exposed portion of the spur is so tiny you can barely manipulate it with your thumb due to the extremely powerful spring, and once that gun is cocked you have a serious problem if you decide not to fire it. You see, it is downright hazardous to attempt decocking a 438 on a live round because it is far too easy for your grip to falter and then it will discharge whether you want it to or not, and there is no way to open the cylinder with the gun at full cock either. The Charter Arms version is a bit safer in that the exposed portion of the spur is a bit longer and the spring isn't quite as powerful. I'd recommend thinking of these as DAO guns and only consider cocking that hammer back under extraordinary circumstances. Which one to get? Up to you, but if you want my recommendation for a new owner's first gun, I'd say get a Taurus or Charter Arms with a concealed hammer. Practically idiotproof.

A lot of guys say Smith & Wesson is the best you can get, and the price certainly seems to reflect that. All I can say is, that is the cost of brand recognition. The fact is, I've owned several Smiths and I didn't think they were all that great. Sure, they were okay, but grossly overpriced and in my opinion over-rated. One reason I don't like Smith is because they have legions of rabid fanboys who insist that any other brand of revolver is crap, and that just ain't so. Smiths are far from perfect. Like any other gun, they do break, sometimes even the first time at the range. Then there is the ugly "Hillary Hole" trigger lock in the side of the frame from when they sold out in the early 1990s in the name of Political Correctness. Sometimes these locks have been known to break while firing, in a few cases this rendered the gun inoperable. And then there is their weird trigger pull. Some guys love the Smith's trigger pull, and it is certainly unique, but I can't say I'm a fan. But, all that being said, Smith & Wesson does have a solid reputation for making quality handguns. They are good, but expensive. Pre-lock Smiths are even more expensive. If you want to get a Smith, go for it, but be advised that there are less expensive options which are just as good. Airweights are typically about 15 ounces, Scandium framed versions a little over 12 ounces, with steel being about 18 ounces.

Taurus gets a bad rap for making shitty guns that break, but basically they are just a cheap version of the Smiths made under license from them, and most of the guys complaining about them are the aforementioned S&W fanboys. I have owned numerous Taurus revolvers and never had a problem with any of them. From what I have heard, most of the problems were with the magnums and the automatics anyway. The standard model 85UL is perhaps their most reliable piece. It also now comes with an internal lock, but it is less noticeable and less prone to malfunction. They are good reliable guns in the same class as the Smith but about 30% cheaper. Just be careful when buying one of their "Ultra-Lite" revolvers, as some of them seem to weigh as much as steel for some reason. I'm sorry, but if that snubbie weighs 21 ounces it should not be stamped "Ultra-Lite."Be sure to either handle it prior to purchase or look up the weight of that exact model on the manufacturer's website. You do not want to pocket carry anything heavier than a pound, tops. Most of their Ultralites weigh in at 17 ounces, including the pricy "Total Titanium" version. Steel framed versions are about 23 ounces.

Ruger is famous for overbuilt, heavy-duty revolvers and they do not incorporate the dreaded internal lock. They are new to lightweight guns, but the polymer LCR is quite impressive. It has been around for a few years now and they have held up well and have developed a strong following for good reason. Of all the lightweight revolvers I've owned, the LCR was my favorite. Very light at just under 14 ounces, great ergonomics, and the trigger pull was amazing. A lot of guys hear the transfer bar rattle and think something is broken, but they all do that so not to worry. The only negative is the resale value on used LCRs is poor—but that is a definite plus if you are in the market for one. I have seen used ones with minor scuffs and handling marks selling for as low as $300, which is a great deal. This is the gun I typically recommend, but I understand that the non-traditional profile and plastic frame will turn a lot of potential buyers off, and that's fine. For recoil sensitive shooters, Ruger has just introduced an 8-shot version of the LCR in .22 LR that, loaded with hypervelocity rounds such as CCI Stingers, will ruin any bad guy's day. Their other snubnose, the SP101, is a 26 ounce monstrosity typically chambered for .357 Magnum, and while it is too heavy for pocket carry, it is excellent as a glovebox or nightstand gun, particularly if loaded with .38 Special +P, as the heavy frame will significantly dampen recoil.

Charter Arms is the redheaded stepchild of the firearms industry. They have been around for decades and have changed ownership about 4 times, and during this tumultuous period turned out a lot of poor quality guns that broke. This resulted in everyone saying that Charter Arms was crap. Well, everyone except the old-timers who remembered that their first guns were just as good as a Smith at half the price. The original Charter Arms snubbies had no ejector rod shroud. That ejector rod under the barrel was fully exposed. Looks ugly unless you're into the film noir/Steampunk appeal, but that exposed ejector rod shows that you've lucked onto one of the good ones. These are great guns, and even though they have a steel frame it is a lightweight 16 ounces, which while a few ounces more than an Airweight is still quite pocketable. Even better, they are typically in the $225 price range, which is a bargain. Later steel framed Charters marketed under the names "Charco" and "Charter 2000" were indeed crap—avoid those. Recently, however, Charter Arms changed management once again and is now producing lightweight 12 ounce alloy-framed snubbies with decent quality control. I have heard few complaints about their new guns, and they are pretty much the lightest of the lightweights, in the same weight class as scandium at a fraction of the price. The only caveat is that they tend to have rather stiff DA trigger pulls out of the box, but this tends to lighten up over time. They are a good choice, especially if you are on a budget. They also are marketed in a variety of interesting colors if you're into that sort of thing.

Rossi is a cheap revolver that is comparable to Charter Arms. The older Brazilian made model 68 and model 88 are often found selling for under $200 on the secondhand market with barrel lengths being 2.5" or 3", and the Lady Rossi is a 88 designed for smaller hands. Like Charter Arms, these are steel framed guns, and they weigh a little more than might be comfortable for pocket carry, necessitating a clip-on or snap-on IWB holster. The model 68 weighs 21 ounces. These are good solid guns with 5 round cylinders and slim concealment grips. The new Rossi USA revolvers are heavier, bulkier, and considerably more expensive.

For fuck's sake, BEWARE of Cobra Arms. This company is famous for POS Saturday Night Special jam-o-matics, and recently decided to make a Centennial knockoff that they have dubbed the "Shadow." Shit stain is more like it. These look very similar to the new Charter Arms snubbies and cost about the same. However, unlike Charter Arms, the Cobra Shadow does not work. Numerous reports of these guns malfunctioning or breaking the first time they are fired at the range. That is unacceptable, especially for a $300 gun. One of the most notorious Saturday Night Specials of all, the Zamak-framed Rohm RG-38, is widely considered to be a piece of shit and can be found in many disreputable pawn shops priced well under a hundred bucks—but the RG-38 can reasonably be expected to go bang every time (even if it can't hit the broad side of a barn from the inside).

And that is, basically, all you really need to know about your choices of lightweight snubbies, as only a few manufacturers are using lightweight frames.

Some guys say they want to carry extra ammo, and I guess that's fine if it makes you feel better, but it is unlikely you'll need to fire that gun at all, let alone empty all 5 rounds. Problem is, how to carry the extra ammo and how much do you need? I'll make it easy for you. One reload should be fine, and for most J-frames that means 5 rounds. A lot of guys love speedloaders, but unless you've got a winter coat or some sort of man purse that speedloader will print. Some guys like speedstrips, but let me tell you, it is a huge pain in the ass getting those rounds off that strip in a hurry. Personally, I like ammo wallets. You can find them in plastic or leather, and they do come in half sizes that hold only 6 rounds. Ammo wallets are a lot classier than a ziplock bag and that is how I recommend carrying your extra ammo. In the unlikely event you require a reload, you probably will have ample opportunity to do so behind cover.

In conclusion, the lightweight snubbie is a great concealed carry piece if you are wearing a jacket or cargo shorts, it has a foolproof design that is unlikely to ever jam, and it does not spit shell casings. Loaded up with Glaser Silver projectiles it is perhaps the perfect point blank range killing machine. Beyond point blank range, accuracy from a DAO snub is poor. Nasty weapon that is extremely easy to use and carry. If you can only afford one handgun, I strongly recommend a lightweight .38 Special snubnose revolver.

THE LIGHTWEIGHT AUTOMATIC

If you have a bit more experience handling firearms you may want to go with a pistol instead of an old fashioned wheelgun. Now, pistols do have a few advantages (higher capacity, quicker reloads, rapidfire ability, flatter profile, look cooler, etc.), but there are a couple of significant disadvantages as well. First and foremost, there is a far greater probability that an autoloading pistol may jam, which could prove most embarrassing if it were to occur at an inopportune time. Secondly, there is the fact that automatics have a tendency to spit incriminating shell casings all over your crime scene (and the scene of *any* shooting is deemed a "crime scene" until the DA decides otherwise), and if you are such a dumbass as to have conveniently pressed your fingerprints and DNA all over them, well, Darwin sez you get the Grilled Cheese Sammich and Cartoon Network for the duration. For fuck's sake wear latex when loading those mags, even if you are a good citizen who has your permit and everything, because you never know what the future has in store for you. You might have a very good reason for leaving the scene of your attack. Perhaps the guy you shot has friends and they are angry with you. But I digress . . . .

For simplicity's sake, we're not going to talk about heavy caliber polymer pistols here. If you're a Glock fanboy, you go ahead and stick with what you know, but in my opinion Glock is over-rated. They were marketed as some sort of futuristic supergun, but then after a few years folks started realizing that they can jam or kaboom just like any other pistol, so there. Glock is not perfect, and they have a shitty trigger that has contributed to more negligent discharges than probably all other brands of gun combined.

Fuck Glock. I'm also not going to discuss ultra-compact single-stack 9 millies. The Kel-Tec PF-9 is popular with some folks (even though it is shit), and the Ruger LC9, Kahr PM9 and Kimber Solo have recently been released (with the expected beta phase problems), but the fact that they are subcompact 9 X 19mm Luger / Parabellum pistols means that they will tend to have far harsher recoil and less reliability than a comparably sized .380 or .32, but if you need that extra pop and have the means to fine tune your subcompact 9mm so it runs flawlessly, I'm not going to dissuade you from that caliber—I just do not consider them to be entry level pistols suitable for novices. Ultracompact 9mm pistols kick hard, and if you go for a .40 or .45 instead it will kick even harder. Stick with a .380 ACP or 9 X 18mm Makarov unless you are carrying something full sized.

I really dislike polymer frames in general, and prefer alloy whenever I have a choice. Unfortunately, our choices of quality alloy framed .380s (AKA 9 X 17mm Kurtz or Corto) are few and far between, and some are long discontinued and rather pricy. All of these pistols are based upon the Walther PP design (not the PPK), from which the legendary Makarov was developed. Bar none, the jam-proof Makarov is the finest automatic pistol available at any price. Unfortunately, at 25 ounces, it weighs as much as a brick, as does the Astra Constable and many similar pistols. Your best choice is the SIG P230/P232 in the 17 ounce alloy framed version, but even used that is typically a $500 pistol. Next on the list would be the lightweight offerings from CZ and FEG, and a few were even made in the slightly more potent 9 X 18mm Makarov. But the version which is most popular due to low price and high reliability is the 20 ounce Bersa Thunder (or the similar Firestorm) and the even lighter and smaller 16 ounce Bersa Concealed Carry (which, at a half inch shorter than the Thunder is also less reliable). These are all DA/SA automatic pistols with decockers. They are a bit at the larger size for pocket carry, but it can be done in a jacket, vest, or cargo pockets. Can't be done with jeans unless you're carrying IWB under a shirt. These are my favorite style of concealed carry pistol and I highly recommend them.

A lot of 1911 enthusiasts love the Colt Mustang, which is a pocket sized 1911 style pistol without a grip safety chambered in .380. This pistol had been discontinued for decades, but was recently reintroduced by Colt in a 13 ounce alloy framed version with a stainless slide. While these can be carried cocked and locked, most guys I know carry them with the hammer down on a loaded chamber. There are numerous versions of this pistol, each with their own quirks, including the 22 ounce Government .380 and the original 19 ounce steel framed Mustang, as well as a +II version with an extended grip. Short recoil system combined with a plastic guide rod caused some problems, and while many of these guns were reliable out of the box, some needed a break-in period and a bit of tinkering to make them run well. The 13 ounce Pocketlite was a lightweight alloy framed version designed for pocket carry. The 15 ounce SIG P238 is very close copy of the Mustang, which also has had its share of reported issues. The Colt Pony was a poorly designed DAO version of the Mustang that most shooters agree is a real POS. The Colt .380 Government and the Llama IIIA / Micromax .380 are both medium sized steel framed pistols that are a little bigger and heavier than the Mustang, but still significantly smaller than a Colt Officer Model or Star BM. Speaking of Star, the Starfire .380 has an excellent reputation as a pocket pistol if you can find one, with the DK version having a lightweight aluminum frame. Personally, I love the Mustang Pocketlight and think that it may be the perfect pocket pistol . . . but SAO action, reliability issues, and price make this a true enthusiast's gun that I do not recommend for the novice shooter.

But of course polymer wins the popularity contest. Quality just can't compete with the convenience of subcompact size combined with ultralight weight—and hey, a few of them actually work. As a general rule, the shorter the recoil system and more powerful the cartridge the more problems you will have. Larger .380s like the 23 ounce Browning BDA and Beretta Cheetah run flawlessly, as do smaller .25s and .32s. Trying to run a .380 through a .25 sized pistol requires a level of engineering expertise that we have not yet seen in the firearms industry. These pistols tend to have long mushy trigger pulls and no trigger reset in the event of a hard primer, but that is the trade off for .380 power in a .25 package. Speaking of power, please remember that none of the polymer subcompacts are rated for +P ammunition, and they will break if you run hot ammo through them. Furthermore, they tend to have uncomfortably snappy recoil and can be a major pain in the ass to strip down for cleaning. Undisputed king of the polymers at this time is the 10 ounce Ruger LCP. Very reliable with a high consumer satisfaction record and few complaints of breakage. The biggest problem with the LCP seems to be that the frame pins tend to gradually work their way free under recoil, but that happens with the Kel Tec P3AT as well. The Kel-Tec is the next most popular, probably because it was made first and is cheaper. They are good guns and a lot of guys love them, but unfortunately they tend to break a lot.

They also have a tendency to jam. This can be corrected by sending it back to the factory for an optional "fluff and buff" treatment, which entails polishing the innards and swapping the springs and extractor, but why should that be necessary on a new gun? Kel-Tec also makes a .32 ACP version which seems so cheaply constructed it is practically a Saturday Night Special, but tends to run more reliably out of the box than the .380 version.

The new Smith & Wesson .380 Bodyguard is in its beta testing phase and, as expected, there have been problems, although it does have a true DAO trigger with second strike capability. Plenty of serious complaints about the Taurus TCP. The "micro Glock" Diamondback has had problems with the plastic guide rod breaking, but these can be made to work if you're willing to tinker with it, although they do have the hazardous Glock trigger, as does the older Sigma SW380 that pops up at gun shows and pawn shops every now and then—personally, I'd be scared to carry either with a round in the chamber, but a lot of folks do. A relatively unknown company DBA InterOrdinance is making an inexpensive LCP/P3AT knock off they call the "Hellcat" which does not appear to be a bargain at all. And then you could go high end and pay twice as much as an LCP for a Kahr P380, which also has been reported to have reliability issues. It seems like the compact polymer .380 is a difficult design to get right, so if you decide to go this route, stick with the LCP unless you really have your heart set on another brand and are willing to have it shipped back to the factory a couple of times or are able to work on it yourself. In my opinion, reliability should never be secondary to convenience or ease of carry.

One thing that I really hate about the polymer micro pistols is the way they are designed, which is more for ease of carry and convenience than reliability or combat. Think of them as autoloading derringers with an effective range of 15 feet. They tend to have horrendous plastic triggers with long mushy pulls, and the internal hammer typically will not reset until the action of the slide pulls it back—which means if you have a dud round due to a hard primer you have no second strike capability and need to rack the slide to clear it and reset the hammer. An external hammer or true double-action capability would improve these pistols greatly.

Now, if you want to pocket carry a polymer .380 you need a pocket holster. Best possible choice is the Desantis SuperFly, which is an improved version of the ambidextrous Nemisis with stickier texture and a removable anti-print panel. Another option for the more adventurous is the wallet rig, which is custom made by several leathersmiths and sold at gun shows and on eBay. Now, while some of you may be aware that the ATF prohibited "wallet guns" a while back, these rigs circumnavigate the ban by leaving the slide of the weapon fully exposed. Not only does this expose enough of the pistol to make it legal, it also reduces the risk of friction based jams which occurred with ultra-reliable Jetfires and Seecamps in the prohibited fully-enclosed rigs. Furthermore, the design of these rigs was vastly improved by several well thought out modifications such as an additional stabilizer hole as well as a foam insert which enables the pistol to be simply pushed into place without any need for snaps or velcro. Looks just like a wallet or PDA when it prints in your front pocket and is a very useful device for the LCP

or P3AT owner (but for fuck's sake, DO NOT use one of these rigs on a Diamondback!).
There are a few other subcompact .380s you should be aware of because they are crap. These being the Walther PPK (particularly the Smith & Wesson and Interarms versions), the NAA Guardian, the MPA Protector, the AMT Backup, and the Magnum Research Micro Eagle. They are all notorious jam-o-matics that frequently break, and they are significantly heavier than the polymer framed pistols. The Seecamp .380 is more reliable, but it is extremely expensive as well as finicky about ammo. You should also avoid cheapo Zamak framed abortions in this caliber as the .380 cartridge is powerful enough to batter them apart very quickly. Sometimes a Davis, Jimenez, Jennings, Bryco, Lorcin, or Cobra will have the slide shatter before a full box of ammo is run through it—plus they jam. Never even be tempted to buy a Saturday Night Special in this caliber, and if you somehow get one for free do not fire it or give it to anyone you care about. Zamak .25s and .32s may be jam-o-matics but the .380s are potential grenades. No joke. If you are going to carry a .380, your best option is probably a medium sized, alloy frame pistol based on the Walther PP / Makarov design.

There has been a lot of debate on what is the "best" round to fire from your .380 ACP pistol, but they all pretty much suck equally. All everyone can seem to agree on is that you should use brass cased, American made jacketed hollowpoints from a quality manufacturer. A few good choices include: Remington Golden Saber, Speer Gold Dot, and Cor Bon DPX. Be advised that most polymer and alloy .380s are not rated for +P ammunition, which will result in inordinate wear and possible breakage. Be further advised that aluminum cased rounds are a frequent cause of jams in small automatics.

I understand that not everyone can comfortably handle the recoil of a .380 ACP from a lightweight alloy or polymer pistol, and for those folks I recommend the .32 ACP / 7.65mm. Now, most .32 ACP pistols are old surplus military and police pistols from Europe, nearly all of which have steel frames which makes them heavy for pocket carry, and although the pistol itself may be relatively inexpensive finding parts for it is not. While an old Sauer 38H, Mauser HSc, or Beretta 1935 may be great for your collection I would advise against choosing it for everyday carry. I would also advise against choosing a Walther PP or PPK with the lightweight Duraluminum frame as they tend to be valued well over a thousand dollars which is a bit excessive. The FEG AP-MBP, Beretta Tomcat, Taurus 732 TCP, Kel-Tec P32, and Seecamp LWS32 are all decent choices. Bersa once offered a limited run of only a thousand Thunders chambered for .32 ACP, but has recently produced another run due to popular demand. One thing to be aware of is that .32 ACP is a semi-rimmed cartridge susceptible to a difficult to clear jam due to "rim lock" in which ammunition is knocked out of alignment in the magazine binding the shells together via rim overlap. This generally happens with hollowpoint ammunition and can be avoided through careful loading or shimming the back of the magazine to take up extra space. Although specific models of pistol chambered for .32 tend to be more reliable and durable than their .380 counterparts (PPK, TCP, Kel-Tec, Micromax), rim lock is always a possibility. Also know that older milsurp .32 pistols frequently choke on hollowpoint ammunition, and can even be finicky with ball ammo. Another thing to consider is that the .32 slug has approximately half the mass of a .380 slug and travels slower, resulting in approximately half as much stopping power. It is best to think of the .32 ACP as a ".25 Magnum" to avoid overconfidence in its abilities, as it is hardly a manstopper by any stretch of the imagination.

In conclusion, if you are prejudiced against wheelguns and insist upon an automatic pistol, your best choice is certainly the Makarov, although its weight necessitates a IWB holster if not a shoulder rig. For comfortable concealed carry, an alloy medium framed pistol in .380 ACP based upon the Walther PP design is recommended, with the 17 ounce SIG P230/232 at the top of a very short list. If you are on a budget, get the 20 ounce Bersa Thunder. Like a snubbie, these conceal best in the pocket of a jacket or cargo shorts. If you need a pistol to carry in the pocket of your jeans or vest, consider the Ruger LCP which seems to be the most reliable of all the polymer micro pistols, although the DAO trigger adversely effects accuracy, and I tend to think of these guns as multi-shot derringers rather than pistols, as they aren't really durable enough to be range guns and are intended for use at point blank range. Always range test any automatic pistol to ascertain there are no issues with feeding or extraction before relying upon it for personal protection. Make certain the shells are polished before being inserted into the magazine with a gloved hand, and wipe down the magazine itself as well. Most importantly, be certain to hold the pistol firmly, as a loose grip or limp wrist will not provide the support necessary for the action to cycle reliably and it may jam.

THE ULTIMATE POCKET PISTOL

In my opinion, the "ultimate" pocket pistol is the 6 ounce North American Arms mini revolver chambered in .22 Magnum. I say this because it is a proven performer, and is my personal favorite for concealed carry. It weighs half as much as a polymer .380 and hits almost as hard with much less risk of accidental discharge and better fire discipline. The disadvantages are you need to manually cock the single action hammer prior to each shot and it is impossible to reload quickly under stress so don't even bother carrying extra ammo.

Even though much of the .22 Magnum's energy is wasted out of such a short barrel, it does show notable increase over the .22 LR, and the jacketed bullets and ballistic tipped rounds provide far better performance than soft lead. The downside is that the muzzle blast and report is quite severe—but if you set the goblin's shirt on fire that's a bonus!

Don't get one of these in .22 LR unless you really have a serious problem with recoil and muzzle flash. The .22 LR has less kick and flash, but it is also built on a smaller frame with smaller grips and handling it can be awkward. If you want .22 LR you really ought to buy a .22 Magnum with a LR conversion cylinder because the extra bit of grip size makes it considerably easier to use. Certainly don't waste your money on the micro .22 Short, as it is so small you actually need to hold the grip with one hand while pressing the tiny stud trigger with the other. One rare occasions you may stumble upon a .17 caliber version or the black powder Companion, but those are only for collectors as the .17 had so many reliability problems they were discontinued, and the cap and ball version produces less energy than a .22 Short. .22 Magnum is the caliber you need to get the most pop out of these wee derringers, and it will fit your hand the best. Some people say that a powderless Colibri round will be nearly silent out of one of these guns, but they obviously have never actually tried it. Colibri is almost as loud as standard ammo out of a 1" barrel, and so are CB caps. Get the magnum and fire magnum ammo through it.

Your best choice is the 7 ounce Pug with the short barrel, secured cylinder rod, heavy frame, and rubber grip. Unfortunately, Pugs are so popular they sell out quick and I've never seen one resold on the secondhand market. The 10 ounce Black Widow is the gun the Pug was based on, but with a 2" barrel and oversized grips they are difficult to conceal, and frankly the sights suck, so even though the Black Widow is one of my personal favorites, I'm going to advise you to pass on it unless you're willing to tinker with it by, at the bare minimum, installing compact grips and taking a Dremel to the front sight. Avoid the earlier Black Widows with the ball detent cylinder pin, as they tended to have issues. What you probably want to get is the more common standard frame mini with the pushbutton/ball detent cylinder rod and smooth rosewood grips, preferably with the short 1 1/8" barrel. These are not quite as nice as the Pug, but they are widely available and sometimes you can find one for under $150. I strongly advise swapping the slippery rosewood for checkered rubber. Sometimes you'll see one set up with a folding plastic grip, where the mini folds up like a lockblade and can be clipped inside your front pocket. Some guys like that setup, but it has always seemed problematic to me. Far quicker, easier, and safer simply to draw from a pocket holster in a single fluid motion (although sometimes the holster remains stuck on the end of your gun). I have also seen Kydex necker rigs that can be concealed under one's shirt, although some are designed for solid retention rather than quick draw—but heating it up on a cookie sheet in the oven with soften the plastic so it can be stretched out a bit.

Minis made during the past decade have notches between each chamber so the fixed hammer-mounted firing pin does not need to rest on an empty chamber to make it drop safe. Older minis have discharged when dropped as they lacked this feature, but if you have an older mini, you can send it to NAA and they will retrofit it with an updated notched cylinder free of charge. The 5-shot NAA mini is superior to 2-shot derringers (which are often larger and heavier) and similar firearms such as the old Freedom Arms mini (which was not drop safe, had an exposed screw-out cylinder pin, and had a longer barrel) and the "Dixie Derringer"(originally made by Charter 2000 and continued by the new Charter Arms, with a push-button safety to make it drop safe which needs to be switched to fire prior to use). You really do not want a safety on a derringer, but if you have one gifted to you it is a lot better than a Davis / Cobra POS.

There is a lot of disagreement on what is the "best" round to fire out of a .22 Magnum derringer, and some guys on the forum have spent hundreds of hours testing them with chronographs and wetpack target medium. Frankly, just about every .22 Magnum round performs about the same, and almost none of the hollowpoints will reliably expand from a 1" barrel with many "new improved" versions being discontinued within a year of being released. I have found that CCI consistently makes the most reliable rimfire ammo, with nickle plated cases being more resistant to corrosion than brass. The ammo I keep in my CCW is 30g CCI V-MAX ballistic tipped ammo, which has a conical polymer cap over the hollowpoint cavity. Supposedly, it expands easier than other hollowpoint designs, and it looks cool. The new 30g CCI TNT Green ammo is a lead-free copper jacketed hollowpoint filled with granulated copper, which is designed to disintegrate much like a Glaser, and Hornaday fas recently released a 45g "Critical Defense" round in this caliber as well. All of them allegedly will expand explosively within the first few inches of tissue, which is why many experts recommend the flat nose FMJ rounds which will penetrate deeper and tumble. One ammo that you really need to avoid is shotshells. Back in the 1980s a few gun writers who should've known better were recommending loading the first chamber or two with snakeshot in order to "scare" or "drive off" a mugger through less than lethal force. The thing is, these rounds sting a little and can put out an eye, but they have zero stopping power. Plus the plastic cap of the next round can pop forward from recoil jamming the cylinder. Also the DA will still consider it lethal force regardless of the ammunition used, even if it was a rubber bullet or a blank, because the "victim" was being shot at with a gun and felt in fear for his life. If you are going to carry a mini be sure to load it with real bullets.

The mini is considered by some to be nothing more than a "novelty" or a "deep cover piece", but it has been many professional's EDC when they choose not to carry a full sized handgun on their belt. It is certainly far better than no gun at all. Very loud, surprisingly accurate, and nearly as powerful as a .380 according to some studies. The NAA mini in .22 Magnum is a devastating multi-shot derringer which is highly effective at point blank range and can be carried in the pocket of one's jeans (preferably in a quality sticky or rawhide pocket holster) or dropped in one's boot (in a cheapo Uncle Mikes nylon .380 pocket holster) for simple and weightless everyday protection.

THE UNLOVED AND BERATED .25 AUTOMATIC

Now, before I go any further, I feel I need to say a thing or two about the .25 ACP / 6.35mm cartridge. Frankly, it has piss poor performance. The .32 ACP is roughly twice as powerful, if that gives you any indication. It has been said that shooting a man with a .25 is akin to stabbing him with an icepick—except you can do it multiple times from over 10 feet away. Thus, the .25 ACP is clearly superior to a knife or club for personal protection. For those of you who think the .22 LR is somehow better, it is not. The .25 ACP is far more reliable both in feeding and ignition, plus certain cartridges provide better performance. The best possible round in this caliber is the Winchester Xpanding Point (the one with a steel BB in the end). Now, while it doesn't actually "expand" all that well, the steel BB and extra velocity greatly increase penetration, plus the BB usually splits off creating an additional wound channel. Best round available. Another interesting choice is the Glaser Safety Slug. Sure, it penetrates for shit, but it will blow apart a few inches under the surface, resulting in a highly contaminated wound cavity which will mandate an immediate trip to the ER. This is significant when you consider that many criminals shot with .25 FMJ are able to have a friend remove the slug with forceps so they never need to go to hospital at all. If you shoot him in the foot with a Glaser, he'll lose that foot. If you shoot him in the throat with a Glaser it is virtually a guaranteed kill. The Glaser does a lot more damage than ball, but it does not penetrate deeply at all. Ball ammo in .25 is pretty much ineffective unless you get real lucky and rupture a major artery. People shot with the .25 frequently die, but rarely at the scene. Usually they die several hours or even days later. This round has minimal stopping power, but 9 rapidfire shots in the face will stop damn near anyone. Don't be so quick to underestimate the humble .25 ACP. John Moses Browning knew what he was doing when he designed this round for cub automatics.

Now, if you are going into a firefight with a fucking handgun your shit is pretty weak, and once you get below .357 Magnum / .45 ACP, all handguns tend to suck equally. Even though the .38 Special and .380 ACP show far better performance on chronographs and in target mediums such a ballistic gelatin, the fact remains that in some comparative studies of thousands of actual shootings, humans have just as much probability of being dropped by an underpowered .25 ACP. A small pistol with a short barrel is an inadequate manstopper, and the "crappiest" pistol of them all with abysmal performance in scientific tests does almost as well as the "minimal" .380 ACP statistically. If you shoot someone with a gun—any gun—they will probably stop attacking you and end up in hospital, but do not count on that to occur, even with a shotgun. Personally, if I was not expecting to go into a bad situation where a firefight was likely and was simply selecting a small pistol for EDC, I'd choose a Beretta Jetfire or Colt Vest Pocket over a Kel-Tec every time. These old guns have character and feel more substantial than a polymer framed pocket pistol to me.

At the very top of your wish list should be the 10 ounce Beretta 950 Jetfire in .25 ACP. This is the ONLY Beretta pocket pistol you want to keep your eye out for. You don't want a Minx due to reliability issues, the 12 ounce Bobcat in .22 LR also suffers from reliability issues and the Bobcat in .25 ACP has an extremely hard DA trigger pull and is thicker and heavier than the Jetfire. The Taurus PT25 is based on the Bobcat design but there have been complaints about jamming and breakage so you don't want that either. You want the Jetfire. In my opinion it is arguably the finest pistol Beretta ever made. It will fire 9 rounds in under 2 seconds and will never jam. The only negatives about this pistol is the ineffectual caliber and the fact that the hammer must be manually cocked prior to firing the first shot. Because of these facts, Jetfires are no longer popular for concealed carry since polymer .380s are widely available, so not that long ago it was common to find one in very good condition priced under $150 . . . but then a popular youtuber, "nutnfancy", uploaded a video clip of himself rapidfiring a Jetfire so all his fans had to buy one which drove the price up quite a bit on armslist and gunbroker—$300 is not uncommon now for excellent condition, and I have seen like new in box priced higher than $400, so thanks to the internet the only $150 Jetfire you're likely to find will have cracked grips and all the bluing worn off—but it will still work great. The Jetfire is one of the best cheap guns you can buy, and its alloy frame makes it only a tad heavier than the LCP. I carried mine with a round in the pipe, safety off, and hammer at the half cock notch; but that is not how I recommend you carry yours, as I recently handled a LNIB Jetfire whose hammer would occasionally drop from half cock when the trigger was pulled—it is a very unsafe practice to carry these pistols at half cock. The manual and most experts say it is designed to be carried with the hammer all the way down on the inertia firing pin and the half cock notch is intended only as a safety feature when decocking . . . but it also makes it far easier to cock, and it is a temptation if you have an older one with tight dry springs. Just be sure to put a drop of oil on that hammer spring so that it will cock easily.

Next up is the 12 ounce Titan .25 automatic. This is an interesting gun with a lot of history behind it. Apparently, there are well over a dozen versions of the Titan and many parts do not interchange. There are 2 styles of slide, 2 styles of recoil assembly, 3 styles of firing pin, and 3 types of magazine (6, 7, and 8 round). So, if you want to get a spare mag be certain to get one exactly like the one which came with your particular gun. Basically, this is the no-frills version on the Jetfire, based on a Tanfoglio design. The original Tanfoglios and Hermanos were steel framed, but after the import ban on frames, boatloads of parts were assembled on made in USA cast Zamak frames by numerous companies (FIE, QFI, FIE, Excam, and Heritage). Sometimes it is referred to as a GT27 or a Targa. Like the Jetfire it has an open slide and external hammer, but the mag release and safety switch are simpler and there is no comparison in regards to fit and finish. These guns are very reliable and extremely acurate. Best of all, you can often find them for only a hundred bucks, sometimes less. The Titan hammer has a half-cock notch, but unless it is made in Italy with a steel frame I would not trust it. Remember, most of these guns were slapped together from mismatched parts on cast Zamak frames, and the hammer on mine sometimes slipped out of half-cock shortly after being lowered to that position. I would only carry a Zamak

Titan with the hammer fully down on a live round. They are reasonably drop safe. You can avoid dropping your pistol on the hammer, but you cannot avoid the hammer dropping due to shoddy assembly practices. Try not to shoot yourself in the dick. Be aware that there are several foreign companies offering "non-gun" versions of the Titan as well, with the Ekol Tuna being the most commonly seen, which are intended to fire blanks or flares only, but some of these have been converted to fire ammunition although accuracy and reliability are poor—be certain to examine the stampings closely, and if you have never heard of the company and if it appears brand new, assume it may be an inferior knock-off or modified non-gun.

One gun you sometimes come across is the 12 ounce Astra Cub, also imported under license from Colt and sold as the Colt Junior. While these are great pistols, they are usually twice the price of a Jetfire with an inferior design. I rarely see one of these guns sell for under $300, and they are frequently priced considerably higher. After the import ban, Astra Cub parts were imported by F.I.E. to be put on Zamak frames and sold as "The Best," which is a far more economical version. These were all very nice little pistols which are also SAO with an external hammer. Most of these pistols were available in either .25 ACP or .22 Short/Corto, but you want to stick with the .25 for reliability, as the Corto has a tendency to jam. Another similarly styled pistol, the Starlet, is highly collectable and often sold for a substantial sum. I have mentioned this series of pistols not so you would buy one, but so you know that they are quality firearms rather than junk should you inherit or be gifted one. While they certainly will work for concealed carry, these really are more suitable for a collector due to price, weight, and small ejection port. They also have a tendency to discharge if dropped and were recalled for that reason. This pistol is nice, although it is not as reliable as the Jetfire or Titan and costs significantly more, especially if it has Colt markings.

Next gun I'm going to discuss is the 13 ounce Colt 1908 Vest Pocket (and the virtually identical FN 1906, based on John Browning's 1905 design). These are valuable collectors items if you can find one in mint condition, however, most are well worn from years of pocket carry and shooter grade 1908s are not uncommon. I have seen quite a few in pawn shops, and many of your older relatives may have owned one. Nearly half a million are in circulation. Some are probably unsafe to carry, whereas others could continue to provide years of service. The thing that makes me nervous about the 1908 is that it is an antique striker fired pistol designed to be carried fully cocked over a live round. The only thing preventing that striker from flying forward is a tenuous connection between two tiny parts, and if one of those parts fails or if the gun is dropped it may discharge unexpectedly. Now, what makes the 1908 so completely badassed is the fact that it is a hammerless automatic equipped with a grip safety, so it is good to go as soon as it clears your pocket—no need to cock a hammer or flip a switch, which may take an extra second and give an attacker the opportunity to rush you. Still, that striker/sear connection scares me a little. The Astra Firecat is very similar in design to the Vest Pocket but has a few minor differences, such as the position of the safety. Stripping the Vest Pocket down for cleaning is a nightmare and replacement parts are extremely expensive, so these pistols are for serious enthusiasts only.

Even smaller and lighter than the Vest Pocket is the 10 ounce "Baby" (Browning Baby, Bauer/Fraser, PSA-25, and 7 ounce PSA Featherweight, as well as the similar Wilkinson Diane, Bernadelli Vest Pocket, Walther Model 9, Liliput, Haenel, and Duo), which has no grip safety and is even less safe to carry with a round in the chamber as well as being far more awkward to shoot, which is why I cannot recommend it. The best way to carry a Baby is with the striker cocked over an empty chamber, which makes it easier and faster to rack the slide and chamber a round. Both the Vest Pocket and the Baby are enthusiast guns, seldom carried by anyone other than collectors and hobbyists nowadays. Be aware that a number of inferior copies of both pistols were made in numerous countries and are of far lesser quality with no parts interchangeability. The copies referred to above by name are of high quality compared to knockoffs from France, Germany, Spain, and other less civilized countries.

Before the Kel-Tecs came along, many people carried one of the aforementioned pistols as their EDC, and before the NAA mini was introduced in the early 1980s it was your only real option for a hideout piece. These "ineffectual" .25 automatics have probably put as many bodies in the ground as the .38 Special and .380 ACP combined due to their popularity, affordability, and ease of carry . . . they just didn't tend to do it immediately unless you emptied the magazine. Very underrated pistols.

The .25 automatic is reliable and easy to conceal, but woefully underpowered. They have very low knockdown ability—I believe it was estimated that only 10% of recorded shootings with a .25 ACP resulted in a one shot stop. Now, one thing that other instructors never mention is that sometimes low power can be advantageous, say when overpenetration is a concern. One reason why the .25 was favored by gangsters is because, unlike any other caliber excepting the .22 short/corto, you can shoot someone in the leg or arm with a very low probability of fatality if you intended to "send a message" or "make an example." You can also use it to shoot an attacker in a crowded room, center of mass, at contact range without worrying about the slug exiting and striking someone else. Although the .25 can indeed kill, it is not a killing gun . . . it is a fighting gun, designed to punish and injure rather than stop. Shooting someone with a .25 is like stabbing them with a screwdriver. It will slow them down and reduce their ability and motivation to continue attacking you, but you can reasonably assume that after you empty the magazine there will be a need to utilize your hand to hand combat skills. If you put 3 rounds in a man's chest they may not reach the heart, and if they do he may not die until an hour later from a slow internal bleed. It is a lot better than a knife for self defense, but has far less power than a .22 Magnum or even a .32 ACP. If you carry a .25 automatic and use it on an attacker, expect to be fighting him.

Because of its low power and small size, I treat the .25 automatic as a special purpose weapon and do not consider it in the same class as other handguns. I normally recommend a nonreflective black, blued, or matte finish on handguns, but usually choose bright polished nickle when picking a .25 (or "Deuce Papi" as they say in da hood). That is because you really want to avoid shooting anyone with it if at all possible and actually want them to notice it in your hand when you're threatening them, and do not want it mistaken as a cap gun or novelty lighter. Polished nickle will catch and reflect light even in a dark alley. This is the gun I would select for investigating noises in your backyard if you live in a densely populated area—gun is flashy, and if you fire it you don't need to worry about ricochets or overpenetration. Don't be fooled by internet know-it-alls who call the .25 a popgun—it is a lot louder than you might expect, and the sound is obviously a gunshot and will attract attention, especially if you dump the magazine. One shot may work as a warning or as punishment, but it takes the whole magazine to "stop" someone. That is why I do not recommend this caliber for self defense. Again, this is a special purpose weapon that will slow an attacker down and possibly kill him eventually, but not something you want to rely upon as your sole means of protection. You need to be a coldblooded motherfucker to use one of these pimp guns effectively, firing it precisely and repeatedly into your adversary's head at point blank range in order to drop him. Shots to the center of mass generally aren't very effective, especially if he is obese or wearing a thick jacket. Multiple headshots. Preferably directly into the face. 99% of gun owners that CCW are incapable of doing this, and you probably can't do it either, even if you think you can. Adrenaline makes your hands tremble, which adversely effects your aim. As I said, you really need to be coldblooded to pull that off. Best to stick with something that has a bit more pop.

DERRINGERS

Most derringers are crap. Some, like the magnum O/U versions from Bond Arms and American Derringer Company are extremely overpriced crap. Frankly, a derringer needs to meet two basic standards: it needs to be lightweight and concealable, and it better not have a fucking safety switch. I do not care if the manufacturer claims that their push-button hammer block safety will automatically disengage once the hammer is cocked (only American Derringer offers this feature). I do not trust a tiny and unnecessary part to function consistently without malfunction. This effectively eliminates the most commonly seen derringers from consideration (Davis, Cobra, Cimarron). Besides, if the hammer has a properly fitted half-cock safety notch it should be considered drop safe. It is designed as a last ditch, desperation, get-the-fuck-off-me gun, and rest assured you will be likely to be in the throes of a full adrenal dump should ever you need to use it. Adrenaline tends to cloud one's thinking and disrupt fine motor skills. Hence, safety switch on a derringer is fucking retarded. Unfortunately, nearly every derringer manufactured over the past decade is equipped with one, and sometimes they are small and not noticeable upon first glance, so be aware of that commonplace design flaw.

The most commonly encountered derringers are those Zamak POS made by Davis and later Cobra and Cimarron. Most common chambering is either .22 Magnum or .22 LR, although other calibers are sometimes encountered. .25 ACP and .32 ACP are small frame, whereas .38 Special, .380 ACP, and 9mm are large frame. You only want a 10 ounce small frame version, not only are the large frame "big bore" derringers heavier and bulkier, but recoil is savage and reliability has been a problem with them. The only way you should carry one of these zinc nightmares is with the safety OFF and the hammer at the half cock notch. If you drop it the gun may fire. It is not uncommon for one of the internal firing pins to break within the first 50 rounds, especially if it has been dry fired. The only positive thing I can say about the Davis / Cobra small frame derringers is that they can often be purchased used for under $100. Now, Chiappa has released an improved version of this design which they call the Double Eagle, and in lieu of the pushbutton safety switch they have chosen to utilize an internal key lock in order to comply with the laws of certain states and avoid lawsuits which have bankrupted other companies. This internal lock eliminates the need to fumble with a possibly defective safety switch (which often requires considerable force to disengage), but it is still an unnecessary mechanical part in a cheap zinc pistol that can be expected to eventually break. The primary issue I have wiith the Double Eagle is that it is pretty much a novelty gun, being a reproduction of the old .41 derringer in size and weight, yet chambered for .22 LR, and you probably want something smaller with more firepower.

The finest derringer ever made was the NAA Mini, which is discussed in detail above, and since it has a rotating cylinder may technically be something other than a derringer, so we shall not discuss it further in this section.

Second finest derringer ever made is arguably the 11 ounce High Standard DM-101, which was a DAO O/U derringer chambered in .22 Magnum (although a .less popular 22 LR version was also made). In lieu of a safety switch it had a 15 # trigger pull. What makes this particular derringer so badassed is that, not only don't you need to cock it, and not only can it be fired from within a pocket without fear of jamming, but several makers created a wallet holster for this gun which completely concealed it inside, and these "holsters" can still be found on eBay very reasonably priced. The only problem is that once ATF realized just how doublecool wallet holsters were they said average folks couldn't own them anymore unless they were registered with their agency as an AOW "disguised firearm." If you disregard their little law and choose to combine a forbidden wallet holster with a derringer (and by "combine" they really mean "own"—doesn't need to be assembled, just capable of being put together should you so wish), well, you face a penalty of up to 10 years in prison, and there is no parole in the federal system and only POTUS can grant a federal pardon. So fill out the tax stamp form and pay their extortion, or don't get caught breaking the law, or just disregard the notion of wallet guns altogether. Really seems like way too much hassle over a folded piece of leather, especially when you consider that for a few bucks more you could get a LCP and a wallet rig which holds 7 rounds instead of 2 and is perfectly legal (for now). While the DM-101 tends to be reliable, they have a plastic cam which has been known to occasionally break, as well as an alloy frame which loosens up within the first half box of magnum loads, resulting in a disconcerting rattle when you shake the gun—but apparently they all do that. Wallet rig makes the rattle go away, and if you take off the grips it slims the profile by half an inch. American Derringer Corporation also offers a version of this weapon, the DS-22.

Third best choice is almost any one of the slew of cheap derringers that were imported from Germany (and occasionally Italy) during the 1950s and 1960s. Most of these were O/U with a rotating firing pin, but a number of single shots based upon the Butler design (which, in turn, were based upon the Colt Thuer) were included amongst the imports as well, both in .22 short and .22 LR, although they were notorious for weak hammer springs resulting in the occasional light strike. There were a handful of 4-barreled guns based loosely upon the Sharps, but these usually were chambered for the inadequate .22 Short and tend to be overpriced. The Estul Twist-2 was essentially a 2 shot, manually rotated pepperbox chambered for .22 LR that had a good reputation for being lightweight and reliable, and the Sport Arms Tumbler was the same design from another manufacturer. You want a .22 Magnum derringer, but a .22 LR will also do if the price is right, as will a .32 ACP or even a .25 ACP. Although .22 short can be lethal and chronograph similar to .25 ACP, I'd advise passing on choosing one as a carry piece, especially if it is a single shot. I would also urge you to avoid "big bore" derringers chambered for .380 or .38 Special as they tend to have problems. Common brands include, but are by no means limited to: Hawes, Reck, Rohm, Romo, Hy-Hunter, American Weapons Corp, General Precision Corp, Tanarmi, and guns stamped with importer marks (FIE, Excam, etc.) which were probably assembled on Zamak frames after the 1968 ban. These guns tend to be very reliable, are accurate within their effective range of 10 feet, usually have a half-cock notch which makes them drop safe, and are very economically priced, often under $75. They are a hell of a counter-knife defense. Although all of these German derringers are widely deemed "crap," none of them have safety switches, they usually do fire reliably, and I've always been rather fond of them. I would always choose an old German import over a POS Davis or Cobra.

Fourth choice is split between a few rarely seen oddities. First is the HJS "Lone Star" single shot derringer chambered for .380 ACP, which often is found priced over $400. Second is the WSP "Downsizer" with a DAO trigger that fired a single round of either .45 ACP or .357 Magnum / .38 Special, which is rarely seen outside of private collections and when one does hit the market it is typically priced around a thousand dollars and sells quickly. Third choice is the Rossi side by side .22 LR derringer with dual triggers and dual "rabbit ears" hammers which is an interesting piece and usually nickle plated. They sometimes come up as low as $150 and are the only "snake eyes" style derringer I can recommend, although only as a functional novelty as quality control tended to be poor.

Honorable mention goes to the 16 ounce Cobray single-shot "Model D" .410 derringer. These were manufactured in Ducktown, TN by a somewhat disreputable company which changed its name numerous times, with Leinad and FMJ being the most common manufacturer stamps. It is my understanding that these were also offered in kit form which were "sterile" with no serial number or manufacturer stamp. These are very naughty guns that resemble a pocket blunderbuss, which effectively is what they are. They kick like hell and are limited to 2.5" .410 shells. The side-by-side double barrel version will chamber 3" shells, but it is twice as heavy, twice as bulky, and the firing pin selector switch has a tendency to break. If you decide to get one of these abominations insist on the single shot version. On rare occasion you may even find one chambered in .357 Magnum/.38 Special. There is also a seldom seem O/U version with the top barrel chambered for .22 LR and the selector switch being on the hammer itself, which provides an extra shot with no real increase in mass, although the firing pin design is less durable. The .410 O/U version is just as rare but almost as bulky as the side by side. These derringers all have a push-button hammer block safety switch, but none of the ones I've seen seemed to be functional. Recoil is downright unpleasant, and it weighs and prints as much as a J-frame. They can also chamber .45 Long Colt, but accuracy is poor and recoil severe. Stopping power of birdshot from a 1" barrel is practically nil. Don't even bother with slugs or novelty flechettes. The only round you want to fire through this nightmare is Winchester PDX1 personal defense shells. They were designed specifically for .410 derringers and incorporate 3 copper disks followed by a dozen BBs and are absolutely devastating at point blank range. In the event you cannot obtain these rounds, .410 buckshot is a passable substitute. This is a very nasty hideout gun for the garage or bathroom. Loaded with birdshot it is okay for snakes on fishing trips, but it works better on trouser snakes as it can castrate a man through his jeans at point blank range. I bought mine used for $50, but I see new in box Model Ds selling for more than double that. Personally, I wouldn't pay much more than fifty for one. Very few gun shops will carry these, but they do come up secondhand every now and then—usually after a new owner fires it for the first time at the range. Recoil and muzzle blast is brutal. FMJ also made a black powder version as well as an orange "marine flare projector" chambered for short 12 gauge flares—both could be purchased via mail order without any background check, and both could be modified to accept the .45/.410 barrel, which could be purchased from another source. They stopped manufacture of the flare projector when it was determined they would accept Aquila mini-shells, which will cause the device to grenade if fired.

One neat gun I've come across a few times was the Mossberg Brownie, as well as copies made by Advantage Arms or imported by EIG. These are a flat, squared-off 4 barrel pepperbox with a rotating firing pin and an incredibly heavy DAO trigger pull, which is chambered in .22 LR, although the Advantage Arms 422 was also offered in a .22 Magnum version, and bright chrome finish was an option. While a 1920s Brownie is a valuable collectable, the 422 and EIG typically sell for around $150, and frankly you could do a lot worse, especially if you don't care for the single-action NAA minis.

Occasionally a variety of "pen gun" derringers are seen for sale, usually very overpriced. Some of these are as thick as a marker and unsafe to carry, others look like a ball point pen but can be folded into a pistol shape after a few moments. They typically fire a single .22 LR round, but I've seen pen guns chambered in other calibers as well. They should be considered novelty items and avoided.

You will sometimes come across muzzleloading .31 caliber derringers which require a percussion cap. Most of these are distinguished by a brass frame and they typically are of the "snake eyes" side by side double barrel dual hammer design, although Traditions did make a brass barreled single shot roughly the size of the Butler marketed as the "Vest Pocket." These are dangerous, unreliable, and woefully underpowered . . . plus if you fire it indoors you will fill the room with a blinding, acrid smoke screen. These are intended more as curiosities and novelties than actual defensive weapons and were considered obsolete by the 1880s. Do not buy one of these unless you are a reenactor in need of a range toy. Many percussion derringers were converted to fire .22 rimfire ammo, and these vary greatly in quality, with most being little more than zip guns with unrifled bores, although drop-in conversion sleeves were openly sold at one time. Some derringers were actually cap guns or zinc replicas that were modified to chamber and fire ammunition—again, these are zip guns that are unreliable, inaccurate, and dangerous to the user. I have seen dozens of such conversions, and they can be mistaken for a firearm by one who lacks familiarity. Never carry or use anything like this.

MISTER SATURDAY NIGHT SPECIAL

Saturday Night Special . . . what does that phrase mean to you? It was a politically charged phrase created by anti-gun zealots hoping for an outright ban of affordable handguns, and in 1968 they did succeed in banning their import. As urban legend would have it, cheap handguns were notoriously unreliable and often would blow up in people's hands, and they were the preferred weapon of robbers and pimps needing something shiny and disposable. However, like non existent "cop killer bullets" and "undetectable plastic Glocks" there is little substance to these hysterical and prejudicial claims. The fact is, while many cheap guns were no bargain, a few actually would outperform far more expensive name brands when it came to reliability and sometimes even accuracy. I'm going to share with you a few of the better ones here. I'll also list a few you definitely want to avoid—after all, not everything cheap is a bargain.

If you really want a bargain, let me introduce you to the notorious Raven. The 15 ounce Raven MP-25 not only has a zinc frame, it has a zinc slide. Furthermore, the steel barrel is actually cast within the frame and is unremovable. Everyone says the Raven is the worst POS ever made . . .

everyone except the few folks who'll actually admit to owning one. The fact is, these guns are extremely reliable. They are considered the Hi-Points of the 1980s, but unlike a Hi-Point they are actually small enough to carry in your pocket. Being striker fired with a trigger safety, it is unsafe to carry with a round chambered, and there are many accounts of these guns discharging in people's pockets. There are several versions of the Raven. The one you want to look for is the final version with the rotary (up/down) safety, as the earlier sliding safeties had problems (although most sliding safety Ravens did not develop this problem, which usually amounted to the safety switching on while firing, and it can be fixed). As long as you keep them clean they will feed and extract reliably, and they can last for thousands of rounds. As an added bonus, Zamak does not rust. The only notable issue with these guns is the strikers can break from repeated dry firing, but they are cheap and easy to replace. If you do find a Raven that jams, the cause is typically very simple and easily corrected by scrubbing the extractor, polishing the chamber, or replacing the magazine. I frequently see Ravens on the secondhand market in the $50 to $70 price range, and they are certainly worth it. In fact, I would pay as much as $120 for a chrome rotary safety Raven Arms with wood grips in like new condition with the original box, just to use as a cool paperweight / conversation piece. Over 3 million Ravens are known to be in circulation, and many of these can be found in states which virtually prohibit civilian ownership of handguns as the black market profit on these was immense since they would typically sell for triple MSRP, and could be resold for even more. There is an online forum for Saturday Night Special enthusiasts who all agree that the Raven was the first zinc .25 and the best. I have owned several, and all had adequate close range accuracy and were extremely reliable. As long as you keep the extractor claw free of gunk and replace the recoil spring every 500 rounds you can count on a Raven to run flawlessly. They are just fat and heavy and unsafe to carry with a round in the chamber. Like similar striker fired pistols, it is best to carry the Raven with a cocked striker over an empty chamber, which makes racking the slide easier and quicker. They hold 6 rounds in the magazine which must be carefully loaded to avoid rim lock as the internal dimensions of the magazine seems nearly a quarter inch longer than the semi-rimmed cartridges. Load it with Winchester X-Panding point ammo for best results. It is advised not to store one of these pistols with a round chambered, and certainly never to carry it in that condition, as these are cheap pistols with a safety that only prevents the trigger from moving but does nothing to prevent the cocked striker from flying forward in the event of mechanical failure due to metal fatigue, and I've heard stories of these guns firing if dropped or even firing spontaneously after sitting in a drawer untouched for years. While this probably won't happen to you, it can and has happened due to the inherently unsafe design.

Some guys love the sleek and pocketable 13 ounce Jennings J-22 and J-25, whereas others refer to it as the "Jammings J-22." If you get a good one, these are nice little pistols. Unfortunately, they were made in over a half dozen factories and quality control was never a priority. A few other names this pistol was stamped with as ownership changed include: Calwestco, Bryco, and Jimenez. Later versions, particularly in .22 LR, tend to require polishing of the feed ramp, modification of the magazine lips, modification of the extractor, and replacement of the springs to ascertain that they will cycle reliably. This requires patience and talent, and is a huge pain in the ass unless tinkering with things is your hobby. If you find an original J-22 or get a great deal on a J-25, or have one gifted to you, don't believe the internet experts who claim it is a garbage fishing weight that will blow up in your face (that is the .380 version), but don't be surprised if you have at least one failure to feed jam for every magazine fired. The Jennings J-22 / J-25 is an enthusiast's gun, and you probably will need to work on it quite a bit to get it to run well, but if you're okay with that go for it. If you can fire 2 magazines without a jam you got a good one. If it jams, keep tinkering with it until it doesn't before you rely upon it as a possible backup piece, with the understanding that some of these guns never run well, even with expert attention. Never carry a pistol that cannot empty a mag without jamming, as many Jennings tend to do. The great thing about these guns is you can often find someone so frustrated with theirs that they are willing to practically give it away—then you can fix it and have a nice plinker. The Jennings needs to be kept exceptionally clean or it will jam, and it is so sensitive to crud the jams will usually start once the third magazine is being fired, but a polished and clean Jennings that will fire 2 mags without a jam can be considered reliable. If the sear wears out or becomes gunked up these pistols sometimes go full auto, which can be embarrassing if it occurs at a public range. Like the Raven, they are unsafe to carry with a round in the chamber, and they are best carried cocked with an empty chamber and full 6 round magazine. Probably twice as many Jennings style pistols are in circulation as the Raven, and they are frequently found in the pockets of teenaged punks, drunk rednecks, and barroom brawlers. A used J-22 in good condition typically sells between $50 and $70, which is cheaper than the average used Raven, making it the most inexpensive pistol on the market. The J-25 is slightly more reliable, but outnumbered by J-22s 10 to 1. I cannot recommend this pistol at all, and it is considered by many to be the worst pistol ever commercially produced.

A lot of guys talk about the Hi-Point pistols and what pieces of crap they are. The Hi-Point is available in a number of calibers, and even though it is a striker fired pistol similar to a Raven on steroids, the safety mechanism is so overbuilt it is considered safe to carry with a round chambered (although I wouldn't). I have heard numerous verified reports of people buying a used Hi-Point 9mm for under a hundred bucks and firing 500 rounds of cheap ammo through it without a single jam—and that is what I call a real bargain. The biggest problem with Hi-Point pistols is that they are huge, fat, heavy monstrosities which are impossible to carry concealed. Their .380 ACP pistol is the same size as their 9mm and weighs 2 pounds, so while it is an adequate truck gun or home defense gun, you ain't gonna fit it in your pocket . . . it is practically as bulky as a MAC.

The Iver Johnson TP-22 / TP-25 is a Zamak copy of the Walther TPH based on an Erma design and built on a Zamak frame using imported parts. The .25 ACP version is more reliable, but rarely seen. TP-22s come up for sale occasionally. The design is good, but the materials and quality control is substandard and these pistols often suffer from broken safeties and cracked frames, especially is hypervelocity ammo is used. Some folks claim to have fired over a thousand rounds through theirs with no problems, other folks report catastrophic failure within 300 rounds. These guns are more reliable than a Jennings but less reliable than a Titan and often are found priced higher than a Jetfire.

They are DA/SA, but have an extremely heavy DA trigger pull. If buying used, be certain to check the frame and slide for cracks and test the safety to see if it is jammed. This is a fair choice if you want a pocket sized DA/SA pistol that is cheaper than a Bersa, although I really can't recommend it.

Sometimes you'll see an ugly little revolver with no cylinder release switch, and then you discover that in order to open the cylinder you need to pull the cylinder pin right out of the frame. These guns were made by Harrington Richardson (H&R) and New England Firearms (NEF) and were available in a variety of calibers, with .22 Magnum and .32 H&R Magnum being the most popular, although older versions like the 732 Sidekick were chambered in .32 S&W Long. They are solid and reliable guns with a loyal following. Unfortunately, they usually cost as much as a better quality Charter Arms, which is lighter and fires a more potent round.

Antique revolvers in .32 and .38 S&W are sometimes found fairly cheap. One thing you need to be aware of is that .38 S&W is not the same as .38 Special, being shorter and lower powered; and there were about a half dozen types of .32 revolver cartridge, and while some will interchange others will not. Fortunately, the most common version was the .32 S&W Long which is still available via commercial channels today. Most of these were crap, but if you find a top-break Harrington Richardson or Iver Johnson you are in luck because they were very well made. .32 Long is, frankly, a rather impotent cartridge, really not much better than the .25 ACP . . . but for defensive purposes you can load it with .32 ACP ammo. I need to state that this is considered unsafe due to the higher pressures of modern ammo combined with the questionable metallurgy of antique steel, but it can be done. As .32 Long was originally a black powder cartridge, you do not want to be firing .32 ACP regularly at the range to save money on ammo because your revolver will loosen and eventually break. A Harrington Richardson .32 revolver typically sells for about $75. A modern SNS .32 Long that sometimes pops up is the short lived Kimmel 5000, which had a 7 round cylinder and a heavyweight frame which would easily handle higher pressure .32 ACP cartridges. Please do not ever fire .32 ACP cartridges out of an antique .32 S&W revolver. The .32 S&W cartridge, sometimes incorrectly referred to as the ".32 Short", is roughly the same size as the .32 ACP but has a lead bullet and wider rim . . . it also produces half the pressure of the .32 S&W Long. While it might seem like a great idea to load an antique H&R Vest Pocket Safety Hammer with .32 ACP Glasers, and it might even fire them, at the very least that gun will be ruined, and it is possible that the cylinder could shatter, resulting in serious injury.

Most cheap .38 Specials should be avoided as they tend to have heavy frames and a few brands are notorious for breakage, such as Armscor, Eibar, and Llama. Occasionally you'll see an old S&W Model 10 (or the earlier Military & Police) with scuffs and dings for a fair price, or an even older S&W Victory that was butchered by importers during the 1950s who would chop the barrels (often without crowning the muzzle), put on a cheap bumper chrome finish, and add a set of fake stag grips. An unaltered Victory in excellent condition would be worth quite a bit to a collector, but a chopped chrome one might sell for under $150. There are a lot of obscure brands of revolver chambered for this cartridge, most of which you should avoid. Also be aware that many older .38 revolvers will not chamber .38 Special ammunition (longer than .38 S&W cartridges) or be able to withstand the pressure of +P loads.

The absolute cheapest .38 Special snubbie you can find is the Rohm/RG, as well as several very similar German revolvers marked EIG, Burgo, Regent, Roscoe, Thalco, or SportArms. There were several configurations with different features, but all were similar enough. These were typically 6 shot .38 Special revolvers with plastic grips and heavyweight 30 ounce Zamak frames, although a few have had steel frames. Surprisingly, they tend to go bang every time you pull the trigger, although accuracy is extremely poor due to keyholeing and some owners have mentioned occasional problems with light strikes or timing. The Rohm/RG .38s are a fair deal if you can find one under $100. Unfortunately, most of the ones I've seen on the secondhand market were priced considerably higher, and these guns just aren't worth more than a hundred bucks. Please note that all other guns manufactured by Rohm/RG, particularly their .22 revolvers and .25 automatics, have a well earned reputation for being garbage guns. Avoid them. Another cheapo German .38 Special is the Arminus, manufactured by Weihrauch, which is of better quality than the Rohm with deeper rifling and a heavy steel frame, but is not the same quality as a Rossi 68 or Charter Arms Undercover. They are still being made and imported under license from Bersa. A Polish GWARD revolver is a better investment than most German revolvers, but they only came with a 4" barrel.

As stated previously, do not waste your money on German .22 revolvers. Many of them, particularly those chambered in .22 Short, are simply starting pistols that were converted to fire live ammunition at the factory, and most of the .22 LR versions are based on the starting pistol design. The cylinders often spin freely clockwise, and rapid fire will result in misfires due to faulty timing. While these guns are unlikely to actually blow up, it is common for them to go "click" almost as often as they go "bang" because the chamber failed to come in line with the barrel and hammer mounted firing pin. Furthermore, rifling is often nonexistent, so bullets keyhole as they exit the muzzle, tumbling in random directions rather that flying true. I have fired an RG-14 that literally could not hit a target 10 feet away from a bench rest, and I have heard similar complaints about the Burgo and Omega. You literally are better off with a knife or a rock in a sock than one of these garbage guns. Aside from the Jennings, these are the only guns uniformly considered trash—even by enthusiasts of cheap handguns. As far as Saturday Night Specials go, the German .22 revolvers are the worst of the worst.

There are a LOT of cheap guns that you want to avoid due to reputations as jam-o-matics with an unfortunate tendency to grenade. In reality, only a very few tend to blow their slides at the range, those usually being high powered, compact pistols with Zamak slides, notably the: Talon 9mm, Skyy/Sccy 9mm, Lorcin 9mm, Jennings 9mm, Bryco 9mm, Jiminez 9mm, Lorcin .380, and Davis .380. These guns all have a verified history of actually blowing up in people's hands on numerous occasions. If you own one of these grenade-guns do not shoot it: disassemble and destroy it. I know that gun snobs like to say that about any cheap gun, but in those few cases they're actually right. Other guns you just want to avoid due to excessive problems with jamming and breakage. A few can be made more reliable after extensive tinkering, but unless you really enjoy doing that sort of thing as a hobby and get one of these for practically free, don't even bother. A very short and partial list of specific brands to avoid follows: Talon, Skyy/Sccy, Lorcin, Davis, Cobra, Bryco, Sedco, Jimenez, Sundance, Jennings, Calwestco, Sterling, Phoenix Arms (with the exception of their Raven), Republic Arms, Standard Arms, Liberty Arms, American Arms, Chiappa, Cimarron, Uberti, AMT Backup, FTL Auto Nine, Wilkinson, Grendel, Intratec, Accu-Tek, Sedco, Erma, Armi Galesi, Galena, Bauer, Fraser, Ruby, OWA, Omega, Deutsche Werk, Burgo, Gradoga, Armscor, Eibar, Llama, Norton, Gecado, Gaztanaga, Tanarmi, Rohm, Reck, RG, Regent, Roscoe, Thalco, SportArms, HS, and pretty much any subcompact rimfire pistol. Also avoid gunlike objects which are frequently sold alongside inexpensive pistols and easily mistaken for or misrepresented as actual firearms. Common examples include: gas pistols (Champion, Mondial, and Precise), flare pistols (GECO or FMJ), replica starter pistols (Chiappa, Bruni, Ekol, Zoraki, and Voltran), or even replica pellet or airsoft guns (Umarex). This list is intended as a general guideline and I'm aware there are exceptions. A few of the "Ring of Fire" zinc pistols can be made to run reliably after a bit of polishing and tinkering, and some Llamas run flawlessly for over a thousand rounds, but as a general rule these guns have very poor customer satisfaction ratings and limited lifespans. Many are commonly offered for sale in the $100 to $150 price range, which is a good price for a gun that works reliably but too damn expensive for a non-functional paperweight. Be advised not to waste your money on junk. That being said, quite a few far more expensive guns (like the Walther PPK, and many subcompact .45s) also tend to be jam-o-matics. Do your research.

AMMUNITION

Whether you've got a .38 Special or a .380 ACP, you want to get the best ammunition available for your carry load. What is "best" is open to speculation as none of the self proclaimed experts seem to agree, but you want to stick with commercially loaded, American ammo of recent manufacture. No reloads, foreign ammo, or 30 year old waterstained boxes filled with discolored rounds.

Reloads are frequently put together by inbred alcoholic mongoloids who sell them to Darwin Award candidates at gun shows who are attracted by the low prices. Some reloads are great, but some are overloaded and will destroy your firearm—especially if it is an aluminum framed snubbie or an LCP that is specifically not intended to be loaded with +P ammo. Other reloads may be "squibs" which contain no powder and can result in a slug clogging the barrel, which can result in the gun exploding if a second round is fired. As a general rule of thumb, never buy reloads.

Foreign ammo is typically dirty as well as loaded to higher pressures and, especially in the Communist countries, quality control is notoriously poor. It is best to avoid foreign ammo altogether.

Old ammo may have degraded primers that fail to ignite, or corrosion could have weakened the cases allowing them to split, resulting in a jam, damage to the gun, or even injury. Furthermore, many advances have been made in bullet design over the past decade alone, so newly manufactured ammo is just better quality. Avoid using questionable ammo for anything other than practice at the range.

Occasionally you may come across "Treasury Loads," "FBI Loads," or casings stamped +P+. Never fire these overpressure cartridges through an Airweight. They hark from a benighted era when police were issued .357 Magnum revolvers but were only authorized to carry .38 Special ammunition, so "Treasury Loads" are actually .38 Special cartridges overloaded to .357 Magnum pressures that were never intended to be fired from .38 Special revolvers—even steel framed ones. +P+ ammo will destroy your gun. Don't use them.

Which brings me back to the fact that the LCP is not rated for +P ammo. No reloads, no foreign 380 or 9mm Kurtz, and no high pressure defensive loads from makers like Grizzly, Buffalo Bore, or Double Tap. The LCP cannot handle them and will break, and for that matter so will the even lighter Kel-Tec P3AT. I would not run hot ammo through any polymer micro pistol. Standard pressure ammo only! Corbon DPX is a great choice, as is Remington Golden Saber and Speer Gold Dot.

For the alloy framed snubbie, +P rounds are okay in moderation. Too many will loosen the cylinder and eventually warp or even crack the frame. This happened a lot with the early Airweights, but metallurgy has improved and the new guns are more durable. Still, if you're buying a used Airweight to save money, avoid a paper trail, or bypass a background check, be certain to examine it carefully for signs of looseness, breakage, excessive wear, flame cutting, or hairline cracks in the frame. Airweights are designed to be fired at the range moderately and intermittently, being primarily concealed carry pieces. They are not intended to last for a thousand rounds, and many break before 500 rounds have gone through them, particularly if you're using a lot of +P at the range. These are not meant for target shooting and excessive range time will wear them out. If you insist on putting in a lot of time practicing I advise you to invest in a steel framed snubbie for range use.

As with the .380, Corbon DPX, Remington Golden Saber, and Speer Gold Dot are all great choices for carry ammo. If you want to downgrade to standard pressure, Federal Nyclad is your best bet. Glaser Silver and Air Freedom prefragmented rounds are an option in warm climates where the bullets will not be impeded by heavy layers of clothing—as a bonus, the excessive fragmentation can make ballistic identification more difficult. Occasionally you may stumble across some old exotic rounds with solid aluminum bullets, teflon coated brass bullets, or even vintage "metal piercing" ammo. All have excellent penetration capabilities against auto bodies, hollow core steel doors, metal desks, and obsolete body armor, but even the fabled KTW rounds (which sell for over twenty bucks each on gunbroker) will not penetrate modern soft vests so get that thought right out of your head. Stick to modern, commercially manufactured, American made, top quality defensive hollowpoints and you won't go wrong.

TRAINING

First, I want to state very emphatically that the lightweight concealed carried handguns I have recommended above are NOT target pistols nor should they be treated as such. They are designed specifically for ease of carry, which means size and mass have been minimized, thereby sacrificing strength and durability. I would give these guns a reasonable life expectancy of 500 rounds, after which they will typically develop problems. If you insist on firing a box of ammo at the range every month you really want to invest in a second gun and stick with standard pressure loads. Otherwise, you will have nothing but a scary paperweight.

Realistically, the average shooter does not have the luxury of being able to safely and legally plink in his backyard, nor can he get to the range more than a few times a year, so as an alternative to live fire I'd suggest investing in a small CO2 powered BB pistol for target shooting in your garage or basement. In some places, if a neighbor sees you with a BB gun in your backyard they'll tell 911 to send the SWAT team to your house, and believe it or not in a few places it is actually a crime to possess one of these toys. Research your laws and use common sense. These look like real guns and will frighten people.

Another training aid that I strongly urge you to buy is Snap Caps. These are inert training cartridges that will allow you to dry fire as often as you like without risking damage to your firing pin. They also allow you to practice reloading quickly and clearing jams. Snap Caps are made by several different manufacturers and can be acquired cheaply from most gun stores as well as eBay and Amazon, and you need to get some. Until you are able to acquire Snap Caps, use spent cartridges instead. I understand that some manufacturers claim that their guns can safety be dry fired with no risk of damage, but there is always a risk of damage. I have heard of Ruger firing pins breaking from dry fire, and they are very tough. Antique guns, rimfire guns, and foreign guns like Llama and Star are especially susceptible to damage and should NEVER be dry fired. The only firing pins that are supposedly indestructible are the copper beryllium pins used in the original Charter Arms revolvers . . . but I always used Snap Caps in those anyway. I foresee a time in the not too distant future when it will be impossible to acquire replacement parts, so buy extra parts now and take care not to abuse your guns.

The main thing you need to practice is drawing your firearm from concealment and firing. Start out slow—you can damage your gun if you drop it. There is no need to practice a "quick draw", just draw your weapon in a calm relaxed manner. This should be a single fluid motion, and after a few hundred draws it will start to come naturally to you. Draw and point, but do not fire. Practice aiming. Practice rapid fire. Practice firing at two separate targets. Practice tracking a moving target. Practice moving and firing. Practice firing from behind cover. You can do all of this within the privacy of your home. Be sure to use Snap Caps. However, do remember that excessive dry firing, even with Snap Caps, will eventually wear out your gun. Gunsmiths see many worn out guns come in that may've been fired rarely, but the owner would practice dry firing at imaginary targets daily. Practice regularly, but don't overdo it.

There are a lot of books and courses available to you which purport to instruct one in the art of combat pistolcraft. If you are a policeman or a special operations soldier this information may prove useful to you, but as a civilian whose mere possession of a loaded handgun is barely tolerated and soon to be prohibited by our government, such a course will likely be wasted on you. Do you really need to learn rapid reloads, seeking cover, engaging multiple attackers, and engaging in numerous fanciful scenarios? Even if you want to do this for fun, the snubbie and LCP are not the right tools for the job. Fortunately, the situations you're likely to face in the real world tend to be a lot simpler and easier dealt with.

GUNFIGHTING

There are dozens of books about combat shooting, tactics, pistolcraft, what have you. Some of them are quite good. Some of them contradict one another due to differing opinions on various points. Many shooters have very strong opinions regarding the superiority of their particular system. If you want to learn more about this subject do some research and find books written by instructors who you agree with. Take no-one's word unquestioningly if something does not seem right for you. A lot of these books are written based more on particular styles for particular reasons and may not be applicable to your needs or temperament. As Bruce Lee said, "Absorb that which is useful." I'm not going to go into detail here at all. Don't carry a gun unless you intend to pull it, don't pull it unless you intend to use it, don't use it unless you intend to kill. If you are only hoping to use it as a threat, you're better off leaving it at home. Do not extend your arm so the gun can be grabbed if the threat is close, but instead keep it low and next to your hip. If you need to shoot, do not hesitate, aim for the center of mass, and continue shooting until the threat is on the ground. If you have not practiced firing live ammo at targets without using the sights, you will probably miss if the target is beyond point blank range. That's pretty much all I'm going to say on the matter. You should really listen to what the experts have to say about this, and that ain't me:

"You must force yourself to the belief that your opponent is going to choke up and miss and that all you have to do to win is keep cool and make your shot—the first one—a hit. This is without letting your manufactured contempt get out of hand and cause you to take foolish chances! With the vast majority of us this attitude must be forced. In an occasional rare individual it is natural. He responds to danger by turning into a machine—ignoring the fire of his opponents and placing his shots as though indulging in private target practice. This is your true gunfighter."

William H Jordan, *No Second Place Winner* (p. 107)

"These experts believed that shooting was 20 percent physical and 80 percent mental . . . . Each became one with the weapon. The gun was an extension of the shooter. They let the bullet go down range—they didn't fire it . . . . Surprisingly, these experts do not need to hold their weapons perfectly still to shoot accurately. Under observation, the shooters displayed a great deal of arm movement as they were firing. They mentally controlled the trigger squeeze, and would not allow the bullet to 'go down range' until their sights were on target. This mental control was an unconscious process that allowed trigger squeeze to occur only when the sights were aligned. The expert shooters call their technique 'controlling the smallest arc of movement.' They knew they would be moving and controlled the arc."

The Warrior's Edge, by Col. John B. Alexander, Major Richard Groller, and Janet Morris (pp. 78-79)

"You should neither see the sights nor be conscious of them. The weapon must be a natural extension of your arm; look at where you're going to shoot and think the bullet into the target."

John Minnery, *How to Kill, Vol. I* (p. 51)

"Clear your mind with a black image . . . think black. That is the color of nothingness. If a man is just firing his handgun without thinking about it, he's just doing it. But the moment he thinks, "I might miss," he's lost his focus of concentration. He's listening to a little voice that's saying, 'Can I or can't I?' And the answer will be, 'I can't.'"

Michael Echanis

"Using the suction tipped darts against a full length mirror, where the student can see his own mistakes and aim at the reflection of his own body, will help a great deal. The darts will stick on the mirror at the point of impact, showing where the bullets would've hit if a gun had been used. Basic errors are much more easily corrected with training of this type."

Rex Applegate, *Kill or Be Killed* (pp. 126-127)

Adrenaline is not your friend. It will give you the fumble fingers, and you may either drop your gun or shoot yourself in the dick if you are unable to maintain your shit. No joke, this has happened to many individuals who have undergone professional training, as well as LEOs with years of experience, and it can happen to you too if you aren't careful. Your primary goal is to get that gun into your hand without dropping it or negligently discharging it, then you want to point it at the bad guy and tell him to go away, and if he either closes the distance or reaches for his own weapon, you shoot him until either your gun is empty or he is on the ground. And *that* is really all you need to know about gunfighting.

A FINAL WORD ON GUN OWNERSHIP

Unless you are a collector who never intends to actually fire most of your guns, reliability should be of the upmost concern. Whatever gun you choose—and I know many folks can't afford more than one or two guns—will be used in the event you need to protect yourself, your family, and your home. Buy a gun that you like, a gun that you are comfortable with, and the best quality gun you can afford. Read and understand the manual. Load it with the best quality ammo you can find. Be certain to do a full function check before test firing it at the range on at least two separate occasions before depending upon it to work properly when you need it. If you are experiencing jams try replacing the magazine before sending off for repair, as most jams are the result of defective or damaged magazines. Another common cause of jams is holding an automatic pistol too loosely which inhibits proper cycling, or using low powered ammunition which fails to cycle the slide fully. Once you have fired 100 rounds without a jam you can reasonably assume your handgun is reliable.

If you pocket carry, be sure to use a pocket holster. If it is hot you will sweat, and sweat contains salt, and this will corrode your gun and ammunition. Even stainless steel can rust over time. Zamak does not rust, but it will corrode. Ammunition in a revolver such as a snubbie or mini is partially exposed, thereby especially vulnerable to corrosion, which in the case of a rimfire mini can easily result in a dud round. Always remove your gun from the pocket holster at night and wipe it down with a dry cloth.

Buy a cleaning kit and be certain to use it properly after every session at the range. Clean the gun every 6 months whether you fire it or not. Protect it from dust, damp, and damage. Be certain the springs have a light coat of oil—dry springs can cause the gun to seize up or break (I've seen that happen twice, and luckily soaking them in oil made them functional once again). Be sure not to over oil—excess oil will attract grime and bind with burnt powder to form sludge. A drop or two on each spring and the rails is all you need, making sure to wipe off any excess. Be certain not to get solvent or oil on your ammo as it can foul the primers. It is seldom necessary to detail strip your gun for cleaning, and even a basic field strip can be avoided most of the time if you can just open the cylinder or the action and get in there with brushes and Q-tips. Some guns, like micro .380s, can be troublesome to field strip. The Colt Vest Pocket is a nightmare to strip. The NAA mini is like a Swiss watch and most gunsmiths are not qualified to work on them, so they should never be stripped past removing the cylinder and grips. Other guns, like Walther based mid-sized .380s and most .25 automatics, are very simple to take down once you know how it is done—and easy to put back together as well.

My .38 revolvers typically just got the bore brush down the barrel and through the cylinders before being mopped clean and wiped down. A lot of good guns have been damaged through improper disassembly or use of harsh cleaning products. Some solvents will stain nickle, melt plastic, or dissolve oils and you want to be careful with them. Break Free CLP is a good safe choice for the average gun owner. In the event you somehow fired antique or imported corrosive ammo through your gun you will need to clean the bore with water to dissolve the salts—so use quality American ammo of recent commercial manufacture.

While armorers agree that one of the most common causes of jams is over-oiling, your weapon cannot be left bone dry. You have moving parts rubbing against one another under pressure at incredibly high speed and there needs to be some lubrication there. Only a small amount of oil is needed on the springs and small parts, with a light coating of grease on the slide rails. Which lubricants you use is a matter of personal preference, but they need to be of modern manufacture and made specifically for firearms. Now, if you have an older gun or one that has been stored in a harsh climate, the springs may be bone dry. This gun will probably dry fire and cycle okay, but once you actually start firing it that stress will overwhelm those springs causing them to bind or seize up. This can have different results. In one case I had a slide freeze and was unable to cycle it, and in another case I had the hammer of a revolver freeze at full cock. While these both could have been caused by a small part inside the gun breaking, in these cases it was due to dry springs. Both guns were fixed by soaking the mainspring (and other small springs) in gun oil and allowing it to sit undisturbed for a few days, after which they were miraculously cured and functioned flawlessly. If you do not have gun oil, common penetrating oil such as WD-40 or 3 in 1 machine oil will work in a pinch, but be certain to wipe off any excess before reassembly and use a quality solvent at your earliest opportunity to clean off the residue and oil with RemOil or CLP instead.

Invest in some inert Snap Cap training rounds to practice drawing, dry fire, clearing jams, and reloading. Familiarize yourself with your gun thoroughly. Purchase as much quality ammo as you can reasonably afford and store, because one day soon you may not be able to buy anymore—many politicians have attempted a variety of ammo bans, in some states you need to show an official permit to purchase ammo, and in times of crisis the shelves will be wiped bare within hours. When you need it most you won't be able to get more. Be certain you always have at least a few full boxes for each firearm. I knew lots of guys who had a wall full of military assault rifles with no ammo for any of them, and the baddest looking gun in the world isn't very effective with no ammo. And if you do find yourself in a situation where society has deteriorated to the point that you're hearing gunfire in the streets on a regular basis, one box of ammo will probably seem insufficient to you, especially if supply lines are cut. No need to stockpile thousands of rounds, just a few 50 round boxes will do. Take care of your guns and they will take care of you.

Always remember that gun ownership is a huge responsibility. If you misuse your firearm, you will go to jail. If you have a negligent discharge, someone may be injured but you will probably go to jail regardless. If your loaded firearm is left unsecured in an unlocked drawer and a visiting child or even a trespasser accesses it without your knowledge, you will be held criminally and civilly responsible for that. If a loudmouth knows you own guns blabs about it, they may be stolen. If an enemy knows you carry a gun, they may file a false report that you threatened them with it in order to get you in trouble. And, of course, if you actually use the handgun in self defense, you will very likely be arrested for homicide and considered a criminal until proven innocent.

MANY additional risks involved with gun ownership, including the fact that millions of people in this country are prohibited from owning guns under federal law, as the prohibited person statute can be applied to numerous categories other than felons (and over the past decade many petty misdemeanors have been upgraded to felonies and dozens of laws have been passed creating new felony crimes, all of this with minimal to zero press coverage). If you have been charged with or indicted for a crime, or if you are wanted for questioning about a crime, you are not allowed to have a gun. If you use marijuana occasionally or drink to excess on the weekends you're not allowed to have a gun. If your citizenship status is questionable you can't have one either. If you once spent a week in a psychiatric ward for observation and never had a judge sign off on your release you're prohibited as well. Then, if there is anything questionable about your firearm, such as if you do not have the required license to carry it or if it has a worn sear or a dirty firing pin which sometimes makes it fire 2 rounds with 1 pull of the trigger, well that is a whole other can of worms. People have actually been arrested and charged with federal crimes after having a firearm malfunction at the range, and not only are federal crimes punished severely with up to a 10 year sentence, but there is no parole in the federal system and convicts are frequently transported to facilities in other states to serve their time.

Remember, in a few parts of this country, anyone who is not a policeman that owns a handgun is automatically treated like a deranged criminal, not just by law enforcement but by society at large—and that even applies to permit holders and retired veterans. In the Yankee NorthEast, individuals known to be gun owners are often shunned or ridiculed, blacklisted from employment, or targeted for burglaries . . . and liberal activists sometimes have created websites to post the names and addresses of pistol permit holders (which, since they include policemen and judges, are typically disabled shortly after the domain host or Internet Provider is served with a court order). In some states and counties, individuals with CCW permits are red flagged in LE databases, so if their plate is run it will initially appear as if there may be a warrant out for their arrest or the vehicle has been reported stolen—I have heard stories about law abiding permit holders being pulled over and proned out at gunpoint by asshole cops (who often have an elitist mentality that no-one other than policemen should be allowed to carry guns). These are a few reasons why I try to discourage people from carrying a gun. Gun-fu seems like such an easy solution to all your self-protection needs, but who will protect you from unjust prosecution? Many citizens are more afraid of the courts and the police than being victimized on the street, and it is a legitimate concern. I advise people who want a gun to keep it at home and don't tell anyone about it, only carrying on select occasions when you feel you may be at risk, or keeping a spare gun locked in the glovebox of your car with the registration and insurance documentation in another location. The risks associated with carrying a concealed handgun every single day are just too great for the average citizen—especially if you are not lawfully permitted to do so (as in many NorthEastern states)—but ultimately that choice is yours alone to make.

SPECIFIC RECOMMENDATIONS

Your top choice for a concealed carry piece should be an alloy or polymer framed, snubnosed revolver chambered in .38 Special. I prefer blackened finish over stainless for better concealment, and do not see the value of Tritium or laser sights. My top choice would be a 12 ounce Charter Arms with a DAO concealed hammer. Second choice would be a 14 ounce Ruger LCR. Third choice would be a 14 ounce Taurus Titanium with a DAO concealed hammer. Fourth choice would be a 15 ounce Smith Airweight Bodyguard or Centennial. Fifth choice would be an original 16 ounce Charter Arms Undercover with the hammer spur bobbed off. 16 ounces is the MAXIMUM weight you want for a pocket gun. A Smith Model 10 snub, Rossi snub, or Arminus snub will make a great nightstand or truck gun, but you really need a belt rig or shoulder rig to distribute the weight. Trust me when I tell you that every ounce makes a noticeable difference, and loading the piece and adding a pocket holster will make it even heavier.

Your top choice for a deep concealment piece should either be a NAA mini revolver chambered for .22 Magnum, or a Beretta 950 Jetfire in .25 ACP. Both pieces are extremely lightweight, tiny, and reliable. Which one you choose will be based on your personal preference: would you prefer a 5 shot toy gun that you need to cock prior to each shot, and will probably miss any target beyond 5 feet, but will penetrate heavy clothing and bone, rupture your attacker's eardrums, and set him on fire; or would you rather a 9 shot toy gun that you only need to cock once before emptying in just over a second, which is capable of repeated headshots at 20 feet, but which may well bounce off said head? It depends on whether you prefer cowboys or secret agents, I suppose.

As a general rule, I try to discourage folks from carrying automatic pistols or derringers. I also discourage folks from carrying large heavy guns which are difficult to conceal, deliver punishing recoil, and will shatter your eardrums if you ever fired them indoors without hearing protection. Ultimately, however, one's choice of CCW piece is extremely personal, and you will surely choose what seems right for you.

F.T.W. COMMENTARY

"I want to shoot you so bad my dick is hard."

Ice T, in "New Jack City"

The concealed handgun is the best possible weapon. I love any tool that can make a frail elder or physically disabled person the equal of some muscular thug intent on beating and robbing them. The handgun is the ultimate "point and click" device. It is your "wand of magic missiles" what with one can blow meaty leaking holes in an assailant merely by extending one's arm and flexing a single digit. I love handguns, they make everything so much easier and provide ample peace of mind. That being said, a few traitorous government officials have decided to deny the citizens of certain states their Constitutionally guaranteed

Right to protect themselves against unlawful aggression. In some places, possession of a handgun without an official "permission slip" is punishable as a felony. It is up to you if you decide to violate an unconstitutional, thereby unlawful, statute—just be advised that gun charges are rarely reduced and you may face harsher sentencing than the criminal who attacked you. If you carry a concealed handgun—especially if not permitted to do so—it is imperative that no-one ever know about it. That is Top Secret data on a highly restricted need to know basis. Most family members, friends, and co-workers should never be told this secret.

The only negative about the handgun is it is really LOUD. Even a .22 CB Cap is loud on a quiet evening. Automatics also spit shell casings which can be traced back to your firearm due to unique markings from the extractor claw and firing pin. Even if prints were wiped off the brass, traces of your DNA could remain—so always wear latex gloves before even opening that box of ammo to load the mags, or stick with a revolver. As stated previously, best possible choice of handgun is the alloy framed .38 snubby with a bobbed hammer. If you really need a pistol, my advice would be to get an alloy framed Bersa Thunder .380, but you want the more reliable full-sized version rather than the Thunder CC. If the snubbie and Bersa are too big for you to conceal, get a North American Arms mini-revolver in .22 Magnum with rubber birdshead or slip-on grips. In the event you cannot afford a handgun, the FIE Titan .25 automatic and antique breaktop revolvers chambered for .32 Long can often be found for under a hundred bucks. Never carry a gun unless you intend to pull it, never pull it unless you intend to use it, and if you shoot, keep firing until the threat is on the ground. Afterwards, a tricky individual might decide to run a rat-tail file down the bore and use needle files to touch up the extractor claw and tip of the firing pin to foil ballistic testing, then clean his hands and arms with black coffee and ammonia to remove powder residue, but I would never tell you to do that. I *will* tell you to discard the clothes you were wearing, as powder and blood never really washes out and can be detected months later after repeated washings. Striker fired Saturday Night Specials can NEVER be carried with a round in the chamber. They will fire if dropped and can even discharge unexpectedly in one's pocket. The proper way to use one of these things is to pull it out of your pocket at point it at the other guy . . . he has no way of knowing your shiny little pistol does not have a chambered round. If he continues running his mouth and refuses to leave, rack the slide—that sends a clear message that you are about to shoot him. If he puts his hand in his pocket or goes to pick something up, shoot him repeatedly, preferably in the face. Do not be surprised if he doesn't fall down. A .25 automatic doesn't have much pop. That is why I prefer the .22 Magnum mini—a lot more pop and it doesn't spit shell casings either. The NAA mini revolver in .22 Magnum should be in your pocket or boot every day you cannot carry something larger. Best pocket pistol ever made, and you need one.

Vehicular Defense

> *"Seriously, don't cut people off. If someone needs to get in your lane, let him or her into your lane. If they saw the lane was going to end and sped up, that's different; you cut their ass off and give them the finger. But if they are just trying to get over, don't be a dick. It's not a contest."*
>
> Forrest Griffin, *Got Fight?* (p. 99)

> *"Cars are heavy."*
>
> Christopher Titus

INTRODUCTORY NOTE

Now, the first rule of vehicular defense is, "Cars are heavy and move really fast." The second rule is, "Lock your doors." Remember those rules because they are very important.

Entire books have been written about vehicular defense, so I'm going to keep this chapter relatively brief and will not delve into evasive maneuvers such as the J-turn or aggressive tactics such as the PIT maneuver. If you want to learn those things it will require a beater car and a vacant lot. One book that I recommend to those who ask is *Drive to Survive*, by Curt Rich. I'm going to split this chapter into several sections: The Basics, Road Rage, and Helpful Tips.

THE BASICS

THE CAR:

First, you need to have a car that has been well maintained and is in good driveable condition. Oil must be changed regularly and all fluid levels topped off. Tires cannot be soft, cracked, or bald. Belts and hoses need to be in good shape. Glass and interior must be kept clean. Headlights should be bright and properly adjusted. Engine should run smoothly. Best possible choice is a mid-sized sedan that is low to the ground which Consumer Reports gives excellent reliability ratings to. A few notable examples are the: Toyota Camry, Honda Accord, Subaru Impreza. Never buy a Ford product, and avoid SUVs, trucks, vans, and other off balanced vehicles with high centers of gravity. Choose a non-distinct color and avoid distinctive stickers or vanity plates.

Second, you need to completely familiarize yourself with the car. You need to learn its idiosyncracies and capabilities. You need to learn what it can and cannot do.

Third, always lock your doors, keep windows partway up, and wear your seatbelt. Never let your tank get less than half full, and especially never let it go below a quarter tank.

THE COLD HARD FACTS:

You are far more likely to be attacked by a stranger due to a road rage incident than any other possible reason. Very high probability you will encounter road rage at least several times during your lifetime, even if you are a pedestrian.

Road ragers are a valid threat you need to be aware of, but most of them are nothing more than average citizens experiencing a momentary lapse into hyper-aggression due to multiple stressors. Road rage is usually the direct result of emotional pain which causes a loss of control compelling certain individuals to lash out at random strangers, usually through verbal abuse which escalates. They typically are only a moderate threat and are primarily composed of women and yuppies . . . and how seriously can you really take someone who can't back up their petulant bullshit? Psychopathic road ragers and carjackers are an extremely high level of threat, yet realistically they are rarely encountered. By psychopath, I mean those guys who are deliberately looking for a random motorist to start trouble with, whereas the average road rager is genuinely out of control—both are equally dangerous when behind the wheel. DO NOT DO ANYTHING WHICH GIVES THEM JUSTIFICATION TO FIXATE ON YOU. Any form of provocation, even mouthed words through a closed window or refusing to allow them to cut in front of you can make them focus all that undirected rage on you, specifically. This seldom ends well and can be very bad. Refrain from excessive or inappropriate use of the horn, which is installed in your vehicle as a warning device rather than a substitute for your finger. Unless you see another motorist about to sideswipe you, never lean on the horn or hit it repeatedly. A single sharp tap is all that is generally needed if someone nods off at a green light or is standing in the middle of the road blocking traffic, and is far less likely to provoke someone into attacking you than aggressively beating on it.

Drugs and alcohol are frequently a major factor in road rage incidents. An individual under the influence of cocaine or methamphetamine will be driving at a reckless speed and making rapid and repeated lane changes missing other motorists by inches. An individual drunk on hard liquor will drive carelessly and sloppily, jumping curbs and scraping parked cars as he weaves and careens down the road. An individual who has stopped taking anti-depressants or similar prescription medication cold turkey will be driving in a hyperaggressive and illogical manner. Drugs and alcohol impair judgement and make aggressive personalities extremely dangerous. Anti-depressant withdrawal tends to make some people impulsive, manic, violent, and suicidal. Stay the fuck away from anyone you see driving in this manner. You cannot reason with a demon, and if you think you're going to "win" an altercation by flipping them the bird and calling them a nasty name you are sadly mistaken and will probably die.

However, the biggest threat to your safety while behind the wheel is stupidity—both that of other drivers as well as your own. Everyone makes mistakes, but you need to be particularly careful not to make them while your vehicle is in motion. If your vehicle is in motion, your eyes need to be looking at the road and your hands need to be on the wheel, and there is no excuse ever to behave otherwise—you don't need to fiddle with your stereo, send a text message, or dig through the pile of junk on the seat next to you until you are parked. Taking your eyes off the road while your vehicle is in motion is the cause of most accidents. Now that we have you covered so you'll never do that again, you need to be aware of the fact that the average motorist is just not paying sufficient attention to the driving process. They are eating food, rushing to punch a timeclock, applying makeup in their rear view mirror, smoking a cigarette, sending a text, fiddling with the stereo, yelling at a child in the backseat, and popping antidepressants when they are supposed to be focused on driving in heavy traffic. Often these individuals are so distracted they will blow through a red light or even rear end a stopped motorist. Believe me when I state with authority that you are at FAR greater risk of getting killed by an octogenarian with Alzheimers or a teenaged girl sending a text message than you are of getting chased or bumped in a road rage situation. Stupid people are the PRIMARY threat you will encounter on the road, and you need to be constantly vigilant if you want to avoid colliding with their vehicles. Carelessness kills.

COURTESY:

Generally speaking, you need to obey the rules of the road as well as be courteous to other drivers. This means no tailgating, no cutting people off, no flipping people the bird, no screamed profanities, and no bumping. Furthermore, you should refrain from speeding in residential areas, blowing through yield signs and yellow lights, zipping in and out of rush hour traffic at double the speed limit, recklessly swooping across several lanes at once in heavy traffic, or driving at highway speeds through shopping center parking lots. Many people consider the aforementioned activities to be rude, and may take personal offence, depending upon their degree of emotional stability. Offense may manifest itself through aggressive driving, better known as "road rage." Persons driving aggressively may slam on their brakes to deter tailgating, may attempt to run offending motorists off the road, may decide to follow an offensive motorist home, or may even fire a handgun at the object of their dismay. Passive-aggressive busybodies will simply call the highway patrol on their cell phone and tell them your plate number along with a detailed (and quite possibly exaggerated) description of your violations of the vehicle and traffic code.

Typically, the goal of the typical aggressive driver is to "teach that asshole a lesson." Enraged by another motorist's perceived incompetence, arrogance, or recklessness, the aggressive personality (imbued with a distorted sense of self-righteous indignation) considers the offensive behavior of other motorists to be unacceptable transgressions which must be immediately dealt with by "putting that bastard in his place." These sick people look upon simple lapses of courtesy as personal attacks necessitating retaliation. Common manifestations of retaliatory behavior include: tailgating, "shadowing" (deliberately driving in the blind spot), and overt pursuit. More severe aggressive activity may entail: bumping (from behind), "clipping" (passing close enough to scratch paint and break off the mirror), or cutting in front and suddenly slamming on the brakes. Astonishingly, these deadly menaces not only tend to be "respected members of the community" with clean criminal records, but also truly believe themselves to be justified in their actions! Scary, isn't it?

The moral of this section is that it isn't prudent to blatantly provoke strangers into committing acts of violence against you. The majority of the "victims of road rage" had done something, often deliberately, to antagonize the aggressor immediately preceding the incident. Victims who did not provoke their aggressor via unsafe maneuvers or derogatory gesticulations either were driving slower than the posted limit and were not allowing others to pass (usually by speeding up in the passing zones), or presented an offensive appearance in some way (either by emblazoning their vehicle with obnoxious stickers or by flaunting wealth in an impoverished area). A very small percentage were either random targets or victims of mistaken identity. Do not allow bad behavior or stupidity to make you a target.

While some aggressive drivers are mentally ill psychopaths, consider that nearly anyone can be temporarily deprived of their faculties when subjected to extreme stress, such as the loss of a job or the dissolution of a relationship. Stressful situations can make even the most meek and inoffensive people lose their shit. A weak individual is suddenly transformed into a force to be reckoned with upon sliding behind the wheel, and may choose to abuse his newfound power. Never assume that an aggressive driver can be made to "back down," as this often escalates the situation to an entirely new level.

Not only must one be aware of the fact that one shares the road with potentially aggressive drivers every day, but one must take care to avoid becoming one as well. By viewing one's vehicle as an extension of oneself, it is easy to suddenly become enraged over idiotic behavior which causes one to instantly react in order to narrowly avoid an accident. It is also common to lose one's temper when rushing to an important appointment and finding oneself stuck behind a slowpoke who not only refuses to pull, but speeds up on the straightaways. In such situations, it is important to remain calm and consider why the offending motorist is driving in such a manner. A reckless driver may be: rushing someone to the hospital, fleeing police pursuit, dangerously impaired, or simply a wild teenager who hasn't even considered the possibility of causing an accident. A slow or erratic driver may be: inexperienced, ill, elderly, drunk, or experiencing car trouble. Remain focused and don't irrationally take their actions as a personal insult to be answered in kind. If you've left for your destination early, and have been checking your mirrors frequently, this is much easier to accomplish.

You need to be aware of your surroundings, be wary of unsafe conditions, and use a modicum of common sense. As a rule of thumb, you should always leave for your destination at least five minutes earlier than necessary to allow for traffic and so you do not feel compelled to rush. If someone is impatient to pass you, allow them to do so, even if it means pulling over to the shoulder for a moment . . . never speed up if someone obviously is attempting to pass you, but apply your brakes instead. If you are passing someone, you should be doing at least 10 mph faster than they are (I see idiots trying to pass at exactly the speed limit, often resulting in two idiots driving alongside of each other for several minutes). Once you have passed someone, wait until you are at least 2 car lengths ahead of them before re-entering their lane, use your turn signal, and do not immediately decelerate after having done so. If someone is merging into traffic, do not block their progress. If someone appears frustrated that there isn't an opening in traffic for him to pull out into, provide that opening. If someone looks like they're about to cut you off, apply your brakes. If someone is driving like a psycho, stay away from them, even if it means taking the time to pull into a parking lot or circle the block. If someone is tailing you and won't be deterred, drive to the police station or a well lit parking lot with plenty of witnesses instead of leading them to your home. Simple solutions to common scenarios, but you would be astounded at the vast number of people unable to draw similar conclusions. If you see an unsafe situation approaching, place yourself out of the way.

You should not make a practice of driving like an asshole. Revving your engine and squealing around corners serves no useful purpose but tends to draw adverse attention to yourself and upset the taxpayers. If, through no fault of your own, you have an accident while driving like this on public roads, everyone will assume that you are to blame. You must strive to be a careful, competent, and courteous driver. If you make a practice of leaving early, driving at a reasonable speed, and being polite, it is unlikely that you will incur the ire of your fellow motorists.

THE CARDINAL RULES:

1. AWARENESS—you need to be cognizant of everything happening in your immediate vicinity as well as what is happening far ahead of you. You need to be aware of any vehicles in your "blind spots" as well as vehicles approaching from behind. You need to be prepared for evasive action so you can react instantly without fear of causing an avoidable accident.
2. SMOOTHNESS—all movements of your vehicle must be as smooth and precise as possible, this includes acceleration and braking as well as steering. Lack of smoothness and precision is equivalent to lack of control.

3. EXPERIENCE—it is necessary to have first practiced performance driving under somewhat controlled conditions before attempting to drive at double the speed limit while negotiating traffic. If you are uncomfortable driving at high speeds, you cannot reasonably expect to do so safely in the event of an actual crisis situation (such as evading a psychotically aggressive driver or medevacing someone to the ER). It is imperative that one have confidence in his abilities.
4. DISCRETION—simply stated, it is necessary to be able to differentiate between a calculated risk as opposed to a foolhardy risk. Certain evasive driving techniques—like passing on the wrong side of the road or squeezing between two cars at a high rate of speed—require lightning fast calculating in addition to quick reflexes. A master wheelman will not pass on a blind curve (or rise) with the sun in his eyes, nor will he attempt to squeeze through a gap narrower than the width of his vehicle (including side mirrors). Only drunks, lunatics, and teenaged car thieves drive in such a reckless manner.

FOCUS:

A driver should be concentrating only on the act of driving. Distractions, such as loud music, unnecessary conversation, or even one's own thoughts should be avoided. If the vehicle's interior is uncomfortably warm or cold, that too would qualify as a distraction, and should be remedied (if possible). A moment's distraction, especially when negotiating sharp curves or heavy traffic at speed, can easily result in a potentially fatal wipeout.

After familiarity with a vehicle has been gained, it is possible to notice minor changes (such as vibrations, rattles, odors, or miscellaneous noises) which could give warning of an impending breakdown that can be avoided through preventive maintenance. After intimate familiarity has been achieved, one can have the sensation of "melding" with the vehicle; in this altered state of consciousness, not only is it possible to feel minor imperfections in the road surface through the steering wheel and pedals, but your sense of awareness is drastically heightened, you make adjustments to the wheel to compensate for curves automatically, and you are able to react to the unexpected instantaneously.

At speeds exceeding 120 mph, it is easy to enter what has been described as a "zen trance." Not only do you feel as one with the vehicle, but you have a feeling of total calmness, everything seems to slow down, and you may experience some minor distortion of time and space (like reaching one's destination earlier than possible, or taking a sharp curve in defiance of the laws of physics). This is a true altered state of consciousness in which you feel separate from your everyday persona. Many would be inclined to dismiss what has been stated here as so much pseudo-mystical balderdash, but those of you who have been there will know of what I speak. Some things cannot be adequately explained in words, and thus must be directly experienced in order to be understood.

When the experienced driver is driving his vehicle at speed, whether he be competing in a race, eluding pursuit, engaged in combat, participating in an emergency medevac, or simply driving fast for his own enjoyment, he will be completely calm. Calm does not necessarily mean "relaxed," however, as a keen sense of alertness will be apparent, as will a degree of muscular tension, but all detrimental emotions (such as anxiety, fear, panic, anger, or rage) will be completely eliminated as if a switch had been thrown, disconnecting one's emotions altogether . . . indeed, the strongest emotions a driver in this state might experience are mild annoyance at a given situation or satisfaction that a difficult technique had been performed flawlessly. Such a driver will not lose control of his emotions regardless of the circumstances.

The totally focused driver will be concentrating solely upon the actions required to keep his vehicle on the road. If an accident is unavoidable, he will use his remaining fractions of a second prior to impact maneuvering his vehicle in such a way as to absorb the energy with as little harm to himself (or other occupants) as possible. If he goes flying over an embankment or into a wooded area, he will keep his eyes open and his hands on the wheel in an effort to guide the vehicle to safety. Even if the vehicle is airborne or in an uncontrolled spin, the calmness attained through total focus will effectively prevent panic and reduce the amount of adrenaline released into the bloodstream. Focus is good.

A common misconception is that evasion requires driving at unsafe speeds and ignoring red lights and 'one-way' signs . . . nothing could be further from the truth. Whether on city streets or back roads, you seldom want to exceed 60 mph. If you go too fast, you cannot negotiate sharp turns, nor can you compensate for unexpected obstacles or the stupidity of other drivers. If your vehicle is low to the ground and you are being pursued by a vehicle with a high center of gravity (such as a 'sport utility vehicle'), you can put more distance between your vehicles by accelerating through sharp curves and taking unexpected turns which a more top-heavy vehicle would need to slow down for to avoid tipping. The only time speeds in excess of 100 mph are permissible is when you are being pursued on a well-maintained, multi-lane highway and feel you have a good chance of safely outdistancing your tail (for example, you are driving a new sports car and they are in a rusted out pickup truck with bald tires). You do not want to drive beyond your abilities or your car's capabilities. Once you wreck, the chase has most likely come to an end.

ROAD RAGE

Ah, road rage. Y'all really need to calm down about that, seriously. People become BOLD inside their cars and do not recognize other vehicles as actually having people in them half the time—you are practically an automaton to them, so they feel free to vent their frustration at the world. You see, road rage seldom has anything to do with the incident that triggers it, these folks are just looking for an excuse to blow and may not even be consciously aware of it. As one of Ellis Amdur's instructors once said (paraphrased): "If you ignore the road rager, he will be out of your life in a moment; but if you choose to engage him, the consequences of that act may be with you forever." THAT is life changing wisdom right there. Seriously, when I read that line it was like a flashbulb went off in my head and I was illuminated and realized what a dumbass I'd been, since half of the violent incidents I'd been in were the result of my need to share my feelings with road ragers. Do not ever do this. If the guy is standing in front of you preventing you from leaving, you mess him up good; but if you are in traffic and some stranger is screaming something that amounts to: "I hate my life and blame you", well, you just let him go on his unmerry way. Psychotic break is real and not at all uncommon—and it most frequently manifests in traffic. I have personally been exposed to well over a thousand incidents of road rage, some of which involved firearms being displayed (by the other guy), so this in an area in which I have some expertise. Let it go. If you do not let it go it may escalate to a car chase or degenerate to a demolition derby—and yes, I have been involved in those as well. Speaking as an "expert" in possession of a certificate from the University of Hard Knocks (suitable for framing), I can say with authority that road rage is one of the few self defense scenarios in which your best tactic is to pretend to ignore the threat. You are in your car. Car has locked doors and glass windows. Cars are heavy and move really fast. You have cellphone communication and firearms or other weapons inside. He is very limited in what he can actually do to you unless you are in a convertible stuck in gridlock. IGNORE HIM. DO NOTHING TO PROVOKE HIM. NEVER EXIT YOUR VEHICLE. LEAVE THE SCENE AND TAKE EVASIVE COUNTERMEASURES IF NECESSARY TO ESCAPE.

Why would an aggressive driver decide to pick you as a target, when there are so many other possible choices? A demented zealot may strongly disagree with the statement emblazoned upon your bumper sticker. A criminal may see you as a favorable target for a robbery. A deviant may find you (or a passenger) an attractive target for a sexual assault. An enraged individual might mistakenly identify you as his enemy who happens to drive a similar vehicle to your own. Or, by far the most common reason of all, you did something that really pissed him off. That is the secret to avoiding battles with aggressive drivers—do not piss people off. What sort of behavior is sure to anger and offend fellow motorists? That can vary greatly, depending upon many factors, but a few common offenses follow:

1.) TAILGATING: This typically is defined as "following too closely" (less than a car-length between vehicles at highway speeds, but sometimes the distance can be measured in inches). This is an incredibly dangerous practice, as a collision is practically assured if the vehicle ahead suddenly needs to slam on its brakes.
2.) INAPPROPRIATELY SLAMMING ON BRAKES: Usually done to discourage tailgating, but often causes a minor situation to seriously escalate.
3.) NOT ALLOWING OTHERS TO PASS: Usually accomplished by accelerating in passing zones, but some aggressive drivers will even cut over the centerline to further "make their point."
4.) CUTTING PEOPLE OFF: This usually entails cutting in front of another vehicle, usually without any prior signaling of intention, by less than a full car-length. "Highway swoopers" are fond of zig-zagging through heavy traffic at high speeds, some people like to suddenly cut across three lanes in order to take their exit, and many idiots like to wait until they're less than a yard from a vehicle's rear bumper to pass—then suddenly cut back into their lane less than a yard ahead of the vehicle's front bumper (perhaps they mistakenly believe that doing so will somehow confuse police radar). This can be dangerous, and is often seen as an intrusion into one's personal space.
5.) FAILURE TO YIELD: Most commonly, this entails failing to move to the left to accommodate merging

traffic, but may also entail the ignoring of "yield" signs and failing to yield the "right of way" when appropriate. Failure to yield is extremely dangerous, and can easily result in a major accident.

6.) SPEEDING: Many "good citizens" are outraged by the sight of such flagrant lawbreaking, and may decide to "teach you a lesson" by breaking the law themselves. They may deliberately cut off a speeder (thus possibly causing a fatal accident), may "give chase," or may simply report your crime to the police on their cellular phone. I can see getting flared about people who recklessly speed through school zones and residential areas, but the highways are a different story altogether.

7.) LITTERING: Many "good citizens" (even those who truly do not give two shits about the environment) will get angry if they see you toss a biodegradable banana peel or sandwich crust out your window. However, nearly anyone would get pissed off if a section of newspaper or half-full chocolate milkshake suddenly hit their windshield!

8.) OFFENSIVE GESTICULATIONS AND/OR COMMENTARY: This activity is usually accompanied by repeated blaring of the horn to ascertain that one's nemesis is paying attention. If you flip another motorist "the bird" while loudly suggesting that he fuck his mother, he may become angry—especially if he's been having a really bad day. It is of the upmost importance that all of your passengers be informed that you will not tolerate any such behavior on their part! Please note that he doesn't even need to actually hear your words, as just the sight of your angry face glaring at him and mouthing words he cannot hear behind glass is enough to throw some folks into a blind rage, and they will chase you.

Either deliberately pissing someone off, or appearing to be a tempting target for a certain type of predator, can result in being bumped, sideswiped, or shot. However, it is far more likely that you will be targeted simply for failing to allow an aggressive driver to pass when he obviously very much wants to do so.

THREAT ASSESSMENT:

As with my section on profiling, I could take up a lot of space going into great detail about ways in which one can size up a potential threat with a mere glance, but I am going to keep this as concise as possible instead.

One of the first things you should consider is the overall mass and power of your adversary's vehicle. A commercial truck, such as a semi sans trailer or a cement mixer or a rental box truck such as a U-Haul presents far more danger to you than a SUV or pickup, which presents more danger than a 4 door sedan, which presents more danger than a compact car. Think: how much damage can their vehicle do to yours, and does he have a clear advantage in mass and power? Avoid brake checking giant trucks that can smoosh you.

The second thing you should consider is overall condition and estimated value of your adversary's vehicle. If it is a rustbucket covered in dents, not only will he be unlikely to care about additional damage, but there is a very high probability he might not even be insured. If it is a high value vehicle in excellent condition, such as a new Lexus or BMW, they will probably be far more reluctant to actually initiate contact between your two vehicles and you can reasonably assume they are just a stressed out yuppie acting up in traffic out of privileged petulance.

The third thing you need to consider is make, model, customization, and reinforcements. In some areas the gangsters and thugs tend to prefer very specific makes and models and often customize them as well. Some gangsters favor older muscle cars or big sedans like Monte Carlos. Others prefer luxury cars like Cadillacs or Lincoln Town Cars. Many choose to drive retired police cars like Crown Vics. Some like zippy little 4 cylinder imports like the Civic or Acura, heavily modified with body kits and spoilers. A few are partial to Camaros or Firebirds. And bikers and cowboys tend to favor jacked up pickups with push bumpers and rollbars. Things to look out for include: dark tinted windows, loud thumping music, custom wheel rims, neon underbody accent lights, hydraulic shocks, lifted suspension, push bumpers, diamondplate, expensive custom paint, or flat black primer. If you see more than one of those features on a make and model favored by thugs, you should take heed of that and refrain from provoking them . . . but if they refuse to give up and continue to tail you after you cut through parking lots and make a series of random turns, you'll need to be prepared to take serious evasive action, ready a weapon to unload into their vehicle, or call for law enforcement assistance in hope that they will rescue you, because you are about to face some extremely serious trouble and may be killed.

PSYCHOPATHIC ROAD RAGERS:

Up till now, we've just been discussing the average road rage incident, in which an average citizen suddenly snaps and acts out in an aggressive manner. That will cover about 90% of all cases—just stupid citizens behaving badly—although they can and will hurt you.

Psychopaths, psychotics, drug addicts, raging alcoholics, and predatory criminals all drive cars too. Someday you may encounter one of these special cases. These threats cannot always be ignored due to their high level of persistence and the risk of extreme violence. If you are targeted and engaged by one of these high level threats it can very well end up becoming a high speed chase which involves cars slamming into one another and gunshots being exchanged. I've been in those situations more times than I care to remember. Because these people exist and share the road with us, it is extremely important to always be a courteous driver and avoid pissing other motorists off. Some of them will kill you over nothing.

That being said, sometimes you do everything right and are targeted anyway. Perhaps a minor error such as failing to signal a turn is being used as "justification", or maybe you are driving an expensive car that they are jealous of, or maybe you are driving through some hick town with out of state license plates (New Englanders and Californians take note). Perhaps a political bumpersticker throws them into a rage, or the band you like makes you a "sissy" who deserves a beatdown. Gay rights, environmental, or anti-military stickers can get you run off the road in some towns. Certain brands of cars can get you tailgaited and bumped from behind. Custom paint and rims—especially if done in poor taste—will attract a lot of negative attention, both from locals and police.

The thing you need to know about these situations is that while they might be smiling and acting like it is a big game that they are enjoying very much, they are the players and you are being played, like a cat plays with a mouse before killing it. Terrorizing you is part of the fun. Make no mistake—they have no intention of backing off, things will escalate, and you will wind up with a wrecked and inoperable car at the very least. They may even decide to take it further than that. You cannot reason with a psychopath, so don't even try. In cases like this you have only two choices: escape or combat These are advanced topics beyond the scope of this book which you will need to research and practice elsewhere. Let it suffice to say that if you have not already practiced evasive driving techniques and do not have a large caliber handgun in your vehicle, you are pretty much fucked at this point. Learn those skills and keep a gun in your car if you want to ensure your safety.

THE CARJACKER:

Carjacking used to be a fairly rare crime, limited to victims who were driving expensive cars through urban ghettos. Now it can happen to anyone, anywhere, and you don't even need to have a fancy car to be a target. Basically, carjacking is nothing more than a violent armed robbery that occurs while you are in or near your car. Many occur in parking lots and the carjacker sometimes will use panhandling as a ruse to get closer, or they could simply rush at you from hiding. Sometimes the victim is kidnapped, sometimes they are shot dead. The perpetrator usually uses the victim's car to escape, but sometimes they only take their cash and cellphone. Many carjackings occur because the car in question can be stripped down for valuable parts (imports in particular), but others occur simply because a criminal needs to get somewhere quickly and his car broke down—so rather than calling a tow truck and a taxi he just takes yours. That is the way criminals think, and the car he was driving probably was also stolen and had improper plates. Quite a few criminals have attempted to carjack the first vehicle they spotted in hope of escaping from police or other enemies. Young punks any wannabe gangbangers sometimes carjack a vehicle "to see what it is like," just to feel the rush, or as a rite of passage to be initiated into a gang or gain respect from their peers. Anyone can be carjacked at any time. Recently, one young lady was actually "carjacked" in her bedroom when a home invader kicked in her door, pointed a gun in her face, and demanded the keys to her Jeep. If you own a car you are a potential target.

Carjacking is an ambush. If your doors are locked and your windows are up you can usually just drive away very quickly. Always be suspicious of groups of young men walking up to your car in traffic—I have pointed guns at people for doing this in certain neighborhoods on Saturday nights, and they just laughed and complimented me on my quick draw before dismissing me as a target and moving on. Always be suspicious of vehicles which bump you from behind, which is a common ploy to get you to exit your vehicle, whereupon you will be attacked. Always be suspicious of individuals who are not dressed in uniforms or safety vests attempting to stop your vehicle. Do not be afraid to back away and turn around. Do not hesitate to run certain people down if you have no other choice. Can you see their hands? Do they have a weapon? Are you being surrounded? Humans are big bags of fluid on a fragile framework—they break open real easy if you run over them. Sometimes you just need to do what you need to do and that's it. If they bust your windshield it will usually hold together due to the way safety glass is constructed. If you cannot see well, lean over to look through a section of unbroken glass until you can park somewhere safe enough to bust a hole through it and peel it back. Number one rule is: *Don't get out of your car.* Number two rule is: *Step on the gas and get the fuck out of there right now.* Carjackers are looking for an easy mark and although they may fire a round or two through your back window it is unlikely they will give chase. Don't worry about them hitting your gas tank and making your car explode, as that only happens in the movies.

Another variant on carjacking is the hitchhiker or person standing next to a broke down car who flags you down, then, once you graciously offer to give them a ride they pull a gun or knife and demand your car keys, wallet, and cellphone before leaving you stranded on the side of the road . . . unless they decide they don't want any witnesses and just kill you outright. I have been in this situation several times, and fortunately was able to see what they were thinking about doing and dissuade them from doing it. The best way to avoid this sort of situation is to not stop for hitchhikers or stranded motorists. If you are such a nice fellow that you just can't do that, I strongly recommend keeping a change of clothes, some Simple Green spray and several rolls of paper towels in the trunk of your car in the event you need to shoot a hitchhiker in the head, because that shit sprays all over.

IMPORTANT TIPS

1.) Lean back in your seat with your seat belt tight. If you need to lean forward, for whatever reason, immediately retighten your seatbelt. Your seatbelt should never become loose, nor should its use ever be neglected . . . not only is it proven to significantly reduce risk of serious injury in the event of many types of accident, but it also keeps you in your seat when subjected to the high G-forces generated during evasive driving techniques (if you were to attempt a "bootlegger's turn" sans seatbelt, you could easily find yourself flung into the passenger seat, from which controlling the vehicle would be difficult). Your seatbelt should never become twisted, nor should it rest over something uncomfortable like a pen, which could puncture flesh in the event of an accident.

2.) Let your head rock freely. You should be relaxed rather than tense, even under stressful circumstances.

3.) When necessary, brace yourself against G-forces by pressing your elbow against the right side of your seat for sharp right turns and grabbing the roof through your window for sharp left turns. You may want to use your knees for support as well.

4.) While maneuvering through extremely sharp right turns, like hairpin curves, it is often necessary to view the road momentarily through the driver side window rather than the windscreen.

5.) It is often helpful to brace one's elbows upon the armrests when driving at high speeds. When driving at speeds exceeding 100 mph, it is neither necessary nor recommended that one move the steering wheel much more than an inch in either direction, and bracing one's elbows both assures stability and enables one to better relax.

6.) Gripping the wheel at the 9 and 3 o'clock positions (or just above them) gives excellent control. Avoid crossing your arms or palming the wheel when turning . . . if it becomes necessary to crank the wheel sharply (as when taking a U-turn), one should instead allow the wheel to be "passed" from hand to hand. One should always keep both hands on the wheel (with very few exceptions). Never permit the wheel to slip from your grasp.

7.) Move the steering wheel as little as possible. If you begin compensating for a curve before you reach it, it is seldom necessary to move the wheel more than an inch in either direction.

8.) Try not to oversteer or understeer when negotiating curves at speed. Different vehicles take the same curves much differently.

9.) Whenever feasible, drive in as straight a line as possible to reduce G-forces, increasing both speed and control. By crossing over the centerline, it is possible to drive through a shallow S-curve as if it were a straightaway. Edging over the centerline can increase one's speed and stability around sharp left curves. Edging onto the shoulder can increase one's speed and stability around sharp right curves. Never "cut corners" and cross the centerline around blind curves or over blind rises.

10.) When driving in heavy traffic or driving at speed on backroads, keep your left foot poised over, but not touching, the brake pedal. This will require development of the ankle muscle, but will greatly increase your reaction time. Never "ride the brake," as this causes them to overheat and rapidly wear out.

When your left foot is not poised over the brake, it should be resting on the "dead pedal" (the bump in the floor conveniently next to the brake) instead of the floorboards.

11.) Acceleration and deceleration should be a gradual progression. To do otherwise will reduce traction and control. If you feel your tires spinning, let off on the gas; if you feel your wheels locking up, let off on the brake . . . otherwise, you might find yourself going sideways. In the event of slick road surfaces, the slippage factor is multiplied and you will need to compensate accordingly.

12.) Sometimes just tapping or "feathering" the brakes is all you need to compensate for sharp curves. Try to apply the brakes before actually negotiating the curve.

13.) Try to keep a "buffer zone" between yourself and other motorists, both to give you room to maneuver and time to brake. This means that there should always be at least three car lengths between you and the vehicles ahead of and behind you—keep this in mind when passing. Even when stopping at an intersection, be sure to "leave yourself an out." This means that you shouldn't ride up to someone's back bumper or otherwise allow yourself to be blocked in if traffic ahead suddenly came to a halt. If need be, you should be physically able to hop a curb and drive across the sidewalk to avoid a jam or escape an armed attacker.

14.) Check your rear-view mirror frequently, especially when other vehicles are behind you.

15.) Always look over your shoulder to check your blind spot before switching lanes or merging into traffic.

16.) If you see an accident or debris in the road ahead, steer around it—do not lock up your brakes. Locking up one's brakes often results in a collision at only slightly reduced speed.

17.) Remember that you can lose traction in a single puddle, patch of packed snow, or thin layer of gravel—especially at speed around curves. Be especially wary of the long shallow puddles that form along the shoulder . . . you can hydroplane at any speed above 45 mph. Dried dirt clods, wet mud, loose hay, or garbage spread across a road can also reduce traction. Large puddles are especially dangerous, due to the fact that all four tires can momentarily lose contact with the asphalt, resulting in loss of control over the vehicle. If you cannot reduce speed prior to driving across a large puddle, immediately take your foot off the accelerator and keep the steering wheel perfectly straight, so that you skim straight across without spinning your wheels.

18.) When decelerating, going down steep inclines, or maneuvering through a series of sharp curves, it is often helpful to downshift your automatic transmission. If you are driving evasively downtown, along a treacherous stretch of road, or through grass, mud, or snow, you can extract better performance from your vehicle by keeping it in 2nd gear at speeds under 60 mph. By keeping your vehicle in 2nd gear, you increase your vehicle's potential for fast acceleration and gain more control when cornering, but the engine will begin to strain at speeds above 45 mph and may overheat.

19.) Never drive a vehicle if your abilities are even mildly impaired due to the ingestion of alcohol, prescription medication, cold/allergy medication, or illicit substances. If you feel the need to drive a vehicle regardless of the fact that your abilities may be significantly impaired, it is imperative that you take care to obey all traffic laws and use extreme caution. If your abilities are impaired in any way—even if due simply to fatigue or illness—never exceed a prudent speed for the conditions and especially never attempt any form of evasive driving—even techniques you've performed flawlessly in the past; if you take foolish risks while impaired, you have an extremely high risk of failure due to accident.

20.) Be sure to study as many televised police chase videos as possible; although most of the perpetrators are either drunk or inept, a small minority of these videos show evasive driving at its most intense—they also show what happens when you fuck up. Police videos will also show you how far a "disabled" vehicle can be driven before becoming truly immobile.

ENDNOTE:

Driving is one of the most dangerous things you can do. There are so many ways an automobile accident can occur, even if you are cautious, and the resulting injuries are often horrendous. Furthermore, many people are assaulted in, or near, their vehicles. People are frequently beaten up in parking lots and ambushed in their own driveways. Criminals and psychotics regularly victimize people stopped in traffic. People are followed, bumped, or shot at for seemingly minor breaches of etiquette. You can be targeted for reasons as trivial as having a bumpersticker that some mentally unstable person finds offensive. There is no need to let these facts make you fearful or paranoid, but it is stupid to be oblivious of what's going on in the world around you.

Driving is also one of the most enjoyable things you can do. It is pleasant to go for a relaxing drive in the country, and it is exhilarating to push a high-performance car to its limits. As long as certain basic precautions are taken, driving can be relatively safe. Make sure that your car is regularly maintained and that you always have at least half a tank of petrol. Be aware of what's going on around you. Be cautious when driving after dark or in inclement weather. Keep your doors locked and windows up (or cracked) when driving through the city. Don't antagonize other motorists. Don't take foolish risks. Don't allow yourself to become distracted. Take precautions against eventualities. Be prepared. Be careful. Be safe.

F.T.W. COMMENTARY

The most important lesson I hope you got from this chapter is: DON'T DRIVE LIKE AN ASSHOLE. Seriously. Don't speed through rush hour traffic because you left 10 minutes late instead of 5 minutes early. Use your turn signals. Don't tailgate or brake check. This ESPECIALLY applies if you drive a fancy car like a late model Lexus or BMW, because many road ragers will get doublepissed simply due to your ostentatious display of privilege combined with arrogance, and will feel compelled to teach you a hard lesson.

Remember to lock your doors. Remember your car can drive through light barriers and knock other cars out of the way. Take care not to rupture your radiator. As long as the car is still mobile you should take full advantage of that, even if it is smoking, screaming, and not handling very well at all. You can indeed drive on a blown engine and four flat tires—not very well, and not for very long, but it can be done. Pedestrians are crunchy. If a road rager exits his vehicle to attack you, he is extremely vulnerable. If he gets stuck under your car he'll come apart and fall loose after a few blocks.

Vehicular combat is best resolved through the use of high powered firearms, the short barreled, pistol grip shotgun loaded with copper sabot slugs being a favorite, as is the Obrez, which is a pistol made from a sawn off Mosin Nagant bolt action rifle. Both of these are NFA weapons which require BATF approval, licensure, and a valid tax stamp to lawfully possess . . . plus they kick so hard they might as well be considered single shot weapons like a Thompson Contender (which is not a bad choice at all in a light rifle caliber such as .30-30). Trust me when I tell you that you do not want to be inside a vehicle in which an autoloading rifle is being rapidfired, as the noise, hot brass casings, and chunks of safety glass will make it a hellish experience. Pros who fire heavy weapons from cars use brass catchers, goggles, and earplugs which you will not have. In my opinion, the best possible choice is probably a .357 Magnum revolver with a 6" barrel, as it provides accuracy and power without punishing recoil or hot brass bouncing around. The idea location for the shooter should be in the back seat with all the windows rolled down, which will provide an ideal shooting platform compared to the front passenger seat position which is far more limited. Best possible target to take out a pursuing vehicle is between the headlights, right in the radiator. If you are taking fire, be advised that there is no cover in a passenger car and even small caliber handgun bullets can pass through doors and glass with ease. The curved laminated windshield offers limited protection unless the rounds are impacting at a downward angle. The magnum revolver is also useful in the event you flip your vehicle in an isolated area and have turned yourself inside out far from medical assistance. As a bonus, you can even use it for hunting deer.

HOME DEFENSE

Many books have been written about the subject of home defense and there is a lot to say about it—far more than can adequately be addressed in this chapter, so I'm just going to touch on the bare basics.

First and foremost, you need to properly secure your home. It is just common sense to lock your doors, but you'd be surprised how often a back door to a fenced yard or a side door that connects your garage to your house is forgotten. Windows are also neglected. I'll bet that at least one 1st floor window in your home is unlocked right now. Screens will pop open if you wiggle them, or you could just slice them open with a pocketknife. Air conditioners are easy to push out of the way if they are not bracketed and screwed in place. If a criminal can climb up onto the top of your porch or shimmy up a drainpipe he can easily access the second floor windows as well. Glass sliding doors are easily lifted out of track. Basement windows are a popular means of access that often are conveniently hidden behind bushes, and a little duct tape or an old blanket will muffle the sound of breaking glass. It is surprisingly easy to break into the average home, and you do not even need lockpicking skills or heavy duty tools. A stout screwdriver and a set of channel lock pliers will get a criminal through most doors. Don't even think of hiding a "spare"key anywhere on your property, as it is the first thing any semi-intelligent burglar will look for and they know all the common hiding places (if it is absolutely necessary to do this, bury it in a waterproof container). If you can adequately secure all your windows and doors to prevent an unmotivated teenaged addict to get through them it is unlikely you'll be the victim of a burglary. 95% of burglars are unskilled amateurs committing crimes of opportunity, and the pros only target houses that look like they'll be worth the time and effort. If a nosepicking slacker can't get in, you are probably safe. Be certain to lock all doors to your vehicles as well, keeping all valuables out of sight. A bum will think nothing of smashing your window after midnight for a few dollars worth of change or a year old cellphone you got for free, but a GPS or a purse can get your window smashed in a busy parking lot in the afternoon.

Second, you want a good alarm system. Most alarms are, quite frankly, a huge waste of money. If you really want a bell and siren and flashing lights you can save a lot of money by wiring it up yourself. The alarm I recommend above all others has four legs and barks. I recommend getting two large dogs and letting them have the run of your house. The breed you choose is up to you. Personally, I prefer German Rottweilers due to their strength and intelligence, but German Shepherds, Dobermans, Great Danes, and Boxers all are very popular choices as well. If you live in a small house or apartment, a single medium-sized dog of any breed—even a mutt—will do just fine. No need for attack training, as all loyal dogs will instinctively defend their territory and master. Besides, it is unlikely they ever will even get to bite an intruder, as their bark is a great deterrent which will alert everyone in the household as well as neighbors that something is amiss. A dog is far better than any electronic alarm system—and it is entertaining and comforting as well. I also highly recommend the book *Dog Logic* by Joel McMains to give you greater insight into the mind of your dog and develop greater rapport.

Third, you want a big fucking gun. By "big" I mean too large for concealed carry, but small and light enough that you can easily maneuver it around the interior of your home. Ideally, it should have a respectable amount of accuracy, power, and capacity. It also needs to be incredibly reliable. The default recommendation I have for the average household is a good quality .double-action 357 Magnum with a 6" barrel, such as a Smith & Wesson 686 or a Ruger GP-100, as they are incredibly simple to operate and the recoil is quite manageable, especially with .38 Special +P loads. In jurisdictions where civilian ownership of handguns is a non-option or cost is prohibitive, I recommend the single-shot, external hammer, break-action shotguns by Harrington & Richardson or New England Firearms. Put an elastic bullet band on the stock and chop the barrel down to 18.5" and you have a perfect home defense weapon that is simple for anyone to use and costs under $150. Rossi offers an inferior version of this common shotgun which works fairly well nonetheless, and very similar antique shotguns you may come across include several model numbers from: Savage, Stevens, and J.C. Higgins. 20 gauge has half the recoil of 12 gauge but is just as deadly at close range with buck or slug, and that is the caliber I recommend for indoor use, loaded with 2 3/4" #3 Buck. A lot of guys prefer autoloading rifles or high capacity handguns, but that is a very personal choice and you need to decide what is best for you—not what the gun magazine or the internet forum tells you is best. In the right hands a

M1 carbine or SKS is just as good as a customized M4, and an inexpensive Mossberg pump is just as good as a Benelli automatic—you do not need to spend a lot of money, nor do you need the most powerful cartridge available. Get what you feel comfortable shooting. If that happens to be a lever action .30-30, so be it. One of my personal favorites is the MPA-930 "Mini MAC" which is better constructed than the Cobray products and accepts 30 round Sten mags (with a tracer every third round), but you might be happier with a double-barrel Coach Gun or a polymer .45 ACP with a tactical light attached. I have known many folks who relied solely upon .22 rifles such as the Ruger 10/22, and a lot of poor people have purchased a Raven .25 as the only gun in their house and it has served them well. One's home defense armament is a very personal choice that you will need to make for yourself, dependant upon personal preference, your living situation, and what you can realistically afford. Living with small children, having frequent houseguests, or living in a crowded apartment building will place limitations on your choice, or possibly even eliminate a firearm as an option. I hate trigger locks and an empty or disassembled gun is useless if you need it immediately. A bedside gun safe or a locked nightstand works best if you have kids. An improvised nightstand drawer lock can be fabricated by drilling a deep 1/4" hole into the side and inserting a long thick nail. Painted with wood stain it is virtually invisible, but you can feel it in the dark and pull it out instantly.

Okay, in the event you cannot lawfully possess a firearm (for example, an Illinois resident who has chosen not to apply for a FOID card), well, I'm not going to advise you to break an illegal law which is contrary to the Constitution, but I will remind you that the bad guys breaking into your occupied residence will be carrying guns—and they aren't allowed to have them either. But let's say you truly are a good citizen who wants very much to obey all laws, or perhaps you are something like a peaceful Buddhist, or a liberal vegan homosexual hipster who discovered this book at someone's house and is flipping through it out of morbid curiosity. I'm not going to judge you for being afraid of having firearms in your house. Maybe you had a bad experience once, or read some hysterical anti-gun essay, or are afraid that a child or irresponsible relative might access and misuse it. I understand. My prior book, *Hardcore Self-Defense*, covered the topic of non-firearm weapons encyclopedically, and I'm not going to repeat myself here, but I will provide a few suggestions you may not have considered. Swords are great home defense tools, but most inexpensive swords are non-functional decorative wallhangers that will not take an edge and will bend or break if you were actually to hit someone with it—they are little better than an aluminum yardstick but give many ignoramuses false confidence. That samurai sword you have over your mantlepiece is probably zinc alloy or aluminum if you bought it at the mall or a flea market. Machetes are also cheap, but they will take and hold an edge, and they are designed specifically for chopping. I recommend a small one, like a bolo or a Thai Enep. Condor is a good and inexpensive brand, although the factory edge is often lacking and will need to be touched up. But I realize that literally spilling blood is something a few of you just cannot bring yourself to do . . . for you I recommend an aluminum Tee Ball bat, which is short, light, and costs under twenty bucks at Wally World. If having a dedicated weapon seems like it might bring too many "bad vibes" into your abode, just grab a tool like a monkey wrench or hammer . . . and if that is still too "negative" for you, get a rolling pin or small cast iron skillet instead. Now, if you are such a disgusting pacifist weakling that you will refuse to pick up even an innocuous skillet to defend your family from a predator who would invade your home to victimize you, well, you are nothing but food and will soon be put in your rightful place, and Darwin sez it will suck to be you.

Finally, use some common sense. Do not allow strangers into your house under any circumstances. I don't care if you need to use the phone, I can call a tow truck or cab for you. I don't care if you need to take a dump—go in the bushes across the street. If you see a stranger wandering around your yard shine a spotlight on them and advise them they have 5 seconds to make it to the road. Also, avoid the use of WARNING signs of any type, as they clearly tell any prospective burglar that you have good stuff inside that is worth the added risk. All burglars know what fake security system signs look like, and if they think there might be an alarm present a quick look around will show them if you actually have one or if you are lying. Signs proclaiming that you are a gun owner or will shoot trespassers tells them FREE GUNS INSIDE, making your house a prime target worth staking out for a week till they get your routine down. Avoid provocative or obnoxious signs as well, because some individuals who aren't even burglars might decide to teach you a lesson about insulting random strangers, and random passersby might be so shocked that they immediately call 911 to report you for suspicion of being suspicious. In the event an incident does occur on the premises, even if no-one is actually harmed, that sign will make a poor impression on police and a digital photo of it presented to a prosecutor or media source could be extremely damaging to your case.

Consider a locked mailbox or even a PO Box to secure your mail, and be certain to shred financial and other sensitive documents before putting them in the trash, because people DO steal entire trash bags in hope of retrieving this data which they can use to profit from fraud. I have seen it with my own eyes in several states, and the problem is especially bad at urban apartment complexes with community dumpsters, where some evil nerd with a messenger bag and a flashlight will spend an hour inside each dumpster looking for bank statements and canceled checks. This is a far more common and likely way of stealing sensitive data than computer hacking or using high tech methods to steal data from card scanners.

Again, this brief chapter was included as a mere courtesy to fill in what most other books have failed to adequately address. You need to research this matter yourself if you want to learn more, and there is plenty of free information available online and at the public library pertaining to this subject.

F.T.W. COMMENTARY

> *"It is an awful thing to handle the still-warm body of a man you've just killed. It feels like God has you under a powerful microscope, and is minutely examining the wrinkles and hidden recesses of your soul. It is a moment that is sad, solemn, and utterly lonely."*
>
> Eric L. Haney, *Inside Delta Force* (p. 313)

A man's home is his castle. That goes double if he has a family to protect. Due to this commonly held belief, many states have enacted a provision of their self defense law known as the "Castle Doctrine," which means if a bad guy forces his way into your home while it is occupied, you get to shoot him dead without fear of criminal charges by the state or civil lawsuits by his survivors. In some states that lack this doctrine, police will not only arrest you for homicide but actually search your home and seize every firearm they find. My thoughts are that, regardless of whether it is lawfully permitted or not, if someone kicks in your door they need to get shot repeatedly. Knowing that you will be arrested for defending yourself in certain regimes, it is up to you whether you decide to notify authorities immediately after the fact. Many attorneys advice delaying making a statement to police until 48 hours have passed. As they will be very insistent that you make a statement as soon as they arrive, perhaps you might want to delay notifying them until you have calmed down and achieved some modicum of mental clarity. Perhaps it would be best if you had your attorney call them instead. Take a few hours and consider your many options. If the police have not arrived by then, one of those options involves trashbags and luggage. You will need a hacksaw, tarp, and cleaning products as well. Full details can be found in my prior book, *Hardcore Self Defense.*

Special Situations

CANINES

I love dogs. Actually, I prefer dogs to most people. However, I do realize that sometimes a dog can attack someone for no apparent reason. Maybe the dog escaped from another tenant's apartment and is running loose in the hallways, or more likely he escaped from his yard and is wandering the neighborhood at large. In some areas, feral dogs are a very serious problem. I understand that people may be attacked at random by a strange dog, and such cases are not uncommon. I've been attacked by large dogs on numerous occasions and have the scars to prove it.

One of the reasons I advocate pepperspray is to deter dog attacks. It is, in my opinion, the BEST choice available for dealing with dogs. A stick or blade or even a small pistol may not immediately work, but I have successfully used pepperspray against canines dozens of times and it has never failed to stop an attack instantly. You see, dogs rely primarily upon their sense of smell, and their noses are not only far more sensitive than our own but they are covered with moist mucous membranes. Mace completely overwhelms their primary sense organ which results in instantaneous confusion and complete loss of interest in continuing the attack. Sometimes they'll walk in circles sneezing, sometimes they will vomit, other times they'll just walk away—but if you hit them full in the face that attack is over. The best thing about this is an hour later they will be fine with no ill effects, and the owner will not be able to file "cruelty to animals" charges against you because no harm is apparent and he may not even realize his dog was sprayed. If you shoot, stab, or beat a dog it is virtually guaranteed that police will be called.

An "attacking" dog isn't always trying to kill you. Sometimes it is simply presenting a threat display as a warning. A large mean looking dog trotting directly towards you may simply be curious. A large dog bounding towards you may actually be friendly. You need to make that judgement call for yourself and respond accordingly. Many "attacks" start with snapping and light test bites, which indicate you are dealing with a dog who may lack confidence or maturity and as such will be easy to deter. Other "attacks" are the result of a dog being overly territorial (usually due to negligent or overly permissive owners) or biting as the result of fear, (frequently due to abuse). If, however, a dog is enraged, or is attack trained, or has mistaken you as prey which it can eat, you are in serious trouble and that animal will need to be disabled or destroyed.

If you have a gun, aim for the head and shoot repeatedly until it stops attacking. With a stick or other bludgeon, again, aim for the head and strike repeatedly as hard as you can, alternative targets are the spine, kidneys, and knees. If the only weapon you have is a blade you are in a lot of trouble, because dogs are incredibly tough and a knife is usually a slow kill, but a hamstring type attack or a disembowelment will immobilize the dog and prevent it from pursuing you. If you are unarmed, do not even attempt to run—dog is much faster than you and will attack from behind, taking chunks out of the backs of your legs. It is possible to choke out a dog if you are large and well trained, but the thick waddles of fat and loose skin around the throat of certain breeds make this extremely difficult. An untrained dog who is lifted off the ground and suddenly dropped will be stunned and confused—but do not attempt that with an attack trained dog. A dog's legs are vulnerable, and are easily broken if the knee joint is kicked. Remember that although a dog's claws can scratch you very badly, its primary weapon is its teeth. In a grappling situation a human has a huge advantage over a single dog, as once the head is immobilized there isn't much that dog can do. Grasping the collar, if it has one, can greatly assist in this. Faced with two or more dogs, if you are unarmed you need to find a big stick or a few rocks right away, because you will need a weapon of some sort to deal with that.

The following data has been excerpted from an anonymous student's notes from the Special Air Service "Combat Survival" course:

"After detecting an intruder, the dog will operate on command of the handler or on situation stimulus . . . . In either case the dog will retain its grip on its quarry until ordered to leave. In the case of highly aggressive dogs, strict compulsion may be necessary. It is this courage and ability of the dog that makes it vulnerable to the intruder. Pad yourself as described below, encourage the dog to attack, biting in a place that you dictate. Present a target to the dog, thereby placing it in a situation where it can be immobilized or destroyed. Adequate protection can be had from wrapping around the arm any of the following: webbing belt, leggings, rifle sling, ponchos, wrapping from

equipment, scarves, headgear . . . . The dog is far less dangerous if it makes firm contact on the first run in . . . . Throughout its training the dog has always been allowed to succeed . . . . Give it the opportunity to succeed and then destroy. It is most vulnerable when gripping target. Remember: a dog deterred will bark or growl, drawing the attention of the guards . . . . The destruction of a trained dog is by no means a simple matter . . . . It is often easier to take the dog and immobilize, either by tying to a secure fitting, or binding the front legs. Always muzzle, and if possible render it inoperable, example, breaking a leg."

THE PASSIVE AGGRESSIVE ATTACKER

> *"He will find ways to disrupt your family life or damage your standing at work. He will do things like start painful rumors or manipulate people around you through lies and deception. His motive is to get others to harm you for him. He doesn't care if you are harmed physically, emotionally, or financially."*
>
> Edward Lewis, *Hostile Ground* (p. 11)

> *"Criminals are likely to say and do almost anything to get what they want, especially when they want to get out of trouble with the law. This willingness to do anything includes not only truthfully spilling the beans on friends and relatives, but also lying, committing perjury, manufacturing evidence, soliciting others to corroborate their lies with more lies and double-crossing anyone with whom they come into contact."*

Hon. Stephen S. Trott, "Words of Warning for Prosecutors Using Criminals as Witnesses"

On the street, you are most likely to run into passive aggression if you are accosted by muggers who proceed to threaten you, whereupon you reveal that you are armed—perhaps only by pulling back your jacket to flash your holstered sidearm—and they back off and you walk home thinking it is over. Unbeknownst to you, however, the muggers dime you to 911, claiming that you just threatened them with a gun "for no reason," and an APB goes out and you are arrested for a felony and very likely convicted since the prosecutor will claim that you couldn't very well have been in fear for your life because otherwise you would've reported the incident to the authorities like any Good Citizen would do. I am familiar with several cases where this exact thing happened and an honest citizen with no criminal record suddenly became an unemployed felon based on nothing more than the testimony of a couple of scumbag street rats. This is another reason why I love Mace.

The subject of passive aggressive violence is complex, and typically relates to domestic disputes rather than the street, but there are some parallels. Passive aggression is the tool of the weak. One example might be the fellow who you punch to the ground who snivels and begs and curls up into a ball, and in your disgust you turn your back on him and walk away, only to have him suddenly spring up to run behind you to shank you in the kidney and flee. Feigning surrender then attacking, or pretending to go submissive before blindsiding you with a weapon are a commonly encountered tactic when dealing with street people who don't follow any rules and are accustomed to "cheating" in order to win.

Far more dangerous than the surprise attacker are those truly passive aggressive types who will not use violence themselves, but will compel others to use violence against you on their behalf. This involves the use of intricately constructed lies, intended to make you look like an evil person in hope that others will turn against you. Deranged women frequently resort to this tactic. In many cases, those "others" will just be her new boyfriend and his buddies, but sometimes an actual false police report will be filed and you will be accused of felonious acts. In rare cases (as the typical pathological liar is borderline psychotic, which adversely affects their credibility), an offender may try to get you fired from your job, evicted from your home, or vilified in the media or on a number of searchable internet sites. Lies can be extremely destructive if the individual in question already has compiled a bit of verifiable personal data about you, which is why it is important to always treat your girlfriends with kindness . . . especially the crazy ones . . . but sometimes they can pull something like this regardless of how well they were treated. I know of many innocent men who were falsely accused of heinous acts such as rape or battery, simply because a crazy woman was angry with him and wanted to see him hurt or punished in some way. Several of these men I knew for a fact were innocent. On one momentous occasion, a lovely young woman came to me with her tale of woe about some bad guy who had done all sorts of horrible things to her and deserved to be punished . . . but when I went over to his house to discuss the matter with him, he was one of the nicest guys I'd ever met, and he told me how he liked this girl and used to give her rides and loan her cash until she started taking unfair advantage of his good nature and he refused to talk to her anymore, whereupon she became insanely pissed . . . and it turned out he was telling the truth, as she later tried pulling something similar with me. Stay away from crazy women, no matter how hot they are, especially if they happen to be exotic dancers. Seriously . . . some dancing girls genuinely seem to hate men. I've seen them try to provoke fights between patrons on many occasions simply for their own sick amusement. But I digress.

The passive aggressive liar will think nothing of filing a false police report, committing perjury, or even committing felony conspiracy in hope of having you murdered. Again, this typically applies only to females who know you personally, but on the street others will use similar tactics. For example, the minor fender bender or borderline road rage incident which is blown way out of proportion by the other guy, who calls 911 screaming that you deliberately tried to kill him and proceeds to concoct a detailed fantasy story to support his allegation—complete with your accurate description and plate number to identify you. Another example might be the overly aggressive panhandler who is working himself up to an actual strongarm robbery when you either place your hand on the knife clipped to your front pocket or pull your jacket back to reveal your lawfully carried sidearm in its holster. After he backs off and you leave, thinking the incident over, don't be surprised to find out that he immediately went to a payphone to dial 911 with a detailed description of you and how you either drew your weapon and threatened to kill him for no reason, or that you currently were threatening a group of fictitious individuals with your weapon and acting like a crazy person—whereupon that call will get a very high priority with every available officer converging on the scene . . . and guess what, you indeed have a weapon just like the anonymous caller described.

There really isn't much that can be done to defend yourself against something such as this. No-one is immune from false accusations, even the police or pillars of the community. The only thing you can do is be aware that sometimes shit like this happens, so it isn't a total fucking surprise. This is a really good reason to avoid letting people know that you have a weapon, especially if you carry it. If you are known to be a collector of firearms, a tip to the ATF that you have something illegal in your collection is something that an enemy could do (even if you have no such thing), or he could simply tell some local dirtbags known to engage in burglary about all your cool guns.

Bad people don't only attack others or steal from them . . . sometimes they tell lies or spread false rumors in order to get innocent people hurt, arrested, fired, expelled, evicted, or shunned. That can be just as damaging as a frontal attack, but far more difficult to defend against. I cannot tell you how to protect yourself from this sort of thing, only that it happens so you should be aware of it. My personal opinion on the matter is that individuals who bear false witness against others are *worse* than snitches and should be treated accordingly. This is an incredibly dangerous situation to be faced with and there is virtually no defense against it unless you have an excellent attorney as well as solid evidence that will destroy your accuse's credibility. Do not make the mistake of thinking your word will be taken over that of a homeless, cracked out, tranny prostitute in a court of law, because it won't. After all, you are not a policeman and have no political connections, so you are just a nobody who will be through under the bus by the "just us" system to demonstrate that everyone is considered equal and the law is indeed "fair." Anyone willing to lie about you under penalty of perjury can do a great deal of damage to your reputation and even deprive you of your freedom in a worst case scenario—and that outcome is not as unlikely as you might think.

SETUPS, SUCKER PUNCHES, AND AMBUSHES

> *"Don't believe anything they say, especially if they say they don't want to fight . . . especially if they come closer rather than back away. Look out for ones who will touch you or put their arm around you, and never shake hands with them—it's the oldest trick in the book. Look for erratic eye movement, wide eyes, fidgeting, hand concealment, false smile, or pincer movement of companion(s)."*
>
> Geoff Thompson (on precursors to an attack)

> *"You might think that some of the signs, like being set up or stalked by an attacker, might be obvious; however, depending upon the skill and cunning of your attacker, they can be surprisingly subtle. It would be impossible to describe all the indicators here, but one of the key things to look for is the positioning of people around you. Be wary of people trying to flank you, move behind you, place you between them, or cut off your avenues of escape. Look for people whose hands*

are cupped or unnaturally stiff, like something is held in them, or concealed from view behind the back or in a pocket. Most importantly, don't let anyone get too close to you, where they might be able to move on you before you can react."

Michael D. Janich, from Knife Fighting: A Practical Course (pp. 98)

"Telltale signs of a potentially assaultive subject include extreme pacing, the inability to keep his arms or hands in one position, wide stance, jutting chest, erect body posture, fixed eyes, speaking to himself, rapid speech, changes in speech volume, refusing to cooperate, looking at you out of the corner of his eye, the inability to maintain a relaxed facial expression, and leaving the area and then returning to stalk you or another intended victim. Bent legs or a bobbing motion are signs that the subject is preparing to spring at you."

Edward Lewis, from Hostile Ground (p. 15)

Surprise attacks are typically perpetrated by punks looking for thrills, passive aggressive alcoholics with hurt feelings at the pub, desperate addicts in need of immediate cash, or someone who has chosen to specifically target you so as to kill you for reasons of their own. These are all very different types of attackers, with widely divergent motives, who will be using very different tactics. What they have in common is that the attack will generally have little, if any, prior warning. It may very well come from the blindside if not from behind.

Listen to your intuition and follow your instincts. If something feels wrong to you, don't ignore it . . . that is a warning sign. If someone gets too close, blocks your escape, or moves their hand out of sight, immediately call them on it so they realize they have lost the element of surprise—this will demotivate and discourage many attackers, whereas a few will be provoked to immediately attack. It is best to get the preliminary bullshit over with so you know exactly where you stand and what you're dealing with.

Be aware that sucker punches and ambushes are common tactics on the street. Awareness will make you less susceptible to them. Setups are similar, but more involved, in that a trap is being laid and if you can see the signs you can avoid it or choose to initiate a pre-emptive strike. A common setup involves a group of young men maneuvering in such a way that you find yourself diverted into a chokepoint or secluded area, or are suddenly surrounded on all sides. Keep potential attackers at a distance, and if it appears you are being flanked and crept up on, consider it an attack—street people aren't going to surround you for any legitimate reason, they want to isolate you and prevent you from running away.

Bad situations to look out for is one guy approaching you from the front to distract you while his buddy sneaks up on you from behind, usually to grab you in a chokehold or crush your head with a rock in a sock or some other bludgeon. Another common tactic is for two or more people to suddenly converge on you from different directions. If you are out in a parking lot and you notice three guys sudenly making beelines directly towards you very quickly, you are about to be attacked. Remember, while most muggings do start out with an interview followed by an open threat and demand for cash, others have little to no preliminaries at all—they just look at you as an obstacle to getting "their" money and will think nothing of simply bashing you in the head until you stop moving so they can go through your pockets. That level of desperation is most frequently encountered amongst addicts.

Sometimes, street people can get extremely creative with their tactics. I have seen improvised boobytraps like deadfalls set up in alleyways to be activated remotely from hiding—a suitable target walks into the alley, and suddenly a few cinderblocks swing towards their chest at the end of lengths of twine. Improvised barricades fabricated from pallets and sheet metal can be effectively hidden, perhaps behind a dumpster, until needed to cut off an escape route. Their parked car can be positioned too close to yours with both doors on that side open, effectively trapping you in a cage should you be oblivious enough to ignore them and open your own door. The punk you told to shut up at a movie theater goes outside and sends a text to all his contacts, which are immediately retexted on multiple social networking sites, and when you exit the theater you're faced with a flashmob of over a hundred people intent on beating your ass for sheer entertainment. Sure, these tactics are extremely rare, but they are examples of things which have been done. The deeper into the ghetto you go, the more likely you'll be to run into that sort of shit, as you're dealing with generations of deviousness and desperation, and even stupid people can be clever now and then, but mind you that the smartest ghetto thugs tend to visit better neighborhoods to do their hunting, particularly the parking lots of upscale shopping centers and alleyways behind fancy nightclubs, as that is known as a target rich environment with excellent profit potential.

Keep your eyes open. Don't allow anyone to crowd you or cut off your escape routes. Look at the big picture and anticipate their intentions before they get too close. If your intuition is telling you something feels extremely wrong, don't ignore it. Your awareness will keep you safe.

GROUP ATTACKS

> *"When facing multiple opponents, you must attack first and keep attacking until the danger subdues."*
>
> Miyomo Musashi, *The Book of Five Rings*

> *"People in riots tend to act as one organism, the riot becoming some moving, twisting monster that sweeps along those in it in a sea of human emotions. There is a loss of individuality that many find very attractive. The riot itself becomes a cloak, a cover that protects the individual from being identified . . . Riots then become a convenient excuse for some humans to do everything they really wanted to do but never had the nerve to. It's carnival time where the mask of the riot provides anonymity."*
>
> Eugene Sockut, *Secrets of Street Survival: Israeli Style*

"A few punks get out of hand, and the mob goes right with it. Even sheep can kick you to death when they stampede."

Andrew Vachss, *Only Child* (p. 192)

"You have to be real careful when you see a group of guys throwing hard looks around. Because they feel safe in a group, they're more likely to start shit. This belief in their safety leads to some stupid-ass decisions on their parts. It's best not to tangle with them, and this is usually done by avoiding eye contact."

Marc MacYoung, *Violence, Blunders and Fractured Jaws* (p. 264)

"Three men can have a hard time fighting against one. They must train together or their rhythm is off, they get in one another's way, they have to be careful not to attack a friend. The lone man has no such problems. Everyone is an enemy. The thought and the action are one."

James D. Macdonald, from The Apocalypse Door (p. 188)

Bullies, punks, and thugs frequently run in packs of 3 or more, and will attack a single unarmed victim or a man with his girlfriend or child, knowing that they have the advantage and will likely win any confrontation decisively. That being said, in the event you have a woman or child with you for whose safety you are responsible, this becomes a very grave situation indeed. Most bullies and low level predators will not do this out of respect for societal taboos, so if it occurs give and expect no quarter. Be advised that it is far more difficult to de-escalate a group attack, and any attempt on your part to berate or belittle the group can go sideways fast due to their collective fear of losing the respect of their peers. You can often dissuade them from attacking you, but you need to be subtle and diplomatic about it. Insults and shouting will backfire. Show no fear, and indicate that they simply picked the wrong target and they are more likely to allow you to pass without further incident.

As stated in a previous chapter, there are various levels of predatory behavior, and each of those predator types will behave differently. Some will be content just to frighten or intimidate you, whereas others will stomp you into a grease spot on the sidewalk and some will even pull and use weapons. An unarmed man facing a group attack is in serious trouble, but against an armed group attack he is probably dead.

You want to know how to defeat a group attack with your bare hands or with a small folding blade? If you haven't already got a general idea you ain't gonna learn how from this or any other book. They need to be unmotivated and complacent, and you need to be incredibly fast and vicious or it ain't gonna work at all. The only way I'm gonna tell you to defeat a group attack is to draw a high capacity handgun (compact double-stack .380s are recommended) and start firing from left to right, then back in the opposite direction until they are all sitting on the ground bleeding. If you do not have a gun when facing an attack by a group of highly motivated adults who are larger than yourself and familiar with violence, you are probably pretty well fucked, especially if they have improvised weapons or knives. Avoid ANY sort of physical conflict with a group. The risks are simply too high. If you have no other option, go all out with the clear understanding that you are probably about to die.

TACHYPSYCHIA

> *"Instinct is the sum of information collected by your senses that is not readily obvious to your conscious mind. It often produces a "feeling" that something is wrong or right without a logical explanation. When you are uncertain what to do next or how to handle an opponent, rely on your gut feelings. The more experience you have in combat, the more reliable your instincts will be."*
>
> Hanho, *Combat Strategy* (p. 16)

This is a complex and little understood topic which recently has been addressed by a number of instructors, who all have their own views which frequently contradict one another. Basically, the core concept is that adrenaline can make your brain react to stimuli so quickly that it seems as if time has slowed down . . . and for all practical effects, it may as well have. I have literally seen bullets in flight while in this state, and supposedly that is not physically possible. Under conditions of extreme stress, time can slow down for you, especially if you are one of those rare individuals whose wetware seems to be wired specifically for combat survival. Adrenaline affects everyone differently. Upon some folks it seems to bestow superpowers, whereas others simply freeze up and puke on their shoes. Yes, you can train yourself to unfreeze and hold your chuck, and I recommend you do so, but a lucky few get the time stop / super strength / super speed thing. Since this is so rare, and has not been analyzed until fairly recently, few people understand it. Peyton Quinn is one of the few instructors who gets it. In fact, he has designed an entire system around these concepts and was a pioneer in adrenaline based stress training. He is considered to be one of the world's foremost experts on the subject. He once made the following observation, and rather than attempting to rewrite it in my own words I've decided to reprint it verbatim as it was phrased so brilliantly and I could hardly do justice to it:

> *"Now dig this, it seems mystical, but it's just human physiology.*
>
> *I got to where the very instant I perceived (on the non-self aware level many times) that a person was reaching for a weapon, then BOOOM! everything seemed like it was moving in slow motion. And as Mushahi said in his 'Book of Five Rings', "there was no need to hurry, there was plenty of time to get things done."*
>
> *The guy looked like he was moving underwater, and I could jump over the bar to safety or drop him very, very brutally instantly.*
>
> *Now consider this: Have you ever been in car crash and seen things moving in slow motion? Or have you seen your kid on the jungle gym and realized that she was going to fall? And then as she did, she fell in slow motion it seemed? This is the adrenal affect,*

and your hearing turns off totally. It is also called tachypsychia.

Hearing shuts off so that processing power can be used by the visual cortex and, in effect, this 'speeds up seeing' so that makes things look like they are moving in slow motion.

The second part of this is developing total relaxation under this stress in your body so you can move as fast as you're seeing.

I have drifted here a bit into the most advanced combat concepts there are, but it is very real and even reliable once you master it through experience. And that is not easy, but it is possible."

And that was the BEST description of the tachypsychia state I have ever seen anywhere. I highly recommend you obtain copies of his books, and if at all possible seek him out to attend one of his seminars. Truly groundbreaking work which gets my highest recommendation.

THE DEMONIC

"Great danger lies in the notion that we can reason with evil."

Doug Patton

This is a highly controversial subject, often merely alluded to or spoken of in the abstract if at all. Before we begin, I wish to assure you that I have no intent of engaging in some sort of theological monologue as I have never been a religious sort. When I refer to the "demonic" it is simply for want of a better word. This in no way refers to anything from the Christian or any other theology. While this may well be a spiritual phenomenon, it is clearly apparent that it is not well understood, even by the alleged "experts."

Everyone knows that evil men rob, rape, and murder . . . that is nothing extraordinary. What I am referring to can almost be considered nonhuman, or beyond normal human capabilities. These individuals radiate negative energy. You can feel it. You can see it clearly in their eyes. It can actually trigger a near panic reaction in experienced and hardened professionals. Once I knew a fellow who studied comparative demonology, by which I mean he spent most of his life researching supernatural events reported throughout History in an effort to see commonalities and patterns. He told me about a few. One of the primary indicators of possession was the eyes. As he stated on page 139 of his book, *Arcane Lore*, "a huge amount of energy will pour out of their eyes—so much so that it can actually cause you *physical pain* (headache, eyestrain, nausea, chills, anxiety) to look directly into them. Such eyes have often been describe as 'wild' or 'blazing.'" He went on to state, "The drunkard, addict, or psychotic who is possessed will experience a resistance to pain and injury—not only will they seem unaffected by a full-force blow to the head, but it may take over a half-dozen strong men to successfully restrain them."Although this condition can seemingly be brought on by hard drugs or strong drink, the drugs or drink are not the cause of it, nor is it a deep trance state. This is something that is inside a person, often dormant for periods of time, but it will surface given the proper stimuli and appears to be a lifelong chronic condition. Many of these individuals wind up doing something impulsive and illegal during their late teens or early twenties that results in their long term incarceration or secure hospitalization . . . others who have more self control over their urges tend to do quite well in corporate management and sales.

What I am trying to say here is that MOST threats—including high level predators—are nothing at all like this. Even the average drug freakout or blacked out drunk is not like this, as it is clearly a distinct phenomenon from "excited delerium." In my entire life, which included years immersed in deep street subcultures—interacting at times with felons, drug addicts, and freaks—I have encountered this phenomena less than a half dozen times. It is fucking scary and it will chill your blood . . . and that is coming from an individual with an emotional flatline who is considered by many to be utterly fearless. These people scare me, especially when drugs or alcohol are not a factor and they are walking around stone cold sober, seemingly fully in control of what they are doing. Nothing can be done about this. You can't even talk to people about it without sounding crazy. The only thing you can do is be aware of who these individuals are and put as much distance between yourself and them as possible.

I have had conversations with such individuals and been able to reason with them and convince them to go elsewhere in a calm and diplomatic fashion. You can never escalate with these people by insulting, yelling, or threatening. Calm them, speak in a polite and respectful manner, show them that you are not threatening them and you are seemingly "on their side" . . . but do not trust them and NEVER turn your back on them. If they focus on you and present clearly as an immediate threat, you will need to kill them quickly, efficiently, and preferably by surprise. These people are highly dangerous and extremely unpredictable. It is likely that you may go your entire life without ever knowingly encountering such an individual. If you do encounter it there will be no mistake in your mind what you are dealing with. Do not engage this threat unless you have no other choice. Leave the area immediately, or if that is a non option, attempt to pacify it until it tires and leaves. Never agitate such a threat. You do not want to see this threat in an excited and focused state. Oh, and religious icons and formal rites of banishment apparently have no effect either . . . I don't believe anyone has actually tried silver bullets though. Simply stated, certain individuals are just evil in a way the average person is unable to comprehend. If you mingle in certain subcultures long enough you will eventually encounter someone like this. I hope you are able to discern the signs and keep your distance.

VALHALLA BOUND

> *"If he is willing to kill, then he must be prepared to die. It is only right."*
>
> C. W. Nicol

> *"The Way of the Samurai is found in death. When it comes to either/or, there is only the quick choice of death. It is not particularly difficult. Be determined and advance . . . . (if) one is able to live as though*

> *his body were already dead, he gains freedom in the Way."*
>
> Yamamoto Tsunetomo, *Hagakure* (Wilson translation)

Sometimes, you just need to say *fuckit* and go all out. An example of this is when one is faced with overwhelming odds and retreat or surrender are non-options. If you are going to die, die well. Don't go out like a sniveling little bitch. Die on your feet doing as much damage to your attackers as possible. If you can't kill them back, settle for maiming and blinding. Make certain they never forget you and look back on this day with regret. I really haven't got much more to say on this topic. In fact, I doubt there really is much more to be said. This isn't a fucking philosophical discussion after all, and if you fail to comprehend this mindset you are obviously a vile weasel who probably wears a tie and has likely misappropriated this book from a superior lifeform in hope of presenting it as evidence against him, so fuck you. Norms are conditioned to fear death and avoid it at all cost, whereas a warrior is ambivalent about it. A norm cannot understand concepts like sacrifice and boldness aside from mere theoreticals, whereas these values are naturally ingrained in a select few . . . and those are the people you never want to fuck with, because they would rather throw their life away than run like a coward or beg for mercy, and they will do some serious damage. Fortunately for Society such individuals are far and few between. Fortunately for myself, I am able to count several such individuals as friends. I do not expect you to understand.

VENGEANCE

> *"Do you want,*
> *to rise and kill?*
> *To show the world,*
> *an iron will?"*
>
> NON, *"Total War"*

It is seriously illegal in all 50 states to defend yourself after the fact, or to punish someone who has criminally harmed a family member or friend. This is known as "vigilantism" and is routinely punished far more severely than rape, robbery, or even manslaughter. If you take the law into your own hands and are prosecuted for it, the court will feel compelled to "make an example" out of you in order to dissuade others from doing the same. You can reasonably expect to spend the rest of your life in prison for this, whereas the guy charged with burglarizing and butt-raping peoples' grandmas will probably be out on parole within 10 years—even sooner if he joins AA and attends church services while incarcerated.

I certainly never would encourage anyone to deliberately hunt down and punish another human being, as that would be wrong and I could possibly even be held liable. But, hypothetically, if say a character in a novel you were writing intended to do something like this, he certainly shouldn't drive a car traceable back to him. Nor should he choose an autoloading weapon which ejects shell casings. A scoped, long-barreled, magnum revolver would be ideal, especially if the only way to do this is from a vehicle. While galvanized steel pipe fittings, powder, and fuse may seem like an ideal solution to many societal problems, it also results in a lot of unwanted attention from federal authorities, especially in post 9/11 times, so simple arson is generally preferable. Poisons are unreliable and despicable, as are boobytraps of any sort—frequently both end up unleashed on someone other than the intended target anyway. Best way to take someone out quietly and quickly is with a hatchet. Wear disposable overalls, rubber boots, a raincoat, and protective glasses, with a backpack under the raincoat containing trashbags, wipes, and clean clothes. A knife lacks stopping power, with victims frequently fighting back or escaping after multiple deep stabs which should've been lethal, but few survive an ax attack from behind.

Again, wrong to kill an attacker after the fact. If you are so much as suspected of doing so the authorities will make your life a living hell as they interrogate and intimidate everyone who has ever had any contact with you in the hope they can put together the flimsiest of cases to pursue formal charges. It is best not to commit an act of vigilante violence unless you truly do not give a fuck about throwing away your life to make someone else pay for the crime they have committed. But if they are dead they aren't really suffering punishment, are they? A .410 derringer loaded with birdshot and discharged at point blank range into a face or groin will make them suffer a lot worse than a high caliber bullet in the brain, as would half a bucket of gasoline splashed on their chest and set ablaze with a fireplace lighter. A potent corrosive agent such as nitric acid could do the same thing without using fire, but can also corrode the ungloved hands of your fictional character as well as any first responders unfamiliar with the situation, and can contaminate the area indefinitely which would be unethical and possibly even bad for the environment. Perhaps it might be best simply to mace, sap, zip-tie, and abduct your character's target to deal with him in a more leisurely fashion.

The question you, or your fictional character, needs to ask is: is this really worth it? Is it necessary to protect your loved ones from future attacks or valid threats thereof? Can legal means be utilized or have they been exhausted or are they simply not an option? Are you, or your character, ready and willing to die in order to achieve this goal? Honestly, the vast majority of vengeance based attacks are committed by gang members motivated by peer pressure or by mental defectives emboldened by alcohol. Most are clearly unwarranted, with the perpetrators typically being psychopaths or stalkers targeting victims over relatively minor offenses. Crimes of this nature are seldom deemed random and everyone suspected of having a motive will be subject to investigation. You, or your character, may well be implicated—especially if the feds are able to track the GPS coordinates of your cellphone and subpoena CCTV records from the neighborhood the crime occurred in. Assassination is a serious offense which will be treated far differently from a common homicide, with every available resource being used to clear this case. If you, or your character, is believed to have done such a thing evidence may even be manufactured in order to gain a conviction. Furthermore, as G. Gordon Liddy once said, *"There is no statute of limitations on that sort of activity."* These are all factors which need to be taken under consideration. It is probably best that one not embark on such a path.

Outlawry

"There's no way to rule innocent men. The only power government has is the power to crack down on criminals. When there aren't enough criminals, one makes them. One declares so many things to be a crime that it becomes impossible for men to live without breaking laws."

Ayn Rand, *Atlas Shrugged*

"They branded us as outlaws. We know, as you, only outlaws can be free."

excerpted from the introduction of *Hell's Angels Forever*

"Treat me good, I'll treat you better. Treat me bad, I'll treat you worse."

Ralph Barger

NOTE:

This was an incredibly difficult chapter for me to write, for numerous reasons. The words that follow will not be pleasant to most readers, which is why I chose to move this chapter to the end of the book so at least you will have had an opportunity to read everything else before becoming completely alienated and offended. I have tried to keep my own opinions to a minimum here, instead relying upon the words of others to convey these concepts. Due to this, many quotations will be used.

I want to state, for the record, that inclusion of this chapter is NOT intended to encourage anyone to break any law. You need to know why laws are regularly broken by members of certain subcultures and how they can justify this to themselves and others. You also need to be aware of the possible consequences of lawbreaking. It is, for those reasons only, that I present the following information.

This is the longest chapter in the book, because perhaps it is the most important, and outside of a few fringe underground publications you certainly aren't going to hear these viewpoints anywhere else, and certainly not as coherently.

APOLOGIA

> *"Our culture engages historians, sociologists, psychiatrists and the media to . . . impose upon us a common view of reality. The reason for this imposing of socially-approved views is fear: As a culture we are afraid that unless we can force the majority of us to comply with particular givens, everything we have achieved and everything we believe we understand will unravel. The truth is that without the continual reinforcement of commonly held cultural views of 'reality,' most of our beliefs and some of our ways of living would unravel . . . . In fairness, we need to*

> *understand that there can never be a common view of reality because each of us is capable of seeing only so much and no more . . . . a commonly-held world view is not a possibility, not now and not ever . . . . We are stuck with the social illusions into which we are born . . . . From this evolution-of-illusion we get politics, religion, fads and all manner of cultural blindness. We pass our blindness down from one generation to another until it becomes so firmly entrenched in daily life that nobody asks whether this or that aspect of our social belief system might simply be wrong."*
>
> Anderson Reed, *Shouting at the Wolf* (p. 142-143, 148)

> *"I only know that he who forms a tie is lost. The germ of corruption has entered his soul."*
>
> Joseph Conrad, *Victory*

I am certain I am going to upset a lot of readers with what is presented in this chapter, and feel an explanation is in order.

You need to understand that the reality you perceive is not shared by others. People of different cultures and classes will see things much differently from you. I am assuming that my average reader is a white male from the middle class, presumably a Christian with a steady job and supportive family who is respected by the community as a good citizen. I am truly happy for you if that is your lot, and it is for you that I have writ this section. If this applies to you, I need you to make an attempt to set aside your ingrained preconceptions for a few moments and try to look at things from my point of view. I am now going to tell you what you need to know.

You have been lied to. Facts have been concealed from you. Things are not as they seem. Are you still with me, or did your conditioning just shut me down as a "kook" whom you should not be listening to? It is true that there are a lot of kooks out there lying about conspiracies and such, but this is no conspiracy that I am talking about now.

You have been sheltered, coddled, and programmed. You are not in the real world if you wear a tie and work in an office. Sales is not the real world either, nor is retail. If you work in academia, holy fuck, you may as well be on another planet. One of the reasons our nation is so fucked up is because the politicians running it are academics with very little real world experience and even less common sense . . . they may as well be entertainers or clergy.

Public schools are mandated to present curriculums and enforce discipline in a specific manner, which is best suited to turn students into docile and obedient workers and weed out the nonconformists. Television entertainment, popular magazines, and the headline links that pop up on your browser fill your head with meaningless distractions. This country is falling apart and you are blissfully unaware, with your nice house, 2 cars, air conditioning, cable television, and wallet full of credit cards. You are part of it. You don't know anything except what the talking bobbleheads on CNN and FOX tell you, and they've been telling you lies. You've been lied to your whole life. If I told you the truth you'd probably get angry and call *me* a liar. That's okay, Captain Hook doesn't give a fuck about your uninformed opinion and I kinda expected that reaction anyway. This apologia exists solely as a courtesy.

Life is not fair. There is a distinct class structure in this country, even though the politicians and public schools shrilly deny it. If you follow the rules and color inside the lines, maybe you'll get a good job that allows you to have money left over after you pay your mortgage, car payments, insurance, utility bills, groceries, and taxes. You can come home from work 5 nights a week to eat dinner in front of the television, and on weekends you can go to the same places everyone else like you goes. That is the pattern They want to lock you into. That is your "reward" for being a good citizen. I am very happy for your success, but please do not presume to think that you know anything at all about the world outside your little homogenized and sanitized bubble of conformity. You don't know shit.

I have made the decision to include this highly controversial chapter because I want you to understand why I sometimes allude to the fact that the best way to get things done is not always the legal way—and why I make no apologies for that, nor do I think it is wrong. The LAW is frequently wrong, as are those who write, interpret, rule upon, and enforce it. I will spend some time elucidating why many reasonable men believe that to be an undisputed fact of life. As Louis D. Brandeis once said, *"If we desire respect for the law, we must first make the law respectable."* Unfair and unreasonable laws breed contempt for the law, even if it does not encourage criminality. Refusal to meekly abide an injustice does not make one a criminal . . . it makes one an outlaw.

I expect a lot of folks are going to misrepresent what I will say here. They may even go so far as to pull a few things out of context and twist around their meaning in an attempt to use my own words against me. Captain Hook doesn't care.

I learned a lot amongst the lower, under, and criminal classes. They see things differently from us. After a while, I realized that they knew more about how the world really worked than the college educated suits and norms living in the suburbs. Some of the smartest guys I've talked with haven't been PhDs, but janitors and auto mechanics. It would be unwise for you to underestimate the intellect of people you meet based solely upon their social class and lack of a university degree. You will be facing folks from these classes in most self defense situations, so do not automatically assume that you are smarter than them. Predators and con men usually pretend to be a lot simpler than they actually are, because they know you'll be predisposed to categorize them as stupid, which gives them a huge advantage.

Now, I'm going to attempt to share with y'all a few of the things I have learned. I do not expect you to embrace these concepts. Social conditioning will alert you that these concepts are contrary to your deeply held beliefs and I expect many of you will automatically reject them. That's okay, I'm not writing this next part for you. In fact, it may be best for you to just skip this chapter altogether and come back to it when and if you are ready. You don't need to agree with what is said here, you just need to understand *why* it is being said.

THE LAW AS WRITTEN

"Why are the people rebellious?
Because the rulers interfere too much."

Lao Tzu, *Tao Te Ching*, chapter 75

Some folks are outlawed because they had the audacity to defend themselves against unlawful aggression in a manner which was not entirely within the specified parameters permitted by local legislation. You may have done everything correctly, even calling 911 immediately afterwards, remaining on the scene, and providing a full and truthful statement as well as a video recording clearly showing that you were indeed the victim—but then face charges or malicious prosecution because one small thing seemed amiss. Perhaps your handgun holds 12 rounds but local ordinances prohibit magazines which hold more than 10. Maybe you used the same hollowpoint ammo used by local police in their duty weapons, but your state says such ammo is unlawful for civilians to possess. Say you used your trusty lockblade to fend off an attacker, but it turns out the blade is a quarter inch above the legal limit. Maybe your attacker was knocked to the ground and was getting back up when you kicked him in the face, or perhaps after he stabbed you, you beat him so badly the prosecutor feels the force you used was "excessive." And then there is the possibility that several of his friends are willing to testify that *you* were the initial aggressor who started the fight. There are over a dozen other possibilities as well. Regardless, even if you seem to be one hundred percent in the right, there is still a chance you may be charged, prosecuted, and even convicted. This will be on your permanent record, and if it is a felony charge you will effectively be outlawed as far as society is concerned.

Most folks, however, run afoul of some other law—of which there are literally thousands, many of which are relatively unknown, a few of which are punishable with mandatory minimum sentences and enforced under Zero Tolerance guidelines, and they can vary profoundly as one crosses a border from one state to another. The Declaration of Independence guarantees all citizens the right to be secure in their property and papers from unwarranted searches, the right to bear arms, and the right to the pursuit of happiness. It was written on hemp paper by a bunch of dope smoking rebels who clearly didn't give a fuck. Politicians are fond of wiping their arses with copies of this document nowadays. If I may give you a few examples: In one state, marijuana is sold openly to MMJ patients in dispensaries, patients may grow their own, and anyone caught with under an ounce is spared prosecution; but cross a border and possession of one joint is punishable as a felony, a mother who tests positive for cannabis is charged with felony child abuse, and an old hippy growing a few plants behind his trailer in the woods has his door kicked in by armored stormtropopers at 0400 who shoot his dog, ransack his home, and drag him across his yard by the hair. In one state, gays and kinksters can openly congregate at their specialized clubs and shops under the full protection of the law, and even post online personal ads; but in another state homosexuality and other forms of non-traditional sexual activities between consenting adults are prosecuted as felony sex offenses. One state has freedom and privacy, whereas another state criminalizes oral sex, sex toys, or unmarried persons of the opposite sex spending the night together even if no intimate contact occurs. One state permits its citizens to buy and sell handguns at garage sales or via online ads; whereas another state will prosecute both the seller and buyer with felony offenses if the sale is not properly approved and registered between two licensed individuals. A few other bizarre things which have been prosecuted as felonies include: reusing a postage stamp, using someone else's computer without their permission, wearing a helmetcam during a traffic stop or otherwise recording law enforcement's interactions with you, drinking alcohol with a firearm in your possession, touching a girl's buttocks without her express consent, and of course a second DWI. I am not saying that any of these things are appropriate, but turning minor offenses into serious felony charges serves no purpose but to permanently criminalize, ostracize, and disenfranchise a substantial segment of our allegedly free society. Please remember the words of George Bernard Shaw, who once wrote: "*Whilst we have prisons it matters little which of us occupies the cells.*"

APEX PREDATOR

> *"You know the score, if you're not a cop you're little people!"*
>
> "Captain Bryant" from *Blade Runner*

> *"We don't obey the law; we **enforce** the law."*
>
> Officer Friendly, DPD

Top of the food chain. Extreme potential threat to your life and safety, no matter how well trained you are or what steps you may have taken to protect yourself. Who could be so dangerous to you? A terrorist? A gangster? A ninja assassin? While it is true those all are deadly opponents it is quite unrealistic to expect the average citizen to face such a one. No, you probably have close calls with the true Apex Predators several times a week. You walk by them on the street and pass by them in traffic. You may even smile politely and nod your head at them, and they may well respond in kind. But they are different from other men. Our rules do not apply to them. They exist in a closed secretive society and walk amongst us, well armed, and ready to do violence to anyone at any time. Who could this Apex Predator be? Why, it is Officer Friendly, of course.

Yeah, I'm definitely gonna piss off a lot of folks over this chapter, but that's okay. This stuff needs to be said and you need to be made aware of it. I'm not saying it is right or wrong, only that you need to be aware of how some of us perceive things to be so you can make a well informed decision. I'm not one of those jerks who hates the po-lice. Police are clearly an important part of any civilized society. Problems arise, however, when they are permitted to routinely abuse their authority with no oversight or fear of punishment. In many jurisdictions this is not a problem at all. In other places, some departments have "a few bad apples" who abuse citizens and break laws regularly. In a few notorious areas, entire departments appear to be rotten, and you effectively have a small police state with officers gone wild. I shit you not. In a few major cities it has become a national scandal. In some small, isolated rural communities, however, it is far worse. What you need to know is that, regardless of what you were programmed to believe, Officer Friendly really isn't your friend. He will try to trick you. He will tell you lies. He will threaten you. He may even point his weapon at you, beat you, or use chemical or electric weapons to make you comply with his demands. Then he will go into court and lie about it . . . and the judge will be sure to take his word over yours. Try never get in a situation where Officer Friendly has control over your life. You are just a statistic to Officer Friendly, and a citation or an arrest is "a feather in his cap." He cares more about overtime pay, performance evaluations and promotion than he does about potentially destroying your life. You just cannot trust Officer Friendly.

The policeman can do whatever he wants to you, and he knows it. A few bullies and psychos seem to revel in it—indeed, power over others is the primary reason some men choose police work as a profession. A policeman who takes an interest in you, perhaps because of the way you're dressed, or the fact that you are walking by yourself after dark, can demand that you answer questions—some of which you are not lawfully required to answer. He can ask your name and ask to see your ID to run a check for warrants and wants, and that is pretty much all you are required to tell him—but if you give a false name he can and will arrest you. Officer Friendly will want to know all about you: what your home address is, where you are coming from, where you are heading to, if you've had anything to drink, if you have a pocketknife, and what is in your backpack and pockets. You may be subjected to a "Terry Frisk" to check for concealed weapons "for the safety of the officer" but many policemen want to go well beyond what is allowed and demand that you turn your pockets inside out and open any bags or parcels you may have. They may demand that you remove your shoes and socks, then take your wallet and dump the contents on the ground. They know they aren't allowed to

do this, but if you don't know your rights they cease to exist. I advise you to consult with a competent attorney about your protections from unreasonable search under the 4th Amendment, as SCOTUS keeps chipping away at our rights every year and the law is constantly changing.
You see, the policeman is a "Super Citizen," having rights, protection and status well above the rest of us. His badge is a symbol of guvmint, whom he is acting as the representative of. If you fight the po-lice you are, in effect, fighting guvmint—which makes you a traitor to be treated without mercy in the Court as well as the media. Policeman has a veritable license to kill. Policeman can stop any pedestrian or any vehicle, with or without cause, and subject the citizen to interrogation as well as a search. Policeman can even come to your home after dark and kick in your door. Policeman can do pretty much anything he wants, and there's not much you can do about it. If you lie to him, that is a criminal offense. If you run from him, that is a crime too. If you are being arrested or assaulted unlawfully and attempt to resist, yet another crime. So, barring any actual criminal activity on your part—aside from being an asshole—you can be arrested for numerous charges (impersonation, accessory, conspiracy, evasion, escape, resisting arrest, assault) solely based upon encountering Officer Friendly on a bad day . . . and mixing cocaine and steroids can make everyday a bad day. Another benefit of Super Citizen status is no drug tests, and many policemen do indeed regularly abuse illegal drugs and alcohol (as do many doctors, lawyers, schoolteachers, clergymen, and politicians, but I digress).

What I'm trying to convey to you is certainly not that you should hate the police, but that you should distrust them, and perhaps even fear them a bit as well. Try to avoid the police whenever possible (this also means you should avoid calling them unless absolutely necessary), and if you are forced into an encounter with them be polite, be respectful, don't make any sudden movements, and try to say as little as possible. Never volunteer information. Never trust anything a cop tells you—they all lie, it is part of the job description. Even if you believe you have done nothing wrong they will still try to find any possible excuse to arrest you. Anything you say will be misquoted, twisted around, taken out of context and used as evidence against you. They may even claim you said something which you did not. Have an attorney on retainer, or at least consult with an attorney and keep his card in your wallet and his number programmed into your phone. Be sure he specializes in criminal law, as an attorney who specializes in wills and trusts will be absolutely useless at representing you in court.

Now, Officer Friendly is not a normal man. He is a direct representative of guvmint—a "minion" if you will. As a minion, he is not free to make up his mind as to what laws to enforce and against whom. If his overlords mandate that a certain law needs to be enforced in a certain area with zero tolerance, he needs to follow that order and do as he's told, even if those orders are in violation of the Constitution. During a declared State of Emergency this is certain to become apparent very quickly. At times of peace and prosperity Officer Friendly will be a lot easier to reason with than during times of civil unrest, but that should be common sense. Still, you'd be surprised how many citizens might think it is a good idea to walk up to a group of highly agitated policemen during an emergency situation in order to ask a stupid question or even insult them or pelt them with an egg or something. People like that *deserve* to get their asses kicked.

While we are talking about interacting with law enforcement officers, I need to go off on a tangent to talk to you about your cellphone. Neat little bits of cellphone trivia you may be unaware of, but it is relevant and you need to know these things. First off, most cellphones contain cameras nowaday with video and audio capability, and let me tell you, Officer Friendly really does not want his questionable behaviors going viral on the youtube. If you video him behaving badly he is going to confiscate that cellphone and either smash it or take it as "evidence" and wipe the memory. Second, if you are arrested for any reason—as is common in nearly all self defense related scenarios—your cellphone may be confiscated as "evidence" so they can look at your call logs, contacts and texts because they want to know who you were in contact with immediately before and after the incident in question. Of course, they will also try to access all your other files as well while they have your phone in their possession, just because they can (private emails, web browsing cache, image files, etc). This is done routinely at some checkpoints, even if no crime is suspected. Now, let us say you call 911, or perhaps an officer at 911 dispatch decides to call you. Guess what? They have the option of locking up your phone so you are unable to make or receive calls to anyone else, and that is common. Another thing they can do is track your GPS chip to your exact location, even if the phone is switched off. Most city PDs have this capability now. If the Federales are interested in you, they have even more options available to them. For instance, not only can they tap into and listen in on your calls, but they can remotely turn your phone into an eavesdropping device through the speakerphone mic even if the phone is switched off. Only way to disable the GPS tracking and eavesdropping functions is to pop the phone open and remove the battery. Sci Fi Big Brother shit is going on for real. And while we're going off on that tangent, you should also be aware that it is now common for detectives to seize the laptop computer of any suspect they arrest who is under investigation for a felony. They want to access your email messages, see what websites you've been frequenting, and look at the files on your harddrive and USB keys. So don't be surprised if after you shoot a burglar Officer Friendly puts you in cuffs, pockets your cellphone and walks out the door with your computer. Guess what? They'll probably be searching the entire house as well and eating food from your refrigerator.

Remember: the policeman is an important part of a civilized society, but he is not your friend and you can't trust anything he says, and if you try to fight back he can kill you and get away with it. Fear the policeman, for he is at the top of the food chain on the street.

There are only two predators more dangerous than the policeman. Indeed, they are the only two predators that can lawfully victimize such a one, although police are typically not preyed upon by them as a professional courtesy. These predators are the Federale and da Judge.

If a policeman is a "Super Citizen", you can think of a Fed as a "Super Policeman" with super powers, secret gadgets, and the entire Federal guvmint as backup. Everyone is scared of the Feds, because they are lawless stormtroopers who can kill on a whim without having to answer to anyone. They can tap your phones without a warrant, read your emails, do a covert "black bag" search of your house, and pull every bit of data about you from every computer database. The policeman hates and fears the Fed . . . probably out of jealousy. The scariest thing about the Feds is *you don't even need to commit a crime* in order to get busted by them. All you need to do is be a friend, relative or co-worker of someone they're trying to build a case against or "put pressure on." Or, they might just want to increase the number of drug or weapon related busts in order to skew statistics for political reasons, which means they can fabricate cases to the point of using informants and assets to create a crime network where none existed, lure a bunch of ignorant locals into their web with the promise of money, drugs, guns, and sex, then swoop in a few months later to arrest everyone and claim they "shut down" the syndicate they created. There are thick books full of obscure federal statutes most folks have never heard of that they can bust you on. The laws are deliberately vague, with definitions so ill defined they can effectively make them mean anything they want. They are also free to modify these statutes at any time or spuriously re-interpret them to suit their immediate needs. These are the Secret Police who do the dirty work of guvmint, and you need to be scared of them.

Only thing more powerful than a Fed is a Federal Judge, but mind you that a mere County Court Judge is just as powerful to little people like you and me. A policeman can only beat you, arrest you, and maybe even shoot you under certain circumstances. A Judge can send you to prison, seize everything you own, and sentence you to Civil Death. You see, there really is something known as your "permanent record." Whenever you go to court, or even are detained by police for questioning, that record gets a wee bit longer. And it NEVER goes away. You get dinged with a felony conviction and your life is effectively over. You are stripped of all rights of citizenship, including the right to defend yourself against those who would harm you and your family. You are further barred from employment in hundreds of professions, limiting you primarily to manual labor or minimum wage service industry jobs—and you'll need to lie on your employment application to get those. And to make matters worse, if you are released under parole or probation, you have some nefarious truant officer following you around to try and catch you violating the terms of your release—and he can search your house without a warrant and interview your neighbors and co-workers should he so wish. Judge can make this happen. Thing is, if Judges were fair, reasonable and sane this would largely be a non-issue—but that is frequently not the case. Many Judges drink or take mood altering prescription medication due to the stress of their jobs. Some partake of illegal drugs or misuse prescription meds. Most become drunk on power. More than a few end up psychotic. If you are standing before an alcoholic, pill-popping, power-crazed Judge with delusions of Godhood you are in a shitload of trouble and it will not end well. And good luck with your appeal, as most Appellate Courts stamp 75% of all appeals DENIED without even considering them. Judge is more powerful than the Chief of Police, Mayor, or even the Governor. You have a better chance of winning the lottery than you do of having a Judge's decision overturned on appeal. Not technically a predator, but top of the food chain nonetheless. And if you are ever involved in a self defense situation in which a weapon is displayed or someone is injured, you are going to meet him. Try to dress nice and be polite.

THE POLICEMAN IS NOT YER FRIEND

> *"Search and seizure, the Miranda decision, all this kind of stuff, police have never cared about any of that. That's all bullshit. They testify however they want to . . . Who's there to say he didn't give the prisoner the Miranda warning? The prisoner? That's a joke."*
>
> anonymous, from Mark Baker's *Cops* (p. 318)

> *"Police, I learned over the years, are like soldiers, normally good-natured people, but part of a culture of obedience to orders and capable of brutal acts against anyone designated as 'the enemy.'"*
>
> Howard Zinn, *You Can't Be Neutral on a Moving Train*

> *"Because of what appears to be a lawful command on the surface, many citizens, because of their respect for the law, are cunningly coerced into waiving their rights, due to ignorance."*
>
> U.S. v. Minker 350 U.S. 179, 187

I'm really not trying to be a dick here, or be confrontational, I'm just stating a very basic fundamental fact: even if you were the one who called them, never make the mistake of believing that the policeman is on your side. He is there to do his job the way he feels like doing it, and will likely resent and possibly punish anything said or done by you which he finds the slightest bit annoying. Police work is a high stress job and most cops distrust and dislike the citizens they are assigned to protect—a good cop will conceal this fact, whereas a bad cop will make his position unmistakably clear. Whenever you come into contact with police, it is usually in your best interest to be polite, non confrontational, and calm.

You are most likely to come into contact with police via a traffic stop. You do not even need to have violated any law in order for a stop to occur. You might be stopped at a roadblock, or you could be pulled over for what is referred to as a "Pretextual Stop," by which a policeman arbitrarily pulls you over for an insignificant or imaginary offense simply as an excuse to fuck with you. One of the most common justifications for this is that you "failed to signal a lane change" or "did not come to a complete and total stop" at a stop sign (count to 5 then proceed), which everyone knows are bullshit violations. If you are driving on a Friday or Saturday night after 10 PM expect to be pulled over for "weaving within your lane"—often a policeman will drive in an aggressive manner on DWI patrol, such as flying up behind you at high speed with his brights on to tailgate you while weaving back and forth, repeatedly speeding up and slowing down as he alternates between tailgating you and shadowing you a dozen car lengths back, or shadowing you with no headlights or even parking lights—all in an effort to goad you into speeding up out of anger or fear. In some states they can ticket you for talking on your cellphone while driving or failing to wear a shoulder harness seatbelt, and some policemen will actually pull a squealing U-turn in front of oncoming traffic and fly up on you at double the speed limit to pull you over for these minor offenses. The average policeman makes several such stops every shift in hope of seeing evidence of anything he can bust someone for. If you are Black, poor, teenaged, have long hair, or have bumperstickers proclaiming that you are a hippie, a gun owner, or some other social deviant, you can expect to be pulled over by police for bullshit reasons such as, "your car is similar to one we've been looking for" on a regular basis in some areas. A burnt out taillight bulb can get you pulled over several times a month until it is fixed, and some municipalities who aggressively use local law enforcement to generate revenue via predatory policing will have you issued a ticket that costs $75 due to a bulb that costs .50 cents to replace. If you regularly exceed the posted speed limit you can expect to be stopped frequently during your lifetime. I recall the time I acquired a Porsche 914 and received 3 speeding tickets within a month, but I'm not blaming the cops for that.

Intimidation and bullying are becoming too common. Hidden behind the "if you have nothing to hide" speeches that nearly all cops use, it makes you out to be a criminal to insist on your constitutional rights. A policeman will pressure you into waiving your 4th amendment rights so he can perform an intrusive search of your vehicle, which will entail looking in all compartments including the trunk and any containers therein without a warrant or probable cause. If you tell him "No" there is a very high probability you're getting searched regardless. Tiny video and audio recording devices can be hidden inside pens and wristwatches, and they can prove invaluable in the event a policeman starts blatantly disregarding the law by threatening you, using profanity, or otherwise violating various Constitutionally guaranteed rights, but be advised that recording the police has been prosecuted as felony "eavesdropping" via malicious prosecution in a few totalitarian regimes.

Don't count on the kindness of a cop keeping you out of trouble just because you are a "good guy"—that Spyderco police model you carry? It's considered an illegal weapon in many places, and can be worth up to $1,000 to the city that prosecutes you for it's possession. Then you're stuck with a "weapons violation" and the sheriff pulls your CCW permit. In places like NYC the police will arrest anyone they spot with an exposed pocketclip indicating a knife, even though the knife itself is legal the fact that the clip is exposed allegedly "alarms others" under the bullshit municipal statute, and they have a zero tolerance policy which means jail and a criminal conviction are virtually guaranteed. To make things even screwier, the guys doing the arresting are frequently undercover transit cops who look and act like unshaven belligerent thugs intent on mugging you prior to presentation of their badge, possibly in hope of provoking you into a "menacing" or ADW bust, which is a felony instead of a misdemeanor and worth more to the cop statistically when he is due for his next performance evaluation.

Any time you come into contact with police they will ask you your name and date of birth. You are required by law to tell them your legal name. You are not specifically required to tell them the correct spelling or your exact date of birth, but it should be close enough to blame on a typo if it ever becomes an issue. Last name and date of birth is used to track people in the NCIC database, and they will be checking you for wants and warrants before leaving the area, and that contact will become part of your permanent record if the data you provide is 100% accurate. They will always try to trip you up by asking you to confirm that your last name or date of birth is something slightly different from what you just said and he copied into his notebook—if you confirm that difference he will know you are lying and may arrest you for criminal impersonation if it turns out you gave a false name, so don't ever do that.

The policeman is not your enemy, but he is not your friend either. You and your concerns are insignificant to him, other than a check on a tally sheet as he is adding up his monthly quota of "tickets and collars" in hope of an excellent performance evaluation which could eventually result in a promotion. You are nothing to him but a statistic. Never forget that.

INTERACTING WITH LAW ENFORCEMENT

> *"Keep in mind that recent statistics say that it takes a minimum of 48 hours for a trained officer to give an accurate statement after a use of force. Statements prior to at least 48 hours do not have the accuracy or detail."*
>
> Force Science Research

> *"Officer, I will give full cooperation in 24 hours after I have spoken with council."*
>
> Massad Ayoob

> *"The golden rule of police interrogation is: absolutely nothing said by police interrogators will be the truth."*

Ragnar Benson, *Ragnar's Guide to Interviews, Investigations, and Interrogations* (p. 56)

Everything you say will be used against you, especially in regards to a use of force incident. Instead of telling you what little I know about interacting with police after a shooting, I instead shall refer you to the words of a former police officer and expert on concealed carry issues who wishes to remain anonymous:

"I've been there, done that, too. Had to defend myself and had to face the aftermath.

My advice is thus.

1. *There is no law saying you have to STAY in the area the attack took place in, in fact it's quite justifiable for you to drive to the nearest place of safety before calling the police. You're fleeing for your life, and you have NO obligation to inform the police that you just had to fire your weapon IMMEDIATELY. You need to un-ass the area till you feel safe.*
2. *There is no time to determine if you can flee, there just isn't. And the law in Colorado does not require you to do so. There is the 'sufficient time for reflection' standard that I've seen used though. I would never ever indicate that I 'made a decision that I could not flee.'*
3. *The moment the police arrive, you ARE under arrest—consider that this is the case until you know otherwise. They can and WILL charge you weeks or months later with an offense if they want to (happened to me).*
4. *Say nothing. If you feel you have to call 911 to report something, then use the bad-guys phone, if the bad guy does*

not have one, drive to a payphone. Getting away means you avoid any followup attack, and you give yourself time to come down a bit from your adrenaline high, you'll be spouting like a geyser on the phone if you call in the immediate aftermath on a cell phone. If you MUST make that immediate call, then call 911, say there's been trouble at your location, ask for medical and police and hang up. You'll get an immediate call back, don't answer. You don't have to explain a damn thing about why you didn't answer, you're the victim of a violent attack, of course you were not capable of doing anything useful for quite a long while. People who act calm on a 911 call are suspect, people who blather on about the fight will have it used against them, people who try to communicate the maximum amount of information, again, are building a case against themselves.

5. *Do not respond to any commands from a dispatcher. They are not a police officer, and they are not there. Again, you've already hung up so this shouldn't come into play, but keep in mind that you cannot do yourself any good by staying on the phone with them.*
6. *Since you left the area before contacting the police, you can, and should, put your gun (unloaded) in plain view on the hood of your car and stepped away from it before they arrive. Don't put it IN your car, that subjects your car to a cursory search, your car should be LOCKED and parked legally.*
7. *You have nothing to 'clear up' and no 'side of the story' to tell. Your statement should be simple and very, very brief.*

I was driving home from work/school/etc. I was stopping to use the ATM when several (never give a number) threatening men demanded money from me and threatened my life. I drew my weapon and told them to leave me alone. When they attacked me, I shot at them.

Never personalize it, like, 'the guy in the white t-shirt came at me first, so I shot him' ALWAYS 'they attacked me and I shot at THEM.' If it's ONE guy, then it's easier.

This will not please the police officer, by now he's gotten the hint that you are NOT a cooperative victim. He's going to try to get more out of you, and at this point you have only ONE THING you need to ask for.

Medical help, you feel short of breath (you probably do) you feel dizzy and your left arm is aching. I don't care how young you are, you are dizzy and you ARE short of breath—it's the way adrenaline eliminates itself from your system. It causes narrow vision, blurry images, momentary deafness, vomiting and diarrhea. You DO need medical help. They cannot refuse your request, and in the face of this, to continue to question you shouldn't happen. While waiting for medical to arrive, the adrenaline will eliminate itself from your body and you can have a clearer head about what you need to say—which is 'I think I need a lawyer before I talk to you.' If he says you don't need one, then ask him if you are free to go—if you are NOT, then you must consider yourself under arrest (even though you aren't technically at this point).

There is absolutely NOTHING YOU CAN SAY that will make you look like a hero/victim in a self-defense situation. NOTHING. No matter how smart you think you are, when your words are read back to you in front of a jury I can guarantee you that you're going to regret saying them.

Cops are not your friend in this scenario. Never. They are 'clean up' and aside from making sure nothing more bad happens, they are on a search for people to arrest. They often arrest BOTH parties in any kind of self-defense situation, don't count on a cop being sympathetic to you. A large segment of them actually believe that only cops have an absolute right to self-defense, yeah, no kidding. A citizen should 'call 911' or 'try to avoid trouble' or anything else. You don't know if this is the kind of cop you're talking to, so you should shut up.

Call someone to be with you at the crime scene, and immediately give them the key to your car. You should already have put your wallet in the car and any other things of a personal nature. If you're arrested the police CAN seize your car, in many cases as long as there is an adult there to take your car they will let them do it. Unless you like paying 300 dollars to get it out of impound. You do have to ID yourself to the police, but no law requires you to 'produce ID.' Just tell them your name, address and date of birth honestly and you're fine.

The police have a lifetime of indoctrination under YOUR belt. You went to school and learned that you had to have official permission to even go to the bathroom. You got a job and found that you had to tell the government about every penny you earned. You carefully measure the buttstock on that used shotgun you just bought, because if you're even 1/20th of an inch too short, you will go to prison and have your life's savings taken away. When you want to visit your grandmother you've also learned that you must submit yourself to someone groping your genitalia. You're already indoctrinated to 'obey' authority. And the ultimate symbol of that authority is a police officer, you will almost WANT to talk to them at length. If they do the intimidation thing, well, most people cannot resist succumbing to the pressure—and while you're on adrenaline and potentially mentally injured? Forget it, you don't stand a chance. The deck is stacked against you. The chattiest person I ever got a statement out of was someone still high on adrenaline, a normally street-wise gangbanger talks AT LENGTH while under it's influence. Try to get them to even say 'hi' an hour later and they'll just give you that blank empty stare they reserve for the police.

Your only chance to avoid their interrogation techniques is in asking for a lawyer, at that point if you've already identified yourself and your role in the incident—there is nothing more they can talk to you about concerning what happened. If they persist, start collecting business cards and ask for a supervisor. It WILL mark you out as 'one of those people' (you know, those people who know their rights) and it wont make you any friends. But the last time I checked, no cop ever came forward to pay the defense costs of a citizen who defended themselves because they felt friendship for the citizen. You have no obligation to make that cops job one iota easier in this respect.

You should wield your lawyer like a weapon, carry his business card in your wallet and keep a spare in your car. Wave it around like a vorpal sword. You DON'T have to have a lawyer under retainer to use his business card to cut off the police from talking to you."

—L.D.

KANGAROO COURT

> *"Watching the trust we had in the legal system disappear has been a sad, confusing experience . . . In the past, we revered the legal system as the backbone of democracy. Now we quite frankly fear it—its linguistic*

fog, the casualness of the brutal transactions, the sheer density of its unconcern."

Dennis Miller, *The Rants* (p. 15)

"A new tyranny has cast its cold and ugly shadow over the nation, a nation where the rights of the people, criminals and citizens alike exist mostly in myth, where the police have become the handmaidens of power, where trials have become mere window dressing and mockeries of justice."

Gerry Spence, *From Freedom to Tyranny* (p. 77)

"To consider the judges as the ultimate arbiters of all constitutional questions is a very dangerous doctrine indeed, and one which would place us under the despotism of an oligarchy."

Thomas Jefferson

"According to criminal justice experts, many of the people who have been convicted on drug charges are innocent. The pressure to snitch is so great that a large number of informants simply make up accusations against friends, associates—even family members—to escape the long mandatory minimum sentences."

Jim Redden, *Snitch Culture* (pp. 195-196)

"Always take a jury trial. Your chances of a not guilty verdict are always greater, and there is always the chance of a hung jury or a reversal of the conviction

in a higher court . . . . Your only real chance for an acquittal is to take a jury trial . . . . Court appointed attorneys could care less if you go to prison and are only there to make a show on the transcript to make the court records look all legal and official . . . . The system loves guys who sit in the courtroom nice and quiet while a mock-up trial is held right in their presence . . . . Your repeated objections and complaints about your attorney will open the doors for post-conviction relief. Stand up for yourself. You are probably the only one who will."

Harold S. Long, *Making Crime Pay* (p. 29, 34, 36)

"'Jury nullification of the law' is a traditional right dating back to the Magna Carta and was intended by America's founding fathers as the final test a law must pass before it gains the authority to punish violators. John Adams, our nation's second president, in 1771 said of the jury, 'it is not only his right, but his duty . . . to find the verdict according to his own best understanding, judgement, and conscience, though in direct opposition to the direction of the court' . . . Due to special interest pressure, juries have been misinformed of their right to judge law as well as fact for almost 100 years. Jurors now swear in their oaths to judge only the facts of the case according to the law as dictated to them by the judge. The majority of judges will not allow attorneys to tell jurors of their power to say 'no' to unjust laws. In most cases juries are no longer allowed to hear the defendant's motives. Fully informed juries are essential for justice,

rebuilding respect for the law, protection of individual rights and control of the government by people."

The Fully Informed Jury Association (FIJA)

"Care should be taken that the punishment does not exceed the guilt; and also that some men do not suffer for offenses for which others are not even indicted."

Cicero

I don't have much to say about the politicians' One Way Law, in which justice becomes "just us." As a NYC trial attorney once asked a client, *"How much justice can you afford"?* The laws are a web that ensnare the weak and powerless who are crushed unmercifully, whereas the wealthy or well connected get a veritable free pass. The law was intended to be fair and unbiased, yet it quite clearly is not.

One example I've used a few times to illustrate how flawed the legal system in this country can be is a case which involved a brother of mine who was unlawfully searched while traveling across New York state with an antique target revolver in his luggage. He was not prohibited from owning that revolver, and antique firearms are specifically exempted from prosecution under federal as well as state law, but he was arrested, prosecuted, and convicted for a felony offense of possessing an unlicensed handgun regardless. He was provided an inexperienced attorney who was openly hostile to him, denied a jury trial, and not even permitted to speak in his own defense while a senile judge raved and screamed at him from the bench. That judge was later disbarred and the prosecutor who insisted upon "the maximum sentence" now sits on that bench, and has proven to be insane as well as a notorious drunkard. This occurred over 25 years ago, and he has been a good citizen who has since gotten married, been gainfully employed, been active in his community, has a stack of character references from employers and law enforcement officers, and has not resided in that state for 20 years, yet he cannot get his rights restored after numerous requests, nor can he have his unlawful conviction overturned. Why? Because New York state law clearly stipulates that only the sentencing court can restore rights or overturn a conviction—the crazy court of an isolated prison town that is running with zero oversight from the state or the feds. So he is counting on the fact that an unlawful conviction cannot be used to prosecute him as a prohibited person since checks and balances just don't apply in some jurisdictions.

If you think that is insane, I've heard of even crazier rulings. I'm certain most of y'all are familiar with the "Armed Citizen" column in *National Rifleman* magazine in which news clips regarding citizens who display or use a firearm to drive away violent felons are listed. In most states, if a stranger intrudes onto your property or into your home and threatens you with bodily harm you can point a gun at him and tell him to go away . . . but in a few states they will arrest and prosecute you for that. In fact, they will even prosecute you for threatening him with a baseball bat, or just telling him you'll "shoot" him when no gun is present. I have heard stories of individuals who had a worn out firearm malfunction at a public shooting range being arrested and prosecuted for unlicenced possession of a "machinegun" even though it was obvious that it was due to a worn sear or grimy firing pin causing an unintentional slam fire. I have heard of a case where a black powder hunter dressed in traditional clothes was arrested for possessing an illegal double-edged dagger for carrying a knapped obsidian blade which he had made himself. I have heard of a case in which police went into a museum and told them that they would be arrested if they did not immediately remove the springs from a set of mint condition antique switchblades which were displayed in a locked case and had been manufactured in that very town 200 years earlier. The law is not only unfair . . . it isn't even sane . . . and cases which clearly have no merit and wrongfully persecute innocent people are aggressively prosecuted, whereas repeat felony offenders routinely get a slap on the wrist with reduced charges and probation, leaving them free to harm society by victimizing others. In some states an individual with no criminal record and a long history of good citizenship who is found in possession of an unlicensed handgun will face mandatory minimum sentencing and no plea bargaining, which gives him a harsher penalty than the average thief, mugger, or sex offender—and that just ain't right. What part of "shall not be infringed" do these states misunderstand? Mandatory imprisonment and the lifelong stigma of a felony conviction can hardly be construed as a "reasonable restriction on firearm ownership and possession" which they claim trumps the 2nd Amendment. Those politicians and judges are traitors to the Constitution they swore an oath to protect and uphold, and their allies intend to impose those restrictions on the entire country if they can.

Fair, impartial judges are a rarity in this country, and many are downright spooky. There are some courts that local defense attorneys will refuse to represent clients in because they, themselves, are scared of the judge and what he might do to them. In the event a bad judge is discovered, reported, and exposed, it is nearly impossible to get them off the bench unless you have witnesses willing to testify that they observed him swigging vodka and whacking off in open court. A County Court Judge is about as powerful as one can get in this country. Judges are virtually untouchable and off limits to most legal action that might be attempted against them. The only thing that can effect a Judge is a ruling from a higher court, but that seldom happens and only under the most extraordinary of circumstances. A Judge is like unto a god in the eyes of the law, and practically rules by Divine Right as if he were infallible, but I digress.

A kangaroo court is a colloquial term for a sham legal proceeding. The outcome of a trial by kangaroo court is essentially determined in advance, usually for the purpose of providing a conviction, either by going through the motions of manipulated procedure or by allowing no defense at all.

A kangaroo court's proceedings deny due process rights in the name of expediency. Such rights include: the right to summon witnesses, the right of cross-examination, the right not to incriminate oneself, the right not to be tried on secret evidence, the right to control one's own defense, the right to exclude evidence that is improperly obtained, irrelevant or inherently inadmissible, e.g., hearsay, the right to exclude judges or jurors on the grounds of partiality or conflict of interest, and the right of appeal.

The term is often applied to courts subjectively judged as such, while others consider the court to be legitimate and legal. A kangaroo court may be a court that has had its integrity compromised; for example, if the judge is not impartial and refuses to be recused.

Many courts in this country amount to little more than ritualistic show trials. Unless you can afford 50 grand in legal fees, expect to be thrown under the bus if you ever find yourself a defendant in a criminal case. The lessons you learned in school about the Bill of Rights and "checks and balances" is a lot of bullshit that simply does not apply in the real world. If you naively go into a court of law thinking you can sway a jury by telling them the absolute truth and presenting a reasonable and compelling defense you are in for a rude awakening. *"How much justice can you afford"?*

THE GRILLED CHEESE SAMMICH

> *"How would you like to be forced all the days of your life to sit beside a stinking, stupid wino every morning at breakfast? Or for some loud fool in his infinite ignorance to be at any moment able to say (slur), 'Gimme a cigarette, man'! And I just look into his sleazy eyes and want to kill his ass there in front of God and everyone."*
>
> Jack Henry Abbott, *In the Belly of the Beast*

> *"Record number of 6 million Americans incarcerated during 2001. 1 out of every 32 Americans is currently either incarcerated or under court mandated supervision."*
>
> CNN news ticker

> *"While one in 30 men between the ages of 20 and 34 is behind bars, for black males in that age group the figure is one in nine.*
>
> *2008 Pew Report*

> *"30 percent in US arrested by the age of 23".*
>
> 2011 AP news wire

> *"This estimate provides a real sense that the proportion of people who have criminal records is sizable and perhaps much larger than most people would expect."*
>
> Shawn Bushway, Criminologist, SUNY Albany

The United States incarcerates more of its citizens—percentagewise as well as numerically—than any other nation on Earth. This is due in part to harsh mandatory minimum sentences, "zero tolerance" statutes, the elevation of many crimes that were once misdemeanors to felonies, and the continual creation of new criminal offenses.

It is unlikely you will actually get raped in the county jail, but it will suck and you will eat the grilled cheese sammich and listen to cartoons all day and have addicts and pathological liars as your roommates for a few months. This is not intended to make anyone a better person less likely to reoffend. It is intended simply to humiliate you and put you "in your place" with the understanding that guvmint can do anything it wants to you and there is always someplace worse they can put you.

There are many levels of incarceration. For sake of brevity I am not including punishments such as: probation, house arrest, work release, halfway houses, minimum security camps, or military stockades, nor shall I presume to describe the conditions in correctional facilities outside of the United States (which in Canada and Europe tend to be cleaner and safer with less time served and few post release restrictions). I shall only provide a few brief words on each.

HOLDING CELL:

This is your introduction to gaol. After you are arrested and initially processed by law enforcement you will probably be locked in a cage at the police station, probably with numerous roommates, some of whom will probably be very drunk . . . hence the common moniker "drunk tank." There will be one toilet in the back of the cell that probably has not been cleaned that month which is for the use of all occupants. It will not have a seat or lid, there will be no toilet paper, and it will may well be backing up and flooding the cell. Welcome to gaol! You will probably be offered a free hot dog and half pint carton of milk before either being released or transferred to County.

COUNTY JAIL:

This is gaol. Depending on your assessment you may be placed in a dormitory, a cell block, protective custody block, solitary confinement, or even made a "trustee" and expected to assist staff in the kitchen, office, laundry, or with janitorial duties. Gaol sucks. It is boring, cartoons play on the TV all day long, you are fed the grilled cheese sammich, and your neighbors spend most of their time lying about what successful big shots they are on the outside or talking about their dicks. You will stay at gaol until you are bailed out, go to court and are released, do up to one year of a sentence on a misdemeanor or minor felony, or are transferred to a State or Federal facility to do a longer sentence. Approximately one third of the inmates in any County Jail are being held for their court appearances and have not been convicted or sentenced, but they cannot afford to make bail. Some of them are actually innocent and will be found as such. Others are not even charged with a crime but are being held as a "material witness" in order to prevent them from fleeing the jurisdiction and in hope that they will be intimidated into testifying. Most people who are arrested for misdemeanors and minor felonies do all of their time in County Jail after plea bargaining, after which they are released on probation. Most weapon possession charges, menacing charges, and assault charges wind up with a sentence to be served in the County Jail.

STATE PRISON:

If you have seriously stepped on your dick and caught a conviction for assault with a deadly weapon, 1st degree battery, or manslaughter, you are going to spend a few years behind bars in prison. If you are a resident of a totalitarian regime such as New York or Illinois, they can and will throw you in prison simply for carrying an unlicensed handgun, whereas the mugger you pulled it on will simply get a month in County and a year of probation. Prison is bad news. People get raped and shanked there. But at least the living conditions tend to be a bit better than County Jail, you usually get your own cell, and the food is better. In many correctional institutes you can take college courses or earn a dollar a day doing assembly work.

STATE PSYCHIATRIC FACILITY:

So your attorney made it so you were found not guilty by reason of insanity? Congratulations, you have now been "adjudicated mentally incompetent" which in some ways is even worse than a felony conviction. There are few actual institutes for the criminally insane in this country, with those guys just being kept in a secure locked wing of the state hospital where all the non-criminal loonies are kept. As an official loonie, you have no rights, by which I mean less rights than a convict in the state correctional system. As a loonie, the state can drug you against your will. They can strap you down and keep you on a Thorazine drip for 5 years if they want. They can also legally torture you via Electro Convulsive Therapy and other "treatments" such as ice baths and sensory deprivation. I hope you like oatmeal, because you'll be seeing a lot of it. You do not want to go here. This is the bad place.

FEDERAL PENITENTIARY:

The Federal Penitentiary is reserved solely for individuals who have been convicted of violating a Federal statute. In a self defense scenario, this could involve: a "prohibited person" found in possession of a firearm, possession of a restricted NFA firearm such as a wallet gun or defective pistol with a tendency to slam fire, defending yourself at a National Park or in the Post Office parking lot, crossing a state line after defending yourself, or conduct which could be construed as "kidnapping" an assailant. There are various levels of

Federal incarceration, from resort spas for well connected politicians and white collar criminals, to SuperMax facilities intended to isolate the alleged "most dangerous" convicts. Generally, Federal facilities are like state prisons with additional security and more widespread and severe abuses of the convict population. For Draconian and arbitrary reasons of their own, even though there may be a Federal correctional institute in the same town the defendant was convicted in, he will likely be sent to a different facility a thousand miles away where it will be nearly impossible for family or friends to visit. Furthermore, there is no parole in the Federal system so you will serve your entire sentence and the only person who can issue a pardon or restore your rights is the President of the United States . . . and, frankly, that just ain't gonna happen. For all these reasons, I strongly urge you to avoid violating Federal laws as the penalties are unduly harsh, especially in comparison to penalties for similar offenses prosecuted under state law.

SURVIVING INCARCERATION

Numerous books have been written about this subject and there is a lot of useful information out there which I encourage you to research. I'm going to be extremely brief. Frankly, your biggest danger is going to be yourself. How well do you think you'll deal with close confinement while being subjected to alternating extreme stress and extreme boredom over a long period of time? Don't run your mouth and piss other people off needlessly. Don't get involved with gambling, drugs, sex, or escape attempts. Unless you had a strong affiliation before going in, avoid getting involved in any way with the gangs. Be careful of your health. And last but not least, don't take shit from anyone. If someone puts their hands on you, takes your stuff, or threatens you in front of witnesses you have no choice but to take him down hard. Soap in a sock works well for this, as does a couple of sharp pencils . . . or you could just douse him in flammable cleaning fluid and set him on fire while he's in his cell. This will probably extend your stay for a few years, but that is better than getting punked out or snitching to the guards. If—for whatever reason—you have decided that survival is no longer an option, I advice taking multiple steps to prevent resuscitation, such as poisoning, exsanguination, and strangulation simultaneously. Best choice of poison is a brew made from cigarette butts, and if you don't have a sharp edge you can use your incisors, and that is all I'm going to say about that.

CONSEQUENCES OF A CRIMINAL RECORD

A misdemeanor barely counts at all. A felony conviction, however, can outlaw you for life. Even if your rights are restored automatically at the conclusion of your sentence or restored after an official request, there is no guarantee that the Feds will recognize that restoration. The ATF has a long and established pattern of creatively interpreting what constitutes a prohibited person, and they feel that "once a felon, always a felon." In order for the Feds to acknowledge that your right to be in the same building as a shell casing or non functional firearm owned by another person (constructive possession of components), your rights need to have been "fully restored." Many states will specifically restore a felon's right to bear arms, but not his right to hold public office . . . "A-ha!" The ATF says, "Your rights have not been fully restored!" The state of Vermont does not strip felons of their rights upon conviction, and the ATF is of the opinion that these people were convicted of felonies but did not have rights "restored" either. A few states can incarcerate individuals convicted of certain misdemeanors for over a year, and even if they were only sentenced to probation the ATF says that since they *could've* been sentenced to over a year they are indistinguishable from a felon. Believe it or not, ATF has repeatedly pursued arrests and prosecutions under each of those circumstances, as well as against decades old non-violent offenses that everyone else has forgotten about. Federal prosecution under prohibited person status is the primary consequence of a criminal record, next to bars on employment and housing.

Routine background checks, which can be performed by anyone with an internet connection and a credit card, can reveal your record to prospective employers and landlords, who can deny you a job and a place to live. Many states will not allow ex-offenders to hold a variety of professional licenses or permits—even something as innocuous as barber, taxicab operator, or a liquor licence necessary to sell beer in a store or serve wine at a restaurant. Furthermore, many states will deny ex-offenders employment at any state, county, city, or town agency, claiming that being a sanitation engineer or dogcatcher constitutes "public office." But this is not intended to further punish you or drive you into poverty and homelessness, but rather for the protection of society. But should a society be protected which deliberately creates a large underclass through exclusion and officially sanctioned persecution? That is an ethical dilemma for you to ponder.

Finally, any time you come into contact with law enforcement, it is possible they may be notified that you are a convicted felon or someone known to possess weapons—especially if you are currently on probation or parole. This varies from jurisdiction to jurisdiction, and may only be limited to state or local records, but it is becoming more common for street officers to have instant access to data well beyond the standard outstanding warrants and wants, so if they pull you over for a traffic stop and scan your driver license their demeanor might instantly change upon the realization that you are a criminal scumbag whom they probably ought to point their guns at and subject to a full vehicle search. Remember, once you have a criminal record you become part of a societal underclass and are not considered to have the same rights as other citizens, which is why this status is often referred to as "Civil Death." As a result of this, many ex-offenders feel that they can no longer rely upon the police to protect them, and will refuse to call them even if they have done nothing wrong and are clearly the victim. If they choose to take matters into their own hands, that makes them an outlaw. These are all severe consequences which typically last for the rest of one's life.

GUVMINT DOES NOT LUV U

This section shall be extremely brief and comprised primarily of quotations. I do not feel entirely comfortable expressing my personal and private views on government and certainly have no wish to risk being wrongfully labeled as some sort of paranoid conspiracy kook, which I am not. I stopped caring about governmental meddling in my affairs long ago—I'm not doing anything subversive or illegal and don't particularly care what data they dredge up pertaining to me. I stopped giving a fuck about that long ago and have no need for a tin foil hat.

One thing I will say is that many laws, and the ways they are enforced, seem to make absolutely no logical sense unless you consider that they might have been intended solely to destabilize society and emasculate the populace gradually over a period of decades, making them complacent and dependant on government services. That sounds like a bizarre conspiracy theory, but the data has been researched thoroughly and appears to be chillingly valid . . . and that's all I'm going to say about that.

Here are a few meaningful quotes from folks more edjumacated than I:

> *"Intelligence is the capacity to discern, to understand, to distinguish; it is also the capacity to observe, to put together all that we have gathered and to act from that. . . . Intelligence demands doubting, questioning, not being impressed by others, by their enthusiasm, by their energy. Intelligence demands that there be impersonal observation. Intelligence is not only the capacity to understand that which is rationally, verbally explained but also implies that we gather as much information as possible, yet knowing that that information can never be complete, about anybody or anything."*
>
> J. Krishnamurti, *The Network of Thought*

> *"Unfortunately, the rulers of any system cannot maintain their power without the constant creation of prohibitions that then give the state the right to imprison—or otherwise intimidate—anyone who*

violates any of the state's often new-minted crimes . . . . In the name of correctness, of good health, or even of God—a great harassment of the people-at-large is now going on. Although our state has not the power to intimidate any but small, weak countries, we can certainly throw most Americans in prison for violating the ever-increasing list of prohibitions."

Gore Vidal, *Dreaming War* (p. 175)

"Men may be without restraints upon their liberty; they may pass to and fro at pleasure; but if their steps are tracked by spies and informers, their words noted down for crimination, their associates watched as conspirators—who should say that they are free?"

Sir Thomas May

"How can citizens be honestly described as free and equal who are not, who never were 'free and equal' in any reasonable sense of the phrase? How can they even be considered men, whose whole lives are governed by cast-iron regulations, whose every movement circumscribed and restrained by penal threats, even whose secret thoughts are in a constant state of silent repression"?

Jack London, *Might is Right* (p. 61)

"The operation of the 'Law' itself is, also, an apt illustration of the paradoxical nature of Right and Wrong. Citizens who break the written law are hauled before judges, inquisitorially cross-examined

and chained for long years in State dungeons, but the statesmen and legislators may sell their country for gold and break every statute law and constitution in the land without the least fear of legal intimidation."

Jack London, *Might is Right* (p. 137)

"There is no War on Crime. There is no War on Drugs. There is no War on Terrorism. There is no War on Youth Violence. There is only the ongoing effort by the federal government to collect as much information on as many people as possible. Domestic law enforcement initiatives are merely excuses to increase the amount of spying on the American people."

Jim Redden, *Snitch Culture* (p. 60)

"A frequent charge for sentencing innocent people to prison is charging them with the federal crime, misprision of felony. Anyone who knows of a federal crime and who does not promptly report it to a federal judge or other federal tribunal is guilty of this crime."

Rodney Stich, from Defrauding America (p. 487)

"If you resist political indoctrination and the enemy realizes that he is failing in his attempt to 'convert' you to his ideology, he will attempt to obtain obedience through fear. He will try to create this fear through terror. The enemy has developed terror techniques which are very effective . . . . These terror measures are: a. Surveillance of telephone and

letters; b. Establishment of an agent and informer net; c. Arbitrary arrests; d. No public trials except 'show trials'; e. Arbitrary sentences; f. Lengthy prison sentences out of proportion to the offense."

Major H. Von Dach, *Total Resistance* (p. 96)

"Whoever lays their hand on me is a usurper and a tyrant; I declare them to be my enemy . . . government is slavery. Its laws are cobwebs for the rich and chains of steel for the poor. To be governed is to be watched, inspected, spied on, regulated, indoctrinated, preached at, controlled, ruled, censored by persons who have neither wisdom nor virtue. It is in every action and transaction to be registered, stamped, taxed, patented, licensed, assessed, measured, reprimanded, corrected, frustrated. Under pretext of the public good it is to be exploited, monopolized, embezzled, robbed, and then, at the least protest or word of complaint, to be fined, harassed, vilified, beaten up, bludgeoned, disarmed, judged, condemned, imprisoned, shot garroted, deported, sold, betrayed, swindled, deceived, outraged dishonoured, that's government, that's its justice, that's its morality!"

Pierre Joseph Proudhon (1848, Paris)

"The more corrupt the state, the more it legislates."

Tacitus

. . . AND THE CONSPIRACY THEORIST WACKOS HAVE THIS TO SAY:

> *"They who can give up essential liberty to obtain a little temporary safety, deserve neither liberty nor safety."*
>
> Benjamin Franklin

> *"Anyone who surrenders his arms because of a cry for public safety does not deserve freedom . . . No free man shall ever be debarred the use of arms . . . Laws that forbid the carrying of arms . . . disarm only those who are neither inclined nor determined to commit crimes."*
>
> Thomas Jefferson

> *"One of the ordinary modes, by which tyrants accomplish their purposes without resistance, is by disarming the people, and making it an offense to keep arms."*
>
> Constitutional scholar and Supreme Court Justice
> Joseph Story, 1840

> *"I have seen the future and it is a boot stomping on a human face . . . forever"*
>
> George Orwell, *1984*

The Shadow Government has existed for well over a century and has mutated over time, with different sects having opposing agendas squabbling amongst themselves and causing the occasional disruption which sometimes results in a news clipping or a paragraph in a History book attributing the strange event to "coincidence" or "blunder." This cabal involves secret societies within government—particularly the intelligence agencies, as well as industry, technology, medicine, media, publishing, entertainment, and clergy. We will not discuss the particulars as that is well beyond the scope of this project and largely irrelevant—secret societies have propped up most governments since before recorded History, as that is the nature of politics and diplomacy.

A common pattern is for them to deliberately take steps to artificially create a major societal crisis in order to justify stepping in to "correct" it via extreme emergency measures. However, after the emergency has passed they are unusually reluctant to rescind those emergency powers, which tend to be extended indefinitely or worked into official policy. In other cases, the goal seems to be nothing less than the breakdown of society itself: break up the family unit, persecute labor organizations and social clubs, alienate people from each other, artificially increase stress levels which are treated with mind-altering prescription drugs, and deliberately increase the levels of violent crime while punishing citizens who attempt to protect themselves harsher than the recidivist criminals who victimized them. Citizens are encouraged to become docile, placid, and helpless sheep completely dependant upon the government, whereas those who show initiative or individualism are blacklisted or hobbled if they stray too far from the status quo.

It is dangerous to speak plainly of such things, or make accusations which could be classified by some as "baseless" or "paranoid" so I shall do no such thing. What I shall do, however, is reveal that roughly 90% of all available writings pertaining to "conspiracy theorism" are indeed baseless and paranoid, if not downright bizarre. That is because they are funded and promoted by the conspirators themselves. And that is really all you need to know. It is harmful and counterproductive to dig deeper without knowing how to separate falsehoods from truth, as some of the disinformation out there is deliberately intended to harm you, and reading random tracts is akin to navigating a minefield without a map. The government has become the master rather than the servant of the people and looks upon citizens as property if not chattle. "Rights" are a myth, as is freedom and privacy. The controllers have won.

F.T.W. COMMENTARY

Interesting people frequently become "persons of interest." Mind that your reputation doesn't get too far out of hand or some snitch will try to cash in on it.

In addition to associating with gangbangers, bikers, and mobsters, I've also had opportunity to befriend a few attorneys, policemen, and even (*gasp!*) a few Feds. These "good guys" know very well how the system works, and you know what they, invariably, confided to me? They all said that if they had no choice but to kill another man who was attacking them—whether it be during a brawl, a robbery, or a road rage incident—and they thought there was a good chance they could simply leave the scene without being spotted, that's exactly what they would do. Why? The level of bureaucratic bullshit involved with a lethal force incident is so overwhelming and unpredictable their life would be hell for at least a year in a best case scenario. In a worst case scenario, even if they did everything right including calling 911 and cooperating fully with investigators, they could still wind up in prison—even for some completely unrelated matter uncovered during the course of their investigation. But of course these highly qualified experts on police and judicial procedure would never publically admit such a thing—even behind an anonymous username on some internet forum—because nothing on the internet is truly anonymous.

Remember that the policeman can do whatever he wants, to whomever he wants, whenever he wants. That is a fact. Sure, it may not be legal, and sure, he might even get his knuckles smacked with a ruler after an administrative review, but while it is actually happening you need to be extra careful about how vehemently you choose to assert your "rights", because as Jack London once penned, *"all 'rights' are as transient as morning rainbows."* Get too lippy with Officer Friendly with no witnesses around, and you could get beat half to death before getting charged with "assaulting an officer." That shit happens all the time, and the police usually get away with it. The only times you ever hear about it are those extremely rare cases that actually make local or national news—those are less than 1% of all official complaints of abuse, and more than half of those are eventually dismissed. An entirely different set of rules apply to those empowered to enforce them.

If you are stopped by police, be polite. If you are interrogated or arrested by police, shut the hell up and demand to speak with your attorney. Never consent to a search. On extremely rare occasions, evidence may be discovered that truly does not belong to you, it just seemed to magically appear in your car or in your coat pocket. Maybe it was hidden in the cop's hand, maybe a police informant planted it there, or perhaps it fell out of one of your passenger's pockets last week. Regardless, if you did not consent to the search that mysterious item might be ruled inadmissable, whereas if you waive your rights that charge will stick . . . but Officer Friendly might just check a box on a form alleging that you "consented" to the search while you're proned out in the dirt at gunpoint, so this might as well be a moot point.

And if you do wind up sentenced to several months, if not years, of grilled cheese sammich, be sure to do your time standing up—and remember that sharp pencils or a bar of soap in a tube sock are almost as good as a shank for taking care of business or protecting the sanctity of your cornhole.

Afterword

"Violence never settles anything."

Genghis Khan

As I stated at the beginning of this book, what I've written is far from perfect. This was written, in part, during a time of crisis in my life with many distractions. Trust Captain Hook when he says that dating hot artist chicks half your age isn't always as great as you might think—especially if they are bi-polar and fond of Irish whiskey—but I digress. Anyhow, I had a strict deadline and several months of bullshit to unfuck, so editing sorta fell by the wayside a bit. I am certain that, upon rereading this book, I shall be horrified and dismayed by multiple glaring errors and omissions, but at this point I no longer care. Fuck. I'm glad this manuscript has been submitted to the publisher so I can finally start writing the novel I've been researching for the past five years. I wrote *Hardcore Self Defense* in about a month while I was smoking weed and drinking beers, and had thought that the sequel could be knocked out fairly quickly as well. Since I am now sober and gainfully employed, I have not been able to give this project the same degree of focus and type 8 hours every day, although it is somewhat more useful and coherent, and I hope at least equally entertaining. I had wanted for it to be "perfect" but of course it is not. I suggest you keep it in your bathroom to read while you are on the crapper. Oh, and thank you for buying my book.

Acknowledgements

First and foremost, I'd like to thank Marc MacYoung and Peyton Quinn for finally getting through to me that it really is okay to walk away from a fight, and that most of the time it is the smartest thing you can do.

I'd like to thank Henry Rollins for assuring me that it really is okay to hate everyone, and that does not necessarily make one a bad person.

I'd like to thank James Keating for showing me that there really is no shame in being crazy, as long as you keep it under control.

I'd like to thank Ralph Barger for reinforcing the importance of turn signals and courteous driving practices which has helped me to be a safer motorist who gets shot at far less frequently now.

And, finally, love and respect to Cai for putting up with my shit for the past few years and keeping me from being another crazy homeless wandering down Colfax muttering to himself and scaring people. I'd probably be dead if not for you.

Y'all have truly helped me to be much less of an asshole, and for that you have my sincere gratitude.

About The Author

C. R. Jahn, AKA CAPTAIN HOOK, AKA tyr_shadowblade, is a renegade Sociologist who has specialized in studying the behavior of bipedal predators in the wild. Fully immersed in deep street subcultures for about 15 years, he was provided an extremely unique opportunity to observe, befriend, and learn from a number of his subjects. C. R. Jahn is an independent biker who can sometimes be spotted riding a black V8 rat trike around the greater Denver area. Other than that, very little is known about C. R. Jahn . . . and C. R. Jahn prefers to keep it that way.